D0075354

FREE WILL

'A remarkably clear-headed, balanced analysis of free will. Dilman's discussions are marked by exemplary clarity in exposition and a focus on getting to what features of human experience have been captured by each thinker.'

Professor Herbert Morris, UCLA

'There can be no doubting the sustained, high level of scholarship displayed in this detailed study of key thinkers and sources on free will and determinism. The style is pleasant and easy to read, making the work accessible to a wide audience.'

Steve Champlin, University of Hull

What is the place of free will in our lives if all our actions are the result of some other cause? Do our desires and unconscious beliefs make us less free? How do human beings assert their autonomy in a world governed by chance, cause and necessity?

The debate between free will and its opposing doctrine, determinism, is one of the key issues in philosophy. *Free Will: An historical and philosophical introduction* provides a comprehensive introduction to this highly important topic and examines the contributions of sixteen of the most outstanding thinkers across the ages. Beginning with Homer and early Greek thought, İlham Dilman examines the writings of Sophocles, Plato and Aristotle, then moves to questions on ethics and theology as explored in the medieval times by St Thomas Aquinas and St Augustine. The analysis continues with the question of free will in the context of empiricism, as seen in the works of Descartes, Spinoza, Kant and Hume, before it embarks on the treatment of the subject by modern thinkers like Schopenhauer, Freud, Sartre, Simone Weil, Moore and Wittgenstein.

This critical study spans a wide area of philosophy and encompasses diverse views on the subject drawn from literature, psychoanalysis, ethics and theology. İlham Dilman provides a thorough analysis of the continuum between freedom and determinism and offers valuable insights from both sides of the divide.

İlham Dilman is Professor Emeritus of Philosophy at the University of Wales, Swansea.

FREE WILL

An historical and philosophical introduction

İlham Dilman

London and New York

LUTHER SEMINARY
LIBRARY
2375 Como Avenue
St. Paul, MN 55108-1447

BJ1460
.D54

First published 1999
by Routledge
11 New Fetter Lane, London EC4P 4EE

Simultaneously published in the USA and Canada
by Routledge
29 West 35th Street, New York, NY 10001

©1999 İlham Dilman

Typeset in Sabon by Routledge
Printed and bound in Great Britain by T.J. International Ltd, Padstow,
Cornwall

All rights reserved. No part of this book may be reprinted or
reproduced or utilized in any form or by any electronic,
mechanical, or other means, now known or hereafter
invented, including photocopying and recording, or in any
information storage or retrieval system, without permission in
writing from the publishers.

British Library Cataloguing in Publication Data
A catalogue record for this book is available from the British Library

Library of Congress Cataloguing in Publication Data
Dilman, İlham
Free will; an historical and philosophical introduction/ İlham Dilman
p. cm.
Includes biographical references and index.
1. Free will and determinism–History. I. Title.
BJ1460.D55 1999
123'.5'09–dc 21
98-35363

ISBN 0–415–20055–5 (hbk)
ISBN 0–415–20056–3 (pbk)

O: 39633797

CONTENTS

CONTENTS

INTRODUCTION

This book is concerned with sixteen thinkers of the Western world who have had something to say about that condition of human existence in which human beings are in bondage: what it means, whether it is in any sense inevitable and, if it is, how one can turn away from it and move towards greater autonomy and freedom. What is free will and in what way is it distinctive of and grounded in human existence? The thinkers in question thus are (i) those who have had something to say about *human life*, what people have to contend with in it, their capacities and weaknesses, and (ii) those who have had some light to shed on the *concepts* in terms of which we try to understand these things and some of the *problems* they raise for us when we think about them.

It follows a historical order. The first four thinkers belong to early Greece. As far as the problem of human freedom goes their main concern is the way human beings become the plaything of certain common human propensities. What Plato had to say about the way evil enslaves men whereas in goodness they find themselves and hence autonomy in their actions echoes through the thinking of a number of the thinkers considered.

The next two thinkers, St Augustine and St Thomas Aquinas, are steeped in Christianity in their thinking. They are both concerned with what the reality of free will, which they take as a gift of God, consists in and the way we differ from animals in our possession of it. If the possibility of evil presupposes our possession of free will and it is God who has given us free will, does that make God responsible for the evil in the world? If though we fall by our own will we cannot rise except by God's grace, how is free will compatible with God's grace? And if God is omniscient and therefore knows what will happen in the future and so what we shall ourselves do, does that not rob us of our free will? The problem of free will thus assumes a theological dimension in their writings. This is in addition to the ethical dimension it inherits from the period of the early Greeks.

Third we have Descartes, Spinoza, Hume and Kant. Prominent in their thinking about human freedom is a new dimension which comes with the

1

III· rise of the sciences: does the empire of causality leave any logical space for human freedom – freedom of choice and action? Each, in their own different way, tries to find room for it. The book critically considers their different solutions to this problem and the metaphysical framework within which it is offered. It considers the Cartesian dichotomy between mind and body and the way it mars Descartes' account of the will and its freedom, and also the dichotomy between reason and passion and the way it has pushed Kant and Hume in opposite directions. While what Spinoza had to say has more than one strand, the book concentrates on one of these, namely what he had to say directly about human life.

In the fourth and last group we have first Schopenhauer and Freud who the book sees as close in their impressions of the way men are enslaved in their confinement to the repetitive patterns that run through their lives. This is the substantive aspect of their determinism. But they both confuse it with the reign of causality. The book tries to disentangle these two strands in their thinking. It considers critically Schopenhauer's account of human motivation as a form of causality and in the chapter on Freud it argues that what Freud offers in his tripartite divisions of the personality are not immutable structures but dissociations within the personality which it is the aim of psycho-analytic therapy to heal. It is in the wholeness of personality towards which the analysand moves as these divisions are healed and inner conflicts are resolved that the analysand finds greater autonomy and hence freedom.

Sartre has something important to say about the freedom which is an integral part of human existence, the responsibility with which it saddles the individual, and the freedom he loses in trying to evade this responsibility in bad faith. He has criticized and rejected Descartes' dualism and his solipsism, but he still finds something he considers important in Descartes' conception of the will as inalienably free. The chapter on Sartre considers his very interesting development of this Cartesian idea.

In this group of thinkers Simone Weil stands on her own. Her knowledge of history, her love of early Greek literature and philosophy, her profound thought on Christianity and other world religions, her close acquaintance with science and its history, and her personal identification with the oppressed put her in a unique position to talk about the 'necessities' to which human life is subject and the freedom that is possible within their context. What she has to say is inspired by Plato and bears a very close affinity to his views. It also exhibits some remarkable affinities with Spinoza.

The chapter on Moore considers his discussion of the compatibility between the freedom of the will and the general law of causality, and the one on Wittgenstein considers his 'Lecture on Free Will' which is roughly in the same area as the one in which Moore's problem arises. The lecture was delivered in Cambridge in 1945–6 or 1946–7 and constructed from notes taken at the lecture by Yorick Smythies. In it Wittgenstein simply raises some questions about the claim that human behaviour may be governed by laws, whether it is predictable and, if it is, whether this excludes freedom of choice.

The discussions of each chapter are on the whole based on a single short text by the writer, though some references are made to some of his other works. The main texts used are the following:

1 Homer: the *Iliad*, and Simone Weil: 'L'Iliad ou le Poem de la Force'
2 Sophocles: *Oedipus Rex*
3 Plato: the *Gorgias*, the *Phaedo* and the *Phaedrus*
4 Aristotle: *The Nichomachean Ethics*, Books III and VI
5 St Augustine: *On Free Choice of Will* (or *De Libro Arbitrio*)
6 St Thomas Aquinas: *De Veritate*, 'On Free Choice'
7 Descartes: *Meditations*
8 Spinoza: *Ethics* Books IV and V
9 Hume: *An Enquiry Concerning the Principles of Morals*
   Kant: *Fundamental Principles of the Metaphysic of Ethics*
10 Schopenhauer: *On the Freedom of the Will*
11 Freud: *Psychopathology of Everyday Life*, Ch 2 and *Beyond the Pleasure Principle*, Ch 3
12 J-P Sartre: *Being and Nothingness*, Pt IV, Ch 1, 'Being and Having: Freedom'
13 Simone Weil: *Gravity and Grace*
14 G E Moore: *Ethics*, Ch 6, 'Free Will'
15 Wittgenstein: 'Lecture on the Freedom of the Will', *Philosophical Investigations*, Vol 12, No 2, April 1989.

These texts are considered with critical sympathy, but the book itself has something to contribute to the questions raised in them in its own voice. What it argues may be summed up as follows:

1 The problem of freedom and determinism is a cluster of problems and thus has many sources.

2 Broadly speaking some of these sources are *a priori* considerations; others are particular perspectives on human life and the light by which human action is seen when viewed from such perspectives. But the substantive question which actions so seen may raise, 'Are human beings *really* free, as we *normally* assume them to be?' can turn into the *a priori*, conceptual question, '*Can* they be said to act freely? Does not the notion of a free action involve a contradiction?' Thus the question about human freedom may have mixed sources and a mixed character. Equally, in the other direction, a thinker who responds to *a priori* questions about human freedom, even within the framework of an elaborate metaphysics, may manage to say something penetrating about human life and the predicament of human beings in such a life.

3

3 Spinoza is a supreme example of this. His 'solution' is developed in response to Descartes'. It bridges the philosophical divides between body and soul, passion and reason. It argues that the individual can attain a state of freedom not by imposing his will on his passions, as in Descartes, nor by siding with reason at the expense of emotions, as in Kant, nor yet by following passion 'prompted and directed by reason', as in Hume. It can only do so by giving up the will – effort of will – and submitting to an order of which we all are a small part. Here we act in the light of a reason that is at one with emotion: 'active emotion'. It can also be called 'affective reason'.

Spinoza thus engages with the 'modern' problems concerning the apparent conflict between freedom and causality. Yet he uses a highly metaphysical system of concepts, developed to sort out difficulties he finds with Cartesian philosophy, to think about the plight of human beings rooted in an order that is indifferent to their self-centred will. The chapter on Spinoza sees his solution as religious and exhibiting affinities with Simone Weil's contribution as inspired by Plato. In its discussion of his contribution it tries to cut through his metaphysics and to get to what he had to say about human life.

4 The book distinguishes between four sources of the problem of 'freedom and determinism': (i) The roles of 'chance and necessity' in human life and the impotence of the individual's will in the face of it. This is emphasized especially in early Greek thought. (ii) Some theological concepts in Christian thinking constitute an additional source of the problem, notably those of God's grace and His foreknowledge, including His knowledge of each individual's future actions. (iii) A third source of the problem for 'modern' philosophers has been the apparent incompatibility between human free will and the general law of causality. (iv) A fourth source is to be found in the perception of the endless repetition of the same patterns of action and behaviour in individual lives, the impotence of the will to change these patterns, and the degree to which such impotence is rooted in self-division and self-deception. We find this source at work in Schopenhauer's and Freud's determinism; but in *some* ways what we have here are the 'necessities' in early Greek thought in a modern guise.

5 In connection with (i) above the early chapters of the book discuss how moral ignorance or alienation from goodness makes human beings vulnerable to the necessities ingrained in their own nature, and how in the case of Oedipus it takes the form of an individual destiny he cannot evade.

In Plato men are represented as enslaved when they give in to what is part of their nature. We see this clearly in Homer's depiction of the warriors in the Trojan war on both sides in the way they are deceived in their very engagement.

The book tries to bring out how in Plato self-mastery and the kind of

4

virtue which constitutes goodness are inseparable and the sense in which the kind of self-knowledge and moral knowledge presupposed in self-mastery are two sides of the same coin. Plato holds that self-mastery is essential for human freedom, for it takes self-mastery to resist and surmount those inclinations that belong to our nature and threaten to master us.

To yield to them is to feed the ego in us – Kant's 'dear self'. So to surmount them one has to detach oneself from those things in which the ego finds growth or enlargement. Furthermore such enlargement is always at the expense of other people and so promotes a disregard of their needs and welfare and hardens the heart to considerations of justice. That is why Plato sees those natural inclinations in which the ego seeks growth and enlargement as the source of evil in men.

It is in the love of what he sees as constituting goodness, Plato believes, that men turn away from and forego these inclinations. Hence he holds that men come to themselves, to goodness, to self-unity and to self-knowledge all at once, and find self-autonomy – which is another word for self-mastery. They are no longer mastered by those inclinations which confine their vision of any alternative to what they crave.

The book engages with this theme in many of its chapters and its clarification is one of its central contributions.

6 In connection with grace the book argues that what is in question is the transformation which keeping faith with God or remaining loyal to goodness affects in one independently of one's will, but that it takes inner work to maintain such faith. This is discussed in the chapters on Augustine, Aquinas and Simone Weil. As for God's foreknowledge in what He sees as being in store for us, the book argues that what is in question is the inescapability of an absolute moral judgement on our life – comparable with Socrates' judgement that Archelaus *cannot* be happy whatever he does in the life he lives.

Where it comes to God's knowledge of what will befall each individual independently of his will, the book argues in the chapters on Augustine and Aquinas that such knowledge is one with God's will. The believer is thus enjoined to accept it unconditionally and unquestioningly. In the chapters on Spinoza and Simone Weil the book tries to clarify how it is that such acceptance is liberating.

7 With regard to (iii) the book argues that while in its scope the law of causality is limitless within the grammar in which it is applicable and makes sense, that grammar characterizes one form of discourse and the reality to which it is internally related. The concepts in terms of which we make sense of human actions and behaviour have a *different* grammar, and the notion of causality in question is not at home in it. All the same human beings are flesh-and-blood beings and *as such* they form part of the world in which the law of causality holds unrestricted sway. Hence it is in no

way suspended in connection with human beings. The question, therefore, is: how does it relate to human actions?

The book discusses how our choices and actions are responsible to reasons which weigh with us as individuals and how, on the other hand, the bodily movements which they involve are conditioned by physiological processes that are subject to causality.

8 It has been said that we are free when *we ourselves* determine our choices and actions. The book argues that we do so when we are at one with or are ourselves in the considerations in accordance with which we determine our actions. By contrast it is not we ourselves who determine our choices and actions when these considerations are dictated to or imposed on us by what is external to us, by what we have not endorsed or made our own – by fashions or conventions to which we conform, needs or passions that are external to our will so that they remain dissociated from us, or when we have not come to ourselves and have no mind or will of our own.

Though we act as the kind of individual we are and our character finds expression in what we do and the way we behave, and though we owe our character to our upbringing and culture and much else that we meet in the course of our development, it does not follow that we are a 'mere product' of that through which we acquire our individual character. We can participate in our own development *or* we may come to be moulded by the circumstances of our life. Accordingly, we may come to a form of character in which we are ourselves or, on the opposite side, we may come to a form of character in which our autonomy is restricted.

9 Especially in connection with Schopenhauer the book argues – and this applies to Hume equally – that if 'freedom of the will' does not mean 'gratuitousness of willing', it does not follow that our will has to be determined by causes or 'motives' to which we are a spectator. Of course if our will is free it is still responsible to considerations – considerations which weigh with us and which are not open to choice in the course of our deliberations. But in subjecting our choices and decisions to such considerations we are ourselves; indeed we do so willingly – doing so is what we will.

10 Finally, it has been said that we have free will if we can do something different from what we in fact do. But, outside philosophy, this is said and has sense only in special circumstances, not regardless of them. As a general criterion it becomes a piece of metaphysics. Thus, for instance, where a person is under hypnotic suggestion we can say that he could not have done anything different from what he does do – what he has been asked under hypnosis to do. But to ask, 'could he have acted otherwise?', always suggests some abnormality; and the abnormality is abnormal only in contrast with the normal. The question, therefore, makes sense only in special circumstances and against a background of norms which our use of language takes for granted.

It is, therefore, not surprising that all the thinkers considered in this book, whether they stress man's freedom or his subjection to some form of necessity, allow for the distinction between freedom and one form of bondage or another and recognize that each is possible in human life. Where they stress the inescapability of freedom and responsibility the question is: how then do men, in bad faith, lose their freedom, and in what sense is it up to them to regain it? When they are impressed by the necessities to which men are subject, the question is: how is it possible for men to be free despite these necessities, or within their framework?

Thus the book could be entitled 'Human Freedom in a World of Cause, Chance and Necessity'. For (i) reference to human freedom makes sense only in contrast with forms of enslavement and hence in a world in which these are possible, and (ii) it is within an order of which the individual is a small part and which is blind or indifferent to him that each of us has to find our share of the freedom of which we are capable as human beings. Sartre would have probably reversed this title: 'The Bondage of Beings who are Free in their very Mode of Existence'. But even he admits that we are only free in a situation of human life – one that exists independently of the individual's will and to which he has to have regard in making choices and acting.

We are flesh-and-blood beings. As such we are part of the material world and so are subject to its causality. We are social beings and live in a world shaped by the culture to which we belong. We owe our very modes of thinking and assessment to it. We share its form of life and activities with others who exist independently of us and who co-operate as well as oppose us. We have a history, a past and roots in that past, attachments and loyalties. And, last but not least, chance too has a part in the events that confront us in our life and often stand in our way. We do not act in a vacuum and so we cannot be free in a vacuum. Each one of us has to find his freedom, in the sense of autonomy, in a world of cause, chance and necessity.

Part I

EARLY GREEK THINKERS
Moral determinism and individual
responsibility

1

HOMER AND THE *ILIAD*
Necessity and grace

1 War: its hazards and necessities

Early Greek thinkers, whether they be poets, dramatists or philosophers, had a tragic perception of the subjection of human beings to what they themselves initiate. But they thought of it as subject to their own character and of that, in turn, as subject to something in them all, something which belongs to 'human nature'. Some represented this as a subjection to a destiny with which the exceptional individual is in struggle, though as helpless in the face of it as the rest. They thought further that the direction in which he was moving inexorably and where he would end up was accessible to a certain kind of perception or insight, given often to those lacking physical sight – *viz* Teiresias in *Oedipus Rex* – and so not distracted by interests rooted in its vision – *viz* the importance of detachment for the possibility of knowledge in the *Phaedo*.

In Homer's poem the *Iliad* human beings initiate the Trojan war. The poem represents the men fighting on both sides as caught up in and enslaved by it. It is they who wage the war, but they become what the war makes of them. Yet it is because they are human that they become what the war makes of them. They are transformed by their pursuit of victory: both by the nearness of victory before it eludes them and by the nearness of death when victory slips from them. On the crest of its wave they are oblivious of their own vulnerability and are hard with and merciless towards those on the brink of defeat. In this blindness to themselves and to others, in the arrogance which hides their kinship to those at their mercy and makes them indifferent to their plight, they are puppets whose strings are pulled by their fortune in the war. They are not its architect. It is their fortune which makes them arrogant, and that fortune in turn is subject to chance and so open to change. The arrogance which it engenders is thus an empty bubble sustained temporarily by a lie about the human condition.

When it is their turn to be in the trough of the wave they come to know what it is to be at the mercy of others who are as hard with them as they

11

themselves were with others. They come to see that their previous good fortune was not something they could have relied on and that it was not their due or desert. In the face of defeat they experience their impotence and the illusory character of the power they had. It was not really theirs. They and the power they exercised were not one but two, and when it was not theirs to exercise because they came face to face with somebody stronger or suffered a chance set back they were left exposed to the same power in the hands of others. That power was not theirs since it was now wielded by others and they were its object. This is not a grammatical platitude about the way power is individuated. It is a truth to which those who wield power and are drunk with it are blind: while they wield it they really think they are invulnerable and immortal.

Thus power, the poem shows, while it is something which many, perhaps most people, find desirable and seek, is not something anyone can appropriate or make his own. Those who have it are deceived by the idea it gives them that they can overcome any obstacle that stands in the way of what they want and that they are safe against any predatory attack. No one can be that. They are deceived equally by the idea it gives them that it is there to stay with them, that it is something they hold and so something they can keep. In reality not only is it by chance that they are able to exercise the power they exercise, but they are also its slave. It determines their conduct and they do not know how to get on without it.

At home, before the expedition, the Greeks each had their own individual life and character. They had their family, wife and children, and the different preoccupations that filled their lives. On the battleground all this is a memory, almost unreal. The Trojans are, of course, on their home ground, exerting themselves to defend it. But it was they who brought the Greeks to their doorstep. It was Paris, their king Priam's son, who kidnapped Menelaus' beautiful wife Helen. The Greeks are there to reclaim her and avenge the kidnapping. But if that is what leads the Greeks to mount the Trojan expedition, once the catch has been released, the spring which is set free has an inertia all its own. It drags all concerned into a milieu in which they are no longer in control over their actions.

While they act in character, they are cut off from the things that are of importance and interest to them in the life in which they have up to now been themselves. Being in exile from that life their life has been arrested and they have been taken over by the desire to crush the enemy and to defend themselves. It is only in short intervals, during lulls in the fighting, when they can remember and mourn, that their humanity is restored, only to be lost again. Within their one-dimensional life on the battle field, they have no choice but to obey what takes them over: they have to prevail over the enemy, teach them a lesson, avenge their dead. As the scores to settle mount each side is further and further anchored in their determination to prevail, to avenge, to destroy. That is how they are locked in an endless cycle of reaction and counter-reaction, each side bent on destroying the other, whatever it takes to do so, that is at whatever cost to themselves.

In such a scene their physical strength and prowess is the only thing they can count on; it is the only thing on which their sense of self, of being someone to be reckoned with, depends. It is the other side of despair; for without it they have nothing, they are nothing, and they are at the mercy of those who know no mercy. They cling to it and it turns them into things.

This is a powerful picture of human subjection, of the slavery of individuals to a cycle of reactions that are natural but mindless – mindless because in his uprooted state the individual has very little to mind: to care, to respect, to take into consideration. With the rupture inherent in such uprootedness, the natural reactions that take over are those of self-assertion and retaliation to any threats to such assertion, taken as insult to the self, and self-preservation. The reactions of self-assertion are ruthlessly aggressive, while those of self-preservation have their source in near-animal fears. Both sets of reactions are human, but at source they are entangled with the activation of the capacity to survive that is part of all biological life.

When I spoke of 'rupture' just now I meant from the many-dimensionality of human life. A human being is free who can move within these many dimensions and choose within their framework. Anything that severs the individual from access to what is part of his life enslaves him. Thus an individual who is unable to take into consideration any of it in his actions because it has lost its reality for him, temporarily or permanently, is someone driven to what he does.

2 Simone Weil on the *Iliad*: necessity and grace

Simone Weil who has written a very searching and thoughtful essay on the *Iliad* takes a deeper view of what the poem portrays and expresses. She characterizes it as 'le poem de la force'; she says that force is its real subject. It changes, she says, all those it touches, all those who are subject to it, into things: its victims, the weak, as well as those who wield it, the strong – like Achilles. In those it crushes it wipes out all inner life. Those who have been crushed by it, in their affliction, cannot think of either the past or the future, they cannot compare their present state with anything, they cannot rebel or make plans for the future. As she puts it:

> At first war is easy and is loved basely. The day comes when fear, defeat and the death of comrades bring the soul of the warrior to its knees before *necessity*. War then stops being a game or a dream; the warrior comes to see that it is real, that it contains death. Death changes from being a limit imposed in advance on the future to being the future itself. Then one cannot think of anything in the future without passing through the idea, the image

of death. Thus war erases all idea of an end – of something to aim
at – even the aims of the war. ...Those who are there do nothing
that will bring it to an end. Intolerable afflictions of this kind last
on account of their own weight ... because they take away the
resources necessary for coming out of them.

> (Weil 1963, p. 29 my translation)

Force petrifies, she argues, differently but equally, the souls of all those who
are its victims and those who manipulate it (p. 32). Those who manipulate
it become drunk with it. We shall see how this connects with Plato's claim
that those into whose souls evil has entered no longer know what they are
doing and have lost all mastery over themselves. Those who wield force
walk in a medium which offers no resistance to their progress, since brute
force eliminates obstacles. They do not, therefore, feel the need to plan,
consider how to realize their intentions, to attend, give thought to and negotiate difficulties. They become, as we say, 'too big for their boots',
contemptuous of what stands in their way and careless. 'They ignore the
fact that their power is limited and finally they find that things no longer
obey them' (p. 21).

Thus the attraction of power, once one gives in to it, sets off an automatic
chain of reactions: drunkenness with power generates 'hubris', an arrogant
self-confidence, which regards all obstacles and difficulties with contempt.
That leads one to ignore the limits of one's power. Sooner or later one
exceeds these limits and is delivered to fate: one passes to the other side and
becomes the victim of force. The same fate awaits those into whose hands
force now passes and the cycle goes on indefinitely. Men are thus not the
initiators of the events depicted in the *Iliad*; they are the passive or inert
vehicles through which these events take place. They are the cogs in a mechanism of nature which, in tune with the early Greeks, Simone Weil calls
necessity. The battles, she says, are not decided by men who calculate, enter
into deals, take resolutions and execute them, but by men who have become
bereft of their faculties, transformed into the grade of inert matter, which is
nothing but passivity, and so by blind forces (p. 32).

The *Iliad*, she says, gives us a just representation of the empire of force
and, therefore, of the rule of necessity in human life. Men are its slaves.
She further believes that force occupies the centre stage in human affairs:
it is at the centre of all human history (p. 11). It forms part of what elsewhere she called 'moral gravity', a counterpart in the human world of
Newton's gravity which operates in the physical world (Weil 1948). She
compares the way it erases inner life with the way nature does, when vital
needs such as hunger come into play, say, with starvation. That too erases
all inner life, even the pain of a mother – the way Niobé, when she is tired
of tears, thinks of eating, or the way sleep overtakes those crying at the
death of their comrades.

But although necessity thus rules in the human world, the early Greeks had a conception of something with which they contrasted the determinism to which they gave prominence in their literature and philosophy with something else. Simone Weil calls it *grace*:

> The lightness of those who manipulate without respect and without taking any thought the men and things they have or think they have at their mercy, the despair which forces the soldier to destroy, the way the slave and the defeated are crushed, the massacres, all contribute to making a scene of undiluted horror. Force is its sole hero. The result would have been a gloomy monotony, had there not been, scattered here and there, some luminous moments, moments brief and divine in which men have a soul. The soul which thus awakes, for a moment, to be lost soon after because of the empire of force over the souls of men, is awakened pure and intact. In such moments there appears no ambiguous, complicated or troubled sentiment; only courage and love illuminate such sentiments. Sometimes a man thus finds his soul in self-deliberation, such as when Hector in front of Troy, without any help from God or man, tries on his own to stand and face his destiny. The other moments when men find their souls are those in which they love. Almost none of the pure forms of love between human beings is absent in the *Iliad* (p. 33).

'These moments of grace are rare in the *Iliad*,' she says, 'but they suffice to make us feel with extreme regret what violence destroys and will destroy' (p. 35). She then points out the 'accent of inconsolable bitterness which continually makes itself felt' in the poem, a 'bitterness which proceeds from tenderness, one which extends to all human beings equally like the clarity of the sun', one which, however, 'never lowers itself into complaint'.

> Justice and love, which can never have a place in this scene of extreme and unjust acts of violence, bathe them with their light, without ever becoming visible other than by the accent of the verse. Nothing precious, destined or not to destruction, is despised, the misery of all concerned is exposed without dissimulation or disdain, no man is put above or below the condition that is common to all men, everything that is destroyed is regretted. The victors and the vanquished are equally close to the author and the audience and made of the same clay as them (pp. 35–6).

She talks of this as the just expression of affliction (p. 40). For 'the cold brutality of the facts of war are not disguised by anything, since neither victors nor the vanquished are admired, but not despised or hated either'.

They are both represented as the victims of force; it is the gods who decide the changing fate of the combatants. They are like the particles of water that are one moment on the crest of a wave, the next moment at the trough. This is an image Simone Weil uses elsewhere. It is a just expression because it comes from the perspective of love and justice: 'the idea of justice illuminates it without ever intervening in what is depicted' (p. 38). She means that there is no suggestion of any compensation of the injustices depicted, no suggestion that there will be any time when the wrongs that are depicted will be righted or compensated. The poem offers no such consolation.

3 Homer's objectivity: love and detachment

Alexander Pope wrote that 'Nature and Homer were the same' (*Essays on Criticism*, p. 124). In an essay on *Anna Karenina* Lionel Trilling compares Pope on Homer and Matthew Arnold who said something similar about Tolstoy to the effect that *Anna Karenina* is not a work of art but a piece of life. He comments that the 'objectivity' which Arnold finds in Tolstoy's novel and Pope in Homer's poem is an illusion:

> Homer gives us, we are told, the object itself without interposing his personality between it and us. He gives us the person or thing or event without judging it, as Nature itself gives it to us. And to the extent that this is true of Homer, it is true of Tolstoy. But again we are dealing with a manner of speaking. Homer and Nature are of course not the same, and Tolstoy and Nature are not the same. Indeed, what is called the objectivity of Homer or of Tolstoy is not objectivity at all. Quite to the contrary it is the most lavish and prodigal subjectivity possible, for every object in the *Iliad* or in *Anna Karenina* exist in the medium of what we must call the author's love. But this love is so pervasive, it is so constant, and it is so equitable, that it creates the illusion of objectivity ... For Tolstoy everyone and everything has a saving grace. Like Homer, he scarcely permits us to choose between antagonists'
>
> (Trilling 1955, p. 68–9).

Others, such as Kierkegaard, have pointed out that in the kind of judgement that is in question here truth is subjectivity. In other words here we are in the sphere of the personal, and where the person making a judgement does not or cannot speak for himself he has nothing to say at all. But that does not mean that no distinction can be made between different judgements that belong to the personal. Thus Trilling contrasts Tolstoy's 'objectivity' with Flaubert's:

Flaubert's objectivity is charged with irritability and Tolstoy's with affection ... it is when a novelist really loves his characters that he can show them in their completeness and contradiction, in their failures as well as in their great moments, in their triviality as well as in their charm ... What we call Tolstoy's objectivity is simply the power of his love to suffer no abatement from the notice and account it takes of the fact that life usually falls below its ideal of itself (p. 69).

Simone Weil shows the same to be true of Homer. Here what is in question is not so much a case of life falling below its ideal of itself, as life in the raw, in its naked reality, undiluted by any comforting fiction and unsoftened by any consolation. But what makes that possible is the *personal* perspective of Homer's *impersonal* love – 'personal' in the way that Homer stands to it and 'impersonal' in that it makes no distinction between the strong and the weak, the victor and the vanquished, between Greeks and Trojans. As Simone Weil puts it: one can hardly tell that the poet is Greek and not a Trojan (p. 38).

Thus, Simone Weil argues, in the *Iliad* what is presented belongs to the mode and spirit of its presentation: it allows nothing to creep in that will disguise the truth about the empire of force over the human soul. What would disguise it are pride, humiliation, hatred, contempt, indifference, the desire to ignore or forget it. For all this anchors one to a point of view on things from their midst. To be able to see the reality about force in the way the *Iliad* does, one needs to ascend to a detached point of view, which is not indifference, not the detachment of an outsider, nor that of scientific objectivity. It is the detachment of a love which takes no sides in human affairs, without condoning evil, one that recognizes the helplessness and vulnerability of all human beings instead of blaming them. It sees those who perpetrate evil deeds, as Plato did, as acting in slavery to evil, and – to use Simone Weil's comparison – as 'tiles blown off a roof by the wind and falling at random' (Weil 1968, p. 177). It is thus, as we shall see Spinoza also emphasized, detached from all such reactive and retaliatory attitudes which pin one down to the world on which the author of the *Iliad* holds a magnifying glass in its presentation of the Trojan War. One cannot, however, achieve such a love or compassion and detachment, such justice in one's feelings and apprehension, 'unless one knows the empire of force (as Simone Weil puts it in her essay on the *Iliad*) and learns not to respect it' (p. 40).

Simone Weil speaks of such a perspective, 'the light of justice', as not belonging to the world depicted in the *Iliad*. She points out that in the scenes depicted in the poem love and justice appear only in rare moments of grace; they are more conspicuous by their absence. What is for the most part absent in what the poem contemplates, however, appears in the

17

manner in which it is contemplated. It appears in the tone of the poem, in the bitterness and regret in that tone – a bitterness at the way men are transformed by force and the pained love of everything that is lost in the process. Without *that* what is depicted in the poem could not have come to view at all; for it constitutes the perspective from which what is depicted comes to view.

Simone Weil, following Plato, characterizes what is depicted in the *Iliad* as what belongs to 'the social' in the affairs of men, the world of Plato's 'great beast'. What cannot be directly described without mislocating it and so diluting what is described, so that it no longer speaks the truth, lies outside that world. It lies 'outside' in the sense that it cannot be seen or found without detachment from the world of human affairs and so without taking a point of view from outside it – not an outsider's point of view, but that of someone who feels at one with the actions without, however, sharing their tunnel vision.

4 The world of human bondage and the possibility of freedom

In the world depicted by Homer thus it is *necessity that rules*, and this is not meant to be just the case in the kind of extreme situation depicted in the *Iliad*. Homer is certainly writing about the Trojan war. But the way human beings are transformed in that war makes us see the vulnerability of human beings and what they are vulnerable to. That is not confined to the war depicted but pervades the whole of human affairs and human relations. Thus elsewhere Simone Weil writes:

> The reality of this world is necessity. The part of man which is in this world is the part which is in bondage to necessity and subject to the misery of need.
>
> (Weil 1962, p. 221)

This is a form of determinism of which the early Greeks had a very strong sense and which we, in our obsession with scientific determinism, seem to have lost:

> The recognition of might [or force] as an absolutely sovereign thing in all of nature, including the natural part of the human soul, with all the thoughts and all the feelings the soul contains, and at the same time as an absolutely detestable thing; this is the innate grandeur of Greece. Today one sees many people who honour might above all, whether they give it that name or other names possessed of a more agreeable sound ... For to know, not abstractly but with the whole soul, that all in nature, including

18

psychological nature, is under the dominance of a force as brutal, as pitilessly directed downwards as gravity, such a knowledge glues, so to speak, the soul to prayer like a prisoner who, when he is able, remains glued to the window of his cell, or like a fly stays stuck to the bottom of a bottle by the force of its urge towards light.

(*Intimations of Christianity*, p. 116)

The light that Simone Weil speaks of is what would deliver the individual from such necessity to freedom – not to a freedom to do what he wants or as he pleases, but to freedom from the endless cycle of reaction and counter-reaction to which he is a slave.

I believe that it was largely the same determinism which Spinoza articulated in his *Ethics*. But the early Greeks believed, as Spinoza did, that such a determinism does not absolve men from responsibility for the way they live nor, as I said, does it exclude the possibility of freedom of choice. Men may be vulnerable to natural needs and, in extreme cases where they are deprived of all possibility of meeting those needs, all other considerations may lose their hold on them in their lives. There, except for the exceptional individual, we cannot speak of freedom of choice, since none is left. An individual who has grown dependent on some such natural need may be in a similar plight even when he is not deprived of the possibility of meeting it. But here the situation is very different since his dependency is an individual matter and he need not be dependent.

It is the same with power. In the kind of extreme situation portrayed by Homer, only the exceptional individual can renounce power and, if he survives, break the cycle in which he turns into a thing continually tossed up and down while his life lasts. But men are often caught up in the same cycle in their professional and personal lives and then are tossed up and down in a similar way. Without minimizing the difficulties in most such cases, it could still be said that the cycle can be broken.

Simone Weil says that 'the reality of this world is necessity' and I go along with her in that this is a thought we find among the great thinkers of early Greece. She continues: 'The part of man which is in this world is the part which is in bondage to necessity.' But she believes there is a part of man which is not in this world, not of this world, though it may be lost to the individual. She makes it quite clear that Homer was well aware of it and of its preciousness and fragility. She speaks of those rare moments of grace in the *Iliad* when it appears and of the way the poem mourns its destruction. As she puts it:

Everything which, in the interior of the soul and in human relations, which escapes the empire of force is loved, but loved with a pain, on account of the danger of destruction continually threatening it (p. 39).

19

She attributes this to 'the spirit of the only true epic which the West possesses'. It portrays the *necessity* which rules in '*this* world'; the world depicted in the *Iliad*, the world in which we live and cannot escape so long as we deny that there is a part of the soul whose life belongs to 'another world'. If we can find it and keep it alive we shall be free, while we continue to take part in the practices of the world, the social world. Even then we shall remain vulnerable to the needs on which that world threatens to make us dependent. We shall be free though in that our relation to it will have changed.

Our relation to it, however, is not one we can change *at will*. What being able to change it calls for is not the assertion of our will, but faith, trust, attention and patience. That involves, among other things, forgiving those who offend against us which sets us free from the need to retaliate. It involves gratitude for any good that comes out of doing so and humility before it: not 'I did it' but 'it was mercifully granted me'. It is precisely all that is contained in these three words 'I did it' which, Simone Weil holds, ties us into the cycle which the early Greeks spoke of as *necessity*. In the attitude which she contrasts with it and which, if we are lucky, would give us freedom in a world of necessity through our changed relation to it, such a change is attributed to *grace*. We have here a conception of the way that good comes about through an attitude of faith or trust and patience. Such an attitude is the antithesis of 'willing'. In it a person actively gives himself to what he has faith in and trusts, and in that trust he finds the confidence to wait unconditionally. This is the capacity for patience which takes the good it receives as a gift of grace.

2

SOPHOCLES' *OEDIPUS*
Fate, human destiny and individual responsibility

1 The meaning of fate and its way of working in Oedipus' life

The kind of necessity to which the actions of the heroes and combatants of the war of Troy are subject in the way we have seen also hangs over the whole of Oedipus' life. Indeed in Sophocles' play *King Oedipus*, the tragic hero's fate is sealed even before his birth. His parents who know it through Apollo's oracle try their best to escape it and so does Oedipus when he comes to know of it, but in vain. Indeed the play represents Oedipus pitting his individual strength against the fate announced for him by Apollo and only succeeding in precipitating it. The things he does to change that fate – patricide and incest – are the very actions that bring him nearer to the fulfilment of Apollo's prophecy. His very belief and confidence that he can circumvent the fate that the gods had in store for him is an expression of his character. Thus in the play Oedipus' fate works through his character.

What is thus significant is that, first, Apollo's oracle is a prophecy of disaster and so something that Oedipus would struggle to avoid, and secondly that it is fulfilled through Oedipus' efforts to avoid it and so through his own actions – actions that bear the imprint of his character and personality. Without these two conditions there would be nothing dramatic about Sophocles' play and, indeed, no tragedy. But the philosophical interest for us is that the fate prophesied for Oedipus is realized through his own actions so that he bears an individual responsibility for it.

All that Apollo's oracle says is that *he will end up* by killing his father and marrying his mother. Nothing is said about what he will do to end up there. If his actions were determined in any detail, his fate would by-pass his individual responsibility and Oedipus would turn into some sort of puppet instead of the tragic figure fit for Sophocles' play.

But this still leaves open the question of how 'what will be' can be immutably fixed in advance so that nothing can intervene to change it? Surely such an impossibility is ruled out by our whole conception of a future time: the future can only be *predicted* and no amount of truth about

21

the present can ever entail a prediction. Even the *inevitability* of death presupposes truths which are contingent. If we become immortal perhaps our lives would so change that we could not longer think of ourselves and of our identities in the way we do. In that sense the words 'we are mortal' express a logical or conceptual truth, but only on the understanding that all the unspoken background truths which our conception of human life takes for granted remain unchanged.

This said, I am not suggesting that the notion of fate is incoherent. I am only suggesting that one which presupposes the future to be closed in a way that goes against our very notion of time is inevitably incoherent. But there are conceptions of the way the future may be closed – closed not absolutely but relatively or conditionally – which do not clash with our notion of time. Here we talk of 'fatalities'. For instance, prior to the discovery of penicillin tuberculosis was, in most cases, an incurable and so fatal disease. To a person who contracted tuberculosis in those days the future was pretty nearly closed.

'Fate', in the sense relevant to Sophocles' play, has a more specific and poignant meaning which, likewise, presupposes the foreclosure of the future in a *relative* sense. It symbolizes the sum total of things in a human life which the individual can make no sense of in terms of who he is and what he deserves. In Oedipus' case what awaited him was fixed before his birth – in some ways similar to the way a congenital weakness or disability is fixed by the genes we inherit from our parents. What was thus fixed before Oedipus' birth could not have had anything to do with what made him who he is – at least until he became cognizant of it. It could not have been what he deserved. It did not determine his character; rather it provided the opportunity for its acute expression and solidification, once he came to know of it.

What was fixed for Oedipus before his birth was what he had to face, not the way he had to face it – that is his character. His fate, therefore, was something unalterable only in the relative sense. Its unalterability depended on his character – one which involved an arrogant ignorance of itself: a form of self-deception. The particular form of character in question guaranteed, in the relative sense, its own continuance and thus ensured that he would face what was fixed before Oedipus' birth in a way that would lead to disaster. It is thus that Apollo's prophecy for Oedipus was fulfilled.

In setting out to avoid the fate that was prophesied for him Oedipus was saying: 'I do not recognize that I have a fate beyond what I myself make of my life for myself'. It is *this* that Sophocles' play shows to be an arrogant illusion and self-deception with inevitably disastrous consequences.

There are two distinct inevitabilities here, different in character from one another: one independent of Oedipus' character and personality and the other relative to it. They continue to constitute or determine Oedipus' fate. Sophocles is telling us that Oedipus, like any other human being, has to face that there are things in life which go to make up his particular fate, things that are there for no reason that has anything to do with him and which, moreover, are beyond his powers to change. He is *also* telling us that Oedipus' attitude towards them, having its source in his particular character, puts him on course for certain disaster. His character determines this course for him and while he remains on that course certain consequences are inevitable sooner or later. They are inevitable relative to his character which keeps him on that course; but there is no absolute inevitability about his retaining that character.

2 Oedipus' lack of self-knowledge and the way it seals his fate

The play depicts Oedipus as lacking self-knowledge: he does not know who he is and he does not see where he is going. He thinks he is Polybus' son, born in Corinth. So when he comes to hear the oracle he leaves Corinth to avoid killing Polybus, whom he believes to be his father, and marrying Queen Meropé, wife of Polybus, whom he believes to be his mother. His journey takes him to Thebes where his real parents are. On the way he meets Laius, his real father, in a carriage, who orders him out of the way 'with a surly command'.

> It was the driver that thrust me aside, and him I struck,
> For I was angry. The old man saw it, leaning from his carriage,
> Waited until I passed, then, seizing for weapon
> The driver's two-pronged goad, struck me on the head.
> He paid with interest for his temerity;
> Quick as lightning, the staff in his right hand
> Did its work; he tumbled headlong out of the carriage,
> And every man of them there I killed.

This is a terrible interaction between a haughty father and an arrogant and impetuous son. And here we have an instance of fate working through the participants' characters. He feels no remorse for killing the old man, thinking that he had asked for what he got. This is part of his arrogant disregard for those who dare to cross him – as long, however, as they are strangers to him:

> But now,
> If the blood of Laius ran in this stranger's veins,
> Is there any more wretched mortal than I, more hated
> By God and man?

It is with the same arrogant boldness that he answers the Sphinx's riddle, destroying her power over Thebes and becoming its King and in the process marrying the Queen, widow of Laius, not knowing that she is his real mother. It is thus that in his ignorance of his origins Oedipus *himself* fulfils the prophecy of Apollo's oracle and makes his fate his personal destiny.

His ignorance of his origins is certainly an important part of his lack of self-knowledge. The reason for this ignorance is that his parents, in order to spare him and themselves the fate prophesied by the oracle, abandoned him to die. But as a result of a chain of circumstances he escaped death and was brought up by the King and Queen of Corinth. That is how he came to believe, falsely, Polybus and Meropé, King and Queen of Corinth, to be his parents. Another part of his lack of self-knowledge is his arrogant over-confidence in himself, which the Greeks named 'hubris'. He thinks that he can take on the gods or, which comes to the same thing, that there is nothing beyond his control, which is a form of self-deception. When he finds out that this is an illusion, late in the day, he will learn humility.

I distinguished earlier between two kinds of inevitability at work in Oedipus' life: chance contingencies which place a limitation on his will and, secondly, his character. It is the two together that work to determine his fate. The contingencies that limit his will do not limit his freedom. A person, for instance, who suffers from a disability may not be able to do certain things which others do and which he may find attractive and so wish he could do. If, unrealistically, he keeps on trying to do them and fails he will hurt himself. A certain kind of person will find it hard to accept his lot, will resent it, and look for a scapegoat on which to put the blame. He will thus remain fixed facing in a particular direction. Someone who accepts his lot, on the other hand, may say, 'it is no good hitting my head against a brick wall'. He may learn to want different things, things within his reach, and thus making the best of his disability, may live a life in which he has as much freedom of choice as someone who does not have his disability.

I said that the man who keeps on trying to do what is outside his ability, ignoring the limitation it places on him, will hurt himself. It is what makes him ignore his limitations that turns his lot into a fate that pursues him all his life. His fate is not sealed without his collusion. Oedipus thinks he is more clever than Apollo and thinks he can outwit the god – as he outwits the Sphinx. But through chance contingencies and Oedipus' response to them Apollo outwits him. Indeed, his outwitting of the Sphinx is part of Apollo's outwitting of Oedipus. For it is that which makes it possible for him to be King and so marry the Queen who, unknown to him, is his own mother.

The play is the story of the way Oedipus himself comes to fulfil the prophecy of the oracle. It portrays the way it comes to be fulfilled through the interplay of chance, Oedipus' knowledge of the prophecy, the horror it inspires, his ignorance of his origins and his pride. It is also the story of the way he comes to self-knowledge. In fact the two stories are intertwined, for it is what leads him to disaster that at the same time leads him to self-knowledge. The action of the play is Oedipus' coming to self-knowledge and it is in the course of that that we find out how the oracle's prophecy came to be fulfilled.

When the play begins the prophecy has already come true, only Oedipus does not know that it has. He is happy, has his citizens' respect and gratitude, and feels safe and secure. But that happiness and feeling of security is precarious because it is based on ignorance and illusion. As the plays' final words coming from the Chorus put it:

> Then learn that mortal man must always look to his ending,
> And none can be called happy until that day when he carries
> His happiness down to the grave in peace.

What sets Oedipus on the way to the fulfilment of the oracle's prophecy is his hearing of the prophecy. What sets him in pursuit of self-knowledge is what he hears from the blind soothsayer Teiresias when he has him fetched, on Creon's advice, to find out who is the murderer of Laius – unknown to Oedipus, his real father. His death is still unpaid for, unavenged, and constitutes a pollution which is the source of the pestilence gripping the city. Unaware of the fact that he is Laius' murderer he commits himself to finding out who he is and punishing him:

> And it is my solemn prayer
> That the unknown murderer, and his accomplices,
> If such there be, may wear the brand of shame
> For their shameful act, unfriended, to their life's end.
> Nor do I exempt myself from the imprecation;
> .....
> Now that I hold the place that he [Laius] once held –
> His bed, his wife – whose children, had fate so willed,
> Would have grown to be another bond of blood between us –
> And upon him, alas, has this disaster fallen;
> I mean to fight for him now, as I would fight
> For my own father, and leave no way untried
> To bring to light the killer of Laius.

But not only is he unaware of being Laius' murderer, he seems to have forgotten that he has blood on his hands, that he too is a murderer. The words with which he commits himself to look for, find and punish Laius' murderer are prophetic:

> 'Nor do I exempt myself from the imprecation:

> If, with my knowledge, house or hearth of mine
> Receive the guilty man, upon my head
> Lie all the curses I have laid on others.

And

> Now that I hold the place that he once held
> .....
> I mean to fight for him now, as ...
> For my own father, and leave no way untried
> To bring to light the killer of Laius.

He throws himself into doing so with the same zeal as he did into solving the Sphinx's puzzle. What he throws himself into turns out to be his quest for self-knowledge, for the man killed is, as he will find out, his father, and the murderer sought is himself.

He throws himself into it blindly despite Teiresias' warning: 'To be wise is to suffer', 'I mean to spare you, and myself ... I will tell you nothing.' He battles with Teiresias to extract the truth, expressed in cryptic words: 'put your own house in order', '*You* are the cursed polluter of this land', 'you are living in sinful union with the one you love', 'your enemy is your-self', 'this day brings you your birth; and brings you death', 'were you not famed for solving riddles? ... Your great misfortune, and your ruin', 'the killer of Laius – that man is *here*; passing for an alien ... a Theban born' and he cites the oracle.

Teiresias' parting words are: 'Go in and think on this. When you can prove me wrong, then call me blind.' The Chorus is clearly ruffled.

> Who is the man?
> Let him fly with the speed of horses racing the world.
> .....
> And the fates sure-footed close round him.
> .....
> Terrible things indeed has the prophet spoken
> We cannot believe, we cannot deny; all's dark.

But the prophet's words fall on deaf ears with Oedipus. Instead of taking heed he accuses Creon: 'Proved plotter against my life, thief of my crown? ... Was it you that made me bring that canting prophet here?' Yet though Oedipus' ears are deaf, he reacts to what is said and rationalizes his reaction: 'When a quick plotter's on the move ... It's safest to be quick in counter-plotting.' He has no proof for his suppositions, they are in reality an excuse for evading 'thinking on' Teiresias' words. Yet he heeds the Chorus: 'is it right to cast away a friend, condemned unheard upon an idle word?' He lets Creon go, even though, he says, it may mean his death or exile in disgrace:

> Your voice, not his,
> Has won my mercy; him I hate for ever.

Creon comments:

> In mercy obdurate, as harsh in anger –
> Such natures earn self-torture.

From then on every stone Oedipus turns in hope turns out, bit by bit, to substantiate Teiresias' words. With each evasion Oedipus falls into the lap of truth – the truth about himself. From each word spoken to reassure Oedipus there emerges something to trouble him, each piece of good news turns out to herald what Oedipus feared.

When Oedipus says that Creon 'shields himself by using a rascally soothsayer as his tool', Jocasta, the Queen and his wife, says:

> Then absolve yourself at once. For I can tell you,
> No man possesses the secret of divination.
> And I have proof ....

She tells Oedipus that it is common knowledge that Laius was killed by robbers. But the place where she says he was killed turns out to be the very same one where Oedipus killed the old man. She tells him that their child was cast off, barely three days old, to perish on the empty mountain-side. He had, she says, riveted ankles. The messenger he sends for later will tell him: 'The infirmity in your ankles tells the tale ... To it you owe your present name.'

On hearing where Laius was killed Oedipus' anxiety rises: 'O God, what wilt thou do to me!' He enquires about Laius' appearance and age, and on finding out, he exclaims: 'Oh, wretch! Am I unwittingly self-cursed?' Then he finds out that one of Laius' servants accompanying him has survived. Oedipus asks to have him brought without delay. He hopes his suspicions will be proved false, but by now his desire to find out the truth about his origins has gathered strength. Jocasta is clearly alarmed: 'Why? What help do you expect from him [the surviving witness to the murder, a shepherd]?' Oedipus: 'You said he spoke of *robbers* ... If he still says *robbers*, it was not I ... But if he speaks of one lone wayfarer, there is no escape; the finger points to me.' Jocasta replies that that was what the shepherd said, that he cannot go back on it now since the whole town heard it.

> he cannot in any event
> Pretend that Laius died as was foretold.
> For Loxias said a child of mine should kill him.
> It was not to be; poor child, it was he that died.
> A fig for divination!

Oedipus is half-reassured: 'You are right. Still, let us have the shepherd here.'

A little later a messenger arrives with what he calls 'good news': 'You cannot but be glad at the message – though you may also be distressed.' He tells Jocasta that King Polybus, whom Oedipus believes to be his father, is dead. When Oedipus enters, Jocasta, keen to reassure Oedipus, for she is more afraid for Oedipus than for herself, and nearer than him to recognizing the truth, tells him:

> Hear this man's news, and when you have heard it, say
> What has become of the famous oracles.

Oedipus is relieved: 'the letter of the oracle is unfulfilled and lies, like Polybus, dead'. But 'there is the other still to fear ... my mother ... while *she* lives, I am not safe'. Jocasta again tries to reassure him and herself: 'Chance rules our lives, and the future is all unknown. Best live as best we may, from day to day.' Indeed, except that what was in the future, unknown to them, is now in the past. The messenger asks him why he should fear that his mother might be alive. Oedipus then tells him of the oracle, whereupon the messenger, in the hope of allaying his fears, tells him that Polybus is no kin of his, not his father. Oedipus asks him to explain how he can be sure of this. He tells Oedipus that he was given to him by another shepherd, one of Laius' men, with his ankles rivetted.

Alarmed, Oedipus wants to have this man found. Jocasta by now is white with terror: 'Forget what he has told you ... It makes no difference.' But Oedipus is by now on a collision course with the truth: 'I must pursue this trail to the end, till I have unravelled the mystery of my birth.' Jocasta: 'No! In God's name – if you want to live, this quest must not go on. Have I not suffered enough?' Oedipus, bent on following the trail, is at the same time oblivious of where it is leading him and blind to the fact that the truth has already dawned on Jocasta. He is no longer in touch with her feelings:

> There is nothing to fear. Though I be proved slave-born
> To the third generation, *your* honour is not impinged.

The possibility of his finding out that he is slave-born is, of course, much less threatening than the possibility of finding out that he has committed patricide and incest. That is why his thoughts clutch at it.

Jocasta: Yet do not do it. I implore you, do not do it.
Oedipus: I must. I cannot leave the truth unknown.
Jocasta: I know I am right. I am warning you for your good.

He ignores her warning as he had earlier ignored Teiresias' warnings.

Jocasta: O lost and damned!
This is my last and only word to you
For ever!

By now Oedipus is intent on unlocking the secret of his birth come what may:

Let all come out,
However vile!
….. I am the child of Fortune,
The giver of Good, and I shall not be shamed.
…..
Born thus, I ask to be no other man
Than that I am, and *will know who I am*.

He thus goes to meet even his own disaster with 'hubris'.
    The messenger comes with Laius' shepherd. The shepherd, at first reluc-
tant, finally admits to having given Laius' baby boy to the messenger. It
was Jocasta who had given the baby to him, to be destroyed: 'They said
'twas on account of some wicked spell.' All dawns on Oedipus finally:

Alas! All out! All known, no more concealment!
O Light! May I never look on you again,
Revealed as I am, sinful in my begetting,
Sinful in marriage, sinful in shedding of blood!

It is thus that Oedipus drags himself to self-knowledge kicking and
screaming: to the knowledge of his origins, and thus of who he is, and of
his own wretchedness and sinfulness.

3 Freud's Oedipus complex and the play

In his *Introductory Lectures on Psycho-Analysis* Freud likens the way
Oedipus comes to such self-knowledge to the way an analysand comes to
self-knowledge in psycho-analysis. The analysand *resists* what psycho-
analytic interpretations point out to him. Yet they also touch and uncover
in him the desire to drop evasion and subterfuge, come out into the open,
and risk being rejected, so as to be himself: rather be himself and rejected
than be accepted on false pretences.

> The Attic poet's work portrays the gradual discovery of the deed
> of Oedipus, long since accomplished, and brings it slowly to light
> by skilfully prolonged enquiry, constantly fed by new evidence; it
> has thus a certain resemblance to the course of a psycho-analysis.
>
> (Freud 1949a, p.278)

I agree with Freud on this resemblance. That which constitutes this resemblance is used by Sophocles with maximum dramatic effect.

Freud also claims that the deed accomplished by Oedipus without knowledge is unconsciously sought and wished for by him. In all those who do not accomplish it, it remains in the form of an unconscious wish which, if made conscious, would inspire horror. He calls it the Oedipus complex. I am not now interested in the latter part of this claim (see Dilman 1983, Chapter 2). As for the first part, there is little evidence for it in the play. The only evidence is a few words by Jocasta:

> Nor need this mother-marrying frighten you;
> Many a man has dreamt as much. Such things
> Must be forgotten, if life is to be endured.

The best that can be said is that Sophocles, the author of the play, knew that 'many a man has dreamt as much', i.e. that he knew of the existence of what Freud called 'the Oedipus complex'.

What role does it play in the play? Obviously Sophocles thinks of its realization as a morally horrible thing. I think that this is used in the play as an *instance* of moral pollution which the play's hero Oedipus falls into because of the way he is – because in his arrogant confidence he ignores the tricks that chance accidents play on him, because he lacks humility and thinks he is above such things. What drives him to disaster is a combination of circumstances and the way he reacts to them and to the ensuing consequences – being the way he is. He kills his father in anger and is sexually attracted to his mother and marries her; but in genuine ignorance. There is no question of these feelings coming from Oedipus' unconscious memory and finding their original objects. For he was barely three days old when he was cast off by his parents. He had not had any relationship with them. Someone may argue that his adopted parents were the object of the wishes and feelings which constitute what Freud called 'the Oedipus complex', that he was unaware of them and that it was the fear of these that drove him away from his adopted parents, and that at a safe distance from them he could express them safely. He may say that it was this that led to Oedipus' disaster. But this is speculation and there is no evidence for it in the play.

What Oedipus cannot face in the play and tries to evade, in the way I have pointed out, is knowledge of *what he has done*, namely that *he* is the

30

person who has killed his father, married his mother and had children by her – unknowingly. It is *that* that he finds horrible – i.e. that he should have *done* so. The fact that he did not know it at the time does not change that, namely that this is something *he* did. In having done so he has become morally unclean. Whether he wanted to do what he did and whether he knew what he was doing is immaterial to the fact that he *did* it and to what he has *become* as a result. I said that he did it unknowingly and I meant 'in ignorance' and not 'unconsciously'. There is nothing in the play to suggest that he knew who his real parents were or that he was looking for them. He only tries to find this out after the event, when Teiresias has spoken.

4 Oedipus' lack of freedom and his downfall

In fact what is characteristic of Oedipus is how much his actions are *reactions* – reactions to the oracle, reactions to what he finds provocative, reactions to Teiresias – and how *blind* he is in his reactions – in his reactions to the stranger from whose mouth he learns of Apollo's oracle, to Laius, to Teiresias, to Creon. His actions and the direction of his life are thus being decided by circumstances and chance encounters which he does not have the patience and humility to fathom, and by words, deeds and gestures the real meanings of which he misinterprets – misinterprets because of the threat they pose of bringing him nearer to a recognition of what he is set to avoid facing. In his haughtiness he is out of touch with Apollo's deviousness for which he is no match, with Teiresias' detached concern, with Creon's uprightness – notwithstanding the character he is revealed to have in *Antigone*, a later play. It is in this that Oedipus *lacks freedom*, though not responsibility. What makes for his lack of freedom is what constitutes his lack of wisdom: he does not meet the necessities of life with humility.

I said that the fate assigned to Oedipus by Apollo symbolizes those things in his life which set limits to it independently of who he is. The oracle or prophecy in which they are expressed is a gauntlet Apollo throws down to Oedipus. It is in his *reaction* to the prophecy that the fate ascribed to Oedipus is realized and becomes *his*:

> Apollo, friends, Apollo
> Has laid this agony upon me,
> Not by his hand, I did it.

The prophecy and Oedipus' hearing of it is essential to the tragedy and essential too to what Sophocles says in the play, to the wisdom the play imparts.

I said that nothing in the future can be delivered in advance. Apollo's oracle proposes a future for Oedipus which Oedipus disposes. As the

French saying goes: 'Dieu propose, l'homme dispose.' With nothing proposed there is nothing to dispose. But is Oedipus forced to do so? He is forced only because he is blind, lacks the wisdom that is to be found in humility. That is what the play shows and that is what Apollo counts on and, indeed, uses. Does Oedipus have to be blind for the play's purposes: Yes. But outside that, a person who lacks wisdom *can* learn from life, he *can* change in himself. This *cannot* be ruled out *a priori*. The play is a tragedy and Oedipus is a tragic figure; thus what he learns he learns *after* the prophesied fall and in sorrow.

Blindness, lack of light, is lack of knowledge or wisdom. This is partly ignorance in Oedipus' case and partly self-deception: lack of humility or, which comes to the same thing, not recognizing the vulnerability of human life to chance, that is to what lies outside the individual's control and prediction. Oedipus believed that he had earned what he had and so deserved and could keep it. This too is part of his lack of humility and it separated him from other mortals in that he thought he was above them: 'Apollo cannot have his way with *me*. What I have is *mine*, I have earned it; Apollo cannot take it away from me – I know how to keep it.' When 'all is out and all is known', as Oedipus puts it, the Chorus articulates what Oedipus comes to see:

> All the generations of moral man add up to nothing!
> Show me the man whose happiness was anything more than illusion
> Followed by disillusion
> Here is the instance, here is Oedipus, here is the reason
> Why I will call no mortal creature happy.

And after describing Oedipus' greatness and pride, the Chorus goes on:

> Time sees all; and now he has found you, when you least
> expected it;
> Has found you and judged that marriage-mockery, bride-groom-son!
> This is your elegy:
> I wish I had never seen you, offspring of Laius,
> Yesterday my morning of light, now my night of
> endless darkness!

Oedipus had everything, yet it turned into nothing because it was based on a lie and was morally unclean: it had been obtained by patricide, a crime which remained unpunished, and its continuation sustained by incest. We must, therefore, add *this* moral blindness to Oedipus' self-deception: he did not know who he was not only in the sense that he did not know who his parents were, but also in the sense that he did not know that the man he killed was his father and the woman he married and had children with was his mother. Thus his ignorance about his origins was indissolubly bound up with his moral deception. The removal of one, therefore, inevitably brought with it the suffering which is an expression of the knowledge of the other – his knowledge of the moral uncleanliness of his own actions. He could not have had that without suffering.

When earlier he tells Jocasta, on her request, how he killed the old man in a carriage in a place where three roads join, he says:

> If the blood of Laius ran in this stranger's veins,
> Is there any more wretched mortal than I …?

He means wretched *now*, whether he knows it or not, and regardless of the consequences – regardless of what the future brings. Since *we* know that the blood of Laius did run in that stranger's veins we know that Oedipus is wretched now and that he does not know that he is. Here Sophocles is using the word 'wretched' very much in the way that Socrates uses the word in connection with Archelaus in the *Gorgias*. That is, like Archelaus, Oedipus is blind to his own wretchedness, though for different reasons. Not only is Oedipus a very different kind of man from Archelaus – he is a tragic hero – but his moral blindness rests on factual ignorance. This is, of course, part of his tragedy.

The play, as we have seen, shows that while he is morally blind, blind to his own moral uncleanliness, his happiness is an illusion – since in reality he is wretched. It also shows that no man is free, *ie* knows what he is doing and acts on his own behalf, who lacks wisdom, *ie* who does not recognize the humbling truth that his life, like the life of any other human being, is subject to necessities that encroach on it for no reason, that is by chance.

It is the second point which is relevant to what concerns us now: ignore or fight these necessities and you are a slave; accept them, learn to live within their limits, and you are free.

5 Conclusion: was Sophocles a determinist?

In many of his tragedies Sophocles represents the individual's destiny as fixed or determined in advance and human affairs as subject to inexorable laws. Yet though the laws are inexorable freedom is possible within their framework – indeed possible *only* within their framework. This is what counts as wisdom for Sophocles. The man who does not recognize them or who takes them lightly comes to grief. He cannot escape the consequences of ignoring or disregarding them. In that respect he is not free: he is not free to do what he likes and go on from there as he would like to do.

Oedipus' fate is sealed in his lack of wisdom, in the kind of 'self-confidence' that made him blind to his dependence on what lies outside his

control. His fate is a necessity only because he colludes with it unknowingly. Paradoxically he cannot escape the fate the gods have predicted for
him because he thinks he can escape it. His fate thus is the outcome of the
interaction between his character and inexorable laws which for Sophocles
characterize human life.

Sophocles is not a determinist in a modern sense. But should we want to
call him that, then he is one in the sense that his thinking flows along the
following pattern: *if* you go on in such-and-such a way *then* such-and-such
consequences are inescapable for you. He further believes that many
people are set to go in such-and-such ways and so are in a collision course
with the very things they wish to avoid. They cannot avoid them because
they are not prepared to change their course and deceive themselves about
its direction. They do not understand the nature of their obstinacy.

If this is a form of determinism, it does not contain a denial of the
possibility of freedom. I expressed it in the conditional: '*if* you go on in
such-and-such a way ...' This does not imply, 'you *have* to go on in that way'.
But in order not to have to go on in that way, you have to be different in
yourself. There is no denial in Sophocles that you *can* be different. But the
lesson you have to learn may demand a great deal from you. What we
learn from Sophocles is that where pride is great, confidence is blind, and
'rationalism' is deep-rooted, the lesson may only be learned too late – after
the fall and in disaster.

3

PLATO AND MORAL
DETERMINISM

1 Good, evil and self-mastery – the *Phaedrus*

So far we have seen the way early Greek literature – the *Iliad* and *Oedipus Rex* – emphasizes the subjection of human life to what were perceived as forms of necessity to which human beings are vulnerable because of their 'unthinking' responses. How does Plato fit into this picture and what does he have to say about it? His view is that if one lacks moral knowledge or wisdom one will be inevitably subject to evil; and evil then, in the form of the ruthless exercise of power, insatiable greed, malice, envy, an obsession for revenge for some harm suffered, etc., becomes a form of necessity. Such a man, he argues, does not act with intent, and voluntarily, and so is a slave to the form of evil which has taken hold of his soul. When someone is at one with the good, in the moral necessity that informs his actions such a person is free: his actions come from him and he does what he wills. In contrast, when he is at one with evil or, at any rate, makes concessions to it he is in bondage: his actions do not come from him, for his will does not belong to him, it belongs to the evil that is in him.

This is a claim which clearly fits what I have shown both Homer and Sophocles to illustrate in the two works I have considered. I have deliberately put it bluntly to make it easier to see the difficulties it embodies as a general claim. I hope that my attempts to elucidate it will lessen some of these difficulties and will make the truth it contains accessible. In them, I will cover ground that I have covered in my books on the *Gorgias* and the *Phaedo*, but I will rethink the questions I discussed there and so cover that ground anew.

The moral knowledge which Plato has in mind and which I have equated with the wisdom which the combatants of the War of Troy lack, as depicted in the *Iliad*, is a love of the good. What is in question is not intellectual knowledge but an affective orientation which takes the form of a love and respect for others. Such a love, concern or respect involves feeling for them in their pain and grief, being prepared to put oneself out to help them where one can, respecting their differences, forgiving their

35

offences. Plato said that the kind of knowledge he was speaking of is identical with virtue; in other words it is a mode of *being*. The person who comes to such knowledge not only sees things differently, but in the perspective to which he comes he changes in himself. In the new significance which things acquire for him they elicit new affective responses in him. It is in the consistency of those responses that his life changes. In that life he is reborn.

In the *Phaedrus* Plato likens the soul to a chariot being pulled by two horses, one black and one white, with the charioteer in control or not as the case may be. The black horse represents appetite, the white horse stands for love, while the charioteer is meant to represent reason. The horses are what moves the soul while the charioteer tries to guide the horses in the light of what vision he has of reality or the good (see pp. 52–3).

It is clear that the white horse stands for what we call 'goodness' and the black one 'evil':

> One of the horses, we say, is good and one not ... The horse that is harnessed on the senior side is upright and clean-limbed; he holds his neck high and has a somewhat hooked nose; his colour is white, with black eyes; his thirst for honour is tempered by restraint and modesty; he is a friend to genuine renown and needs no whip, but is driven by the word of command. The other horse is crooked, lumbering, ill-made, stiff-necked, short-throated, snub-nosed; his coat is black and his eyes a blood-shot grey; wantonness and boastfulness are his companions, and he is hairy-eared and deaf, hardly controllable even with a whip and goad.
>
> (Plato 1973c, pp. 61–2)

Socrates, Plato's mouthpiece in the dialogue, describes the white horse in words that clearly depict restraint, consideration and obedience, a characteristic of pure love and generosity, and the black horse in words which sum up ego-centricity, a characteristic of greed, lust and appetite.

It is clear that Plato is concerned with questions about the individual's relation to good and evil, the difference which his moral knowledge, knowledge of good and evil, makes to this relation and to his contact with situations in which he acts and lives, and to his capacity to consider the consequences of his actions for others, for himself and for the future – in other words to the extent of his self-mastery. Clearly by goodness he means something he finds inherent in love which is directed outwards, namely respect and concern for others; and by evil he means putting oneself first, thinking only of one's pleasure and gratification – the gratification of one's sensuality and of the ego.

He thinks that a person's nearness or distance to the good admits of degrees and is a matter, at one and the same time, of vision and affective orientation. The nearer he is to goodness the greater his inner unity – the unity in what he wants, the direction in which he moves and the way he lives. The nearer he is to goodness the deeper his contact with others, the greater his recognition of their existence in its own right. The opposite or antithesis of this is a life of impulse or of expediency, a life in which the direction of a person's actions is contingent on changing circumstances. It is an ego-centric life in which the person's gratification and his interests are paramount. It is clear that Plato thinks of evil as ego-centric and as unruly – as abiding by no rule and refusing to accept restraint. For evil the world is there to be plundered; it does not contain anything for which the person may feel affection, sympathy, respect and even awe. Nothing is valued in it except with reference to the self or ego.

One could put what Plato says here as follows. There are two currents in human life which pull the individual in opposite directions, and both stem from what lies in the individual. One of these belongs to love. The desire for the loved one's welfare, the pain felt at any injury to it, blaming oneself when one is responsible for it, preparedness to forgive the hurt caused by others, trust and gratitude, the capacity to co-operate. These are all part of a person's love, friendliness and good feelings and characterize one of these two currents. Thus this current of human life is giving, creative, healing. One can contrast, for instance, the forgiveness which brings together two people who have fallen apart and which frees them to move on in their relationship, with the vindictiveness which freezes all such movement, locks the direction which the injured person faces, fixing his attention on his wounds – real or imaginary. This other current belongs to all ego-centric feelings: greed, envy, hatred, malice, lust for power and other forms of lust. It is thus taking, exploitative and destructive.

A person can thus grow to become good or evil depending on which current gains ascendency in his life. In the one case he has to work through his bad feelings – his hate, resentment, envy and greed. By working through I mean such things as forgiving those one blames for offences, real or imaginary, grieving one's own badness, making reparations and restitutions. It is one's good feelings, one's capacity for love, that enables one to do so, and it involves one actively. As Simone Weil puts it for Plato: 'on ne tombe pas dans le bien' (one does not fall into the good). Whereas moving in the other direction is a form of yielding or indulgence; for ego-centricity is something one indulges in. Love on the other hand involves the practice of generosity and such practice takes thought, consideration, discipline and self-criticism. It is in the reflexivity of such activity that Plato's charioteer comes in.

In the ideal case of the gods, Plato tells us, 'all the horses and charioteers of the gods are good and come of good stock', the charioteer is 'winged' and 'his team act together' (p. 50). When thus 'winged' the soul 'moves on high' and does not 'encounter solid matter'. The wings keep the soul in 'the region above, where the gods dwell' (p. 51). That is, as described in the *Phaedo*, the soul exists in a pure state, that is separate from and uncontaminated with the body, so that it has knowledge of the good. Its being in that state and its moving in the region where the gods dwell is one and the same thing: virtue and knowledge are one. That region is 'the abode of the reality with which true knowledge is concerned' (p. 52). Plato's description of it as 'a reality without a colour or shape, intangible but utterly real' makes it clear that it is the 'world of forms' which he is talking about. Here, he says, it is the 'intellect', that is the apprehension of the forms, 'which is the pilot of the soul' (p. 52). Indeed, the soul grows wings, Plato tells us, when it is nourished on 'beauty, wisdom and goodness'. 'Ugliness and evil cause the wings to waste and perish' (p. 51).

Those who live in the region where the gods dwell, that is who are at one with the good, 'each pursue their allotted task', that is live in harmony and perfect co-operation 'since jealousy has no place in the company of the divine' (p. 52). Jealousy is an ego-centric emotion; it thrives in an ego-centric orientation and reinforces that orientation. That is what the soul becomes when it loses its wings and falls to the sphere of 'solid matter' and partakes of 'the body'. In contrast, in the course of its journey upwards 'it beholds absolute justice and discipline and knowledge' (p. 53) and loses the orientation in which jealousy, greed, vanity, the thirst for power, sexual lust, and the desire for revenge for wrongs received thrive.

This is an idealized state – 'such is the life of the gods' Plato says (p. 53) – and even if it cannot be reached by the immortal soul in 'this life', that is in a life where it is 'associated with the body', the soul can journey towards it and in the process be transformed so as to come nearer to such an ideal state. Presumably this transformation involves the growth of wings, that is the capacity of lifting itself from the sphere of 'the body', of 'solid matter' – the sphere of *natural necessity*. It involves the transformation of appetites – the disappearance of gluttony and its ceding its place to normal, healthy hunger, the transformation of sexual lust to love, of greed into a proper self-regard – a self-regard that is divested of all ego-centricity. When such a transformation takes place the charioteer no longer needs to use a whip on the black horse or tug the reins so violently that he brings both horses down upon their haunches' (p. 62). As Plato puts it, lust for the beloved gives way to reverence (p. 63). Thus, as he says, 'by subduing the part of the soul that contained the seeds of vice and setting free that in which virtue had its birth, they [the people who do so by being guided 'into a way of life which is strictly devoted to the pursuit of wisdom'] will become *masters of themselves* and their souls will be at peace' (p. 65 italics mine).

The self-mastery which Plato has in mind is not achieved by subjugating unruly elements of the soul to control (what is involved in Freudian

repression) but in their transformation. In the course of such transformation conflicts within the soul – represented by means of the two horses
pulling in opposite or, at any rate, different directions – will be resolved,
the charioteer's team will act together – that is the person will come
together and act as one: his soul 'will be at peace'. It is in such self-mastery
that the person will have achieved *autonomy*: what he does will be what
he wants to do, not what he is forced to do, and he will be wholly behind
it. This is Plato's description of how, inevitably living in a world of natural
necessity, a man can be nevertheless free.

2 Freedom and self-mastery – the *Gorgias*

Such freedom comes from goodness, calls for wisdom, and requires moral
discipline. This is part of what Socrates argues in the *Gorgias* too in his
discussion with Callicles. Callicles holds that freedom is the throwing away
of all restraint and indulging every desire. Socrates, on the other hand,
argues that for a person to achieve the kind of freedom that is autonomy,
that is where a person acts to do what he himself wants to do, approves of,
and can wholeheartedly endorse and give his blessings to, he needs to be
whole. He needs to integrate his desires, make them his own, that is what *he*
wants as a person who has come together. Only then will his desires be
responsible to considerations – considerations of consequences in the light
of interests and of values that weigh with him. Otherwise satisfying his
desires is giving in to impulses of the moment, and that is a form of slavery
in which the self is ruled by the contingencies of the moment and, if not
that, then by lasting obsessions – lust for a woman, thirst for power, the
desire for revenge, greed for money, ambition for fame or renown.

But to achieve such wholeness in which a person has self-mastery, that
is mastery over himself in the face of needs and attractions that may otherwise threaten to enslave him – first divide and then rule him – he has to be
prepared to commit himself to the discipline of values which matter to him
because of what he sees in them. While such discipline may impose some
restraint on him in certain circumstances this will be self-restraint. What
he forgoes as a result he will thus forgo willingly and so freely – of his own
accord. In doing so he will be heeding his own counsel. If, for instance, he
resists a temptation, he will be doing what he himself wants to do. Here
we need to distinguish between a genuine conscience in which it is the
person himself who speaks, transformed by his moral beliefs, and the
Freudian super-ego where the voice which speaks to the person is not his
own voice but someone else's, though it comes from within him. The part
in him from which it comes is that part of him in which he yielded to
someone (his father) in fear, took sides with him to disarm and pacify him. It
is a voice which still speaks threateningly to him. If one cannot see any
alternative to such a voice then, indeed, rejecting it, as Socrates brings out

well, is laying oneself open to a different form of tyranny – the tyranny of need, impulse and appetite. That is not any kind of freedom.

It is true that in such a case the discipline rejected is a yoke, because it is imposed on a person who sees nothing in it. It is therefore obeyed only by a part of the person and obeyed out of fear. It makes little difference whether what the person thus conforms to is imposed by a part of himself or some outside 'authority' which he fears and needs to appease or needs to please because of what he wants from it. This is what Callicles rightly rejects in the name of freedom:

> Conventions ... are made ... by the weaklings who form the majority of mankind. They establish them and apportion praise and blame with an eye to themselves and their own interests ... Our way is to take the best and strongest among us from an early age and endeavour to mould their character as men tame lions; we subject them to a course of charms and spells and try to enslave them by repetition of the dogma that men ought to be equal and that equality is fine and right. But if there arises a man sufficiently endowed by nature, he will shake off and break through and escape from all these trammels: he will tread underfoot our texts and spells and incantations and unnatural laws, and by an act of revolt reveal himself our master instead of our slave ...
>
> (Plato 1973b, pp. 78–9)

Here Callicles is not only identifying Socrates' morality with convention but he is also arguing that a man is free who has the courage to take power into his hands and exercise it without regard to the good or harm of other people. Those who have no scruples about exercising power in this way are free and all those whose master they thus become are slaves:

> They are the people who ought to rule states, and right consist in them as rulers having an advantage over the rest, who are their subjects (p. 90).

Socrates asks him: 'Will they be rulers of themselves? ... Or is there no need for self-mastery as long as one is master of others?' He explains that self-mastery involves "being moderate" and being master of one's own passions and appetites'.

Callicles thinks that a man is moderate only because he lacks courage and that moderation involves repression: 'the man who is going to live as a man ought should encourage his appetites to be as strong as possible instead of repressing them, and be able by means of his courage and intelligence to satisfy them in all their intensity by providing them with whatever they happen to desire' (p. 90).

Callicles is right this far: repression is one antithesis of freedom, and to be oneself one has to be independent and oneself, not bow to convention, not kowtow to the expectations of others, whatever one does, whatever direction one gives to one's life, it must be because one believes in it oneself. But he is wrong to think that satisfying whatever one happens to desire is necessarily what a man wants. Someone may need money and on a particular occasion he may be tempted to steal. But, however poor he may be, he may draw the line at acquiring it by stealing. Callicles forgets that we live in a world – a human world – in which things have various forms of significance for us, constituted by the morality and culture to which we stand related. Much of what we want and what we are averse to is shaped by this relation – a relation which involves us individually as thinking beings. What we want is responsible to what we make of ourselves in a way that Callicles' simple-minded dichotomy between nature and convention cannot make intelligible.

Secondly, it is true that a morality can be no more than a convention for a person which, in the conformity it exacts from him, can become a force of repression. In such a case if he is to find himself and be faithful to what he wants out of life he has to change his relation to the morality in question and be clear about what it is he believes in. A morality does not automatically and *as such* have the character of a convention in the sense that Callicles has in mind. To have the courage to defy what is an agency of repression in oneself is not to embrace licence. Repression and licence do not exhaust the alternatives, in fact they are both forms of bondage. It is only through self-mastery – which is very different from repression – that, Plato argues, freedom can be achieved: the freedom of self-autonomy.

In reply to Callicles' questions Socrates says that self-mastery is 'being moderate and in control of oneself and master of one's own passions and appetites'. Callicles replies that the people Socrates calls moderate are 'the half-witted' and sees such people as lacking courage and manliness (pp. 90–91). Socrates knows that this could be the case but is not talking of people where this is true. In the *Phaedo* he explains that temperance can, indeed, be a sort of self-indulgence': 'they refrain from one kind [of pleasure] because they cannot resist the other' (Penguin Classics, pp. 88–9). In the same way he speaks of the bravery that arises out of fear and cowardice. These are not real virtues. In contrast, the kind of 'self-control' required by 'self mastery' involves 'preserving a decent indifference towards the desires'. Such indifference is not, as Callicles supposes in the *Gorgias*, a form of death – a death of the passions. As he says to Socrates: 'at that rate stones and corpses would be supremely happy' (p. 91). No, it is a detachment from the ego. It is a moral orientation in which the significance one sees in certain values, and the significance which in turn they give to certain things, makes one indifferent to what sparks off jealousies, rivalries, anger, feuds, etc., in many people. It is not a death of the passions, but their purification of all ego-centric elements. That, of course, involves losing certain passions and desires, and acquiring new ones.

As I said, Callicles thinks of the kind of self-control Socrates regards as necessary to freedom and autonomy as a form of repression and so opposes it to licence. But they are on the same side; both are forms of 'self-indulgence'. In contrast, the self-control or self-restraint of which Socrates speaks is the antithesis of 'self-indulgence', and self-indulgence, whatever form it takes, never amounts to genuine freedom. It is slavery to the ego. Here the self or person is subject to the needs of the ego. Here the person has not even come to himself. In contrast in self-mastery a person has come to himself and the self to which he has come is master of the ego. That is what it means to have mastery over oneself. Such a person has mastery over impulses which would toss him this way or that, over temptations which would lead him by the nose, needs which would make him dependent on contingencies to which he has constantly to make concessions, or obsessions and ambitions which would blind him to his own good and self-interest. Indeed a person who lacks mastery over himself is either rudderless or is not captain of his own actions.

In view of what we saw in our discussion of Sophocles let me make it clear that I did not say 'captain of his own life'. For we saw that there are many natural necessities and contingencies that impinge on people's lives which a person has to learn to submit to and accept. In that sense no one is captain of his own life. But to accept them in humility, in contrast with trying to circumvent or try to defy them in vain, is to show mastery over oneself, over one's pains and disappointments, and to steer a course for oneself in full awareness of the unpredictable in human life. As we have seen, one's limitations are limitations to one's freedom only if one denies them.

3 Love of goodness and slavery to evil

We see so far that Plato holds that freedom requires discipline, not a discipline imposed on and so external to the self, but self-discipline. Without such discipline the self is fragmented, and a fragmented self has no abiding will, the person does not know what he wants, or if he does his will is subject to what obstructs or deflects it from the direction it faces. He further holds that the discipline in question belongs to the love of the good.

The person who loves goodness is one committed to the values of a morality of love. This means that these values are not open to choice for him. But this is not a restriction or limitation of his freedom of choice, it is a precondition of it. To be able to move at all a person has to be able to lean on something that is fixed and does not move. In his notes *On Certainty* Wittgenstein has argued that it is the same with doubting: to be able to doubt things at all there must be certainties that are beyond doubt for one. This is equally true of choice: to be able to choose what to do in particular circumstances there must be certain things which are *unthinkable* for one there. What is unthinkable for one are actions which violate or infringe values which one believes in unconditionally, values which play the role of absolute norms in one's deliberations and judgements.

One deliberates, of course, when it is not clear to one in which direction the good lies: what would be the just thing to do? Should I be honest and hurt him or omit telling him the truth and spare him the suffering? Often some doubt remains, for such matters are not always clear cut. Yet we take the risk, make up our minds and act. But where we are clear we know what we *must* do. Just as certain things are unthinkable for one, *ie* not open to choice, in certain circumstances, likewise certain things are *morally necessary*, they too are not open to deliberation and choice: we do them not because we choose to do them, but because we *cannot* do otherwise. Our moral beliefs *compel* us to act in certain ways in certain circumstances by ruling out for us alternatives – i.e. what would be alternatives for someone not holding those beliefs.

Given one's moral beliefs, the situation can be compared with that in mathematics. There are necessities within mathematics and the mathematician who recognizes them will not infringe them, he will not be able to make sense of its infringements. Yet these mathematical limits or necessities are not limitations, since in contravening them the mathematician would be departing from what he could make sense of in mathematics. On discovering an error he has made in his calculations or in a proof he is developing, he may say 'I am not free to go that way'. But this is misleading, because the moment he realizes that he has gone wrong in the line he took he will not want to go that way and so will not in any way be constrained.

Similarly the person who realizes that a certain action is ruled out for him by his moral beliefs will no longer want to do it; and one who realizes that it is demanded from him by his moral beliefs will not want not to do it, even if he is afraid to do it because of some danger involved. If he hesitates, this means either that he is not sure that it is really demanded of him, or that his commitment is not wholehearted. Where it is, he will be wholly behind the action and such words he may use as 'I cannot do otherwise' do not signify that his hands are tied or that he is like someone who is acting under duress.

We have seen that in his discussion with Callicles, Socrates contrasts the actions of a man who knows his mind, has made a fair appraisal of the circumstances relevant to his action and does what he himself wants or believes he ought to do, and one who seeks any and every satisfaction. Earlier in the dialogue he described the latter as someone who 'does as he pleases' and the former as someone who 'does what he wills'. He further argues that only the good man, the man who has the kind of knowledge that is virtue or goodness, does what he wills. In his will he is at one with the good, and so what he *must* do is his will. In his service of the good, in following what are *moral necessities* for him, he is himself, autonomous and so free.

In contrast, he argues, the evil man does not know what he does, he does not act voluntarily. In his service of evil he is subject to *natural necessities*; service of evil is a form of bondage. He claims this despite his recognition of the fact that a man may be thoroughly evil and so totally alienated from goodness, so that his will is at one with evil. From this it would seem to follow that in serving evil, like the man who serves the good, he is doing what he wants, doing the only thing that makes sense to him. So what grounds can Socrates have for saying that the evil man is a slave to some natural necessity, that he is not free?

When Socrates speaks of evil action as *involuntary* he has in mind the fact that the evil man does not know the good, lacks moral knowledge, and so does not think of what he does as evil – even if he knows that others call it evil. He may hurt someone voluntarily and maliciously, but not recognize his act as malicious. So, Socrates argues, the malice is not voluntary. If he knew what the good man knows he would not and could not do what he does maliciously. It is in *this* sense that he acts without knowledge and therefore without intent.

Clearly Plato sees an important asymmetry between good and evil, and so between serving the one and serving the other. One can say that while both are forms of compulsion or necessity, they differ in the part of the self or soul which they engage. Earlier I articulated what Socrates was saying in the *Phaedrus* by saying that there are two currents in human life out of which good or evil grow. One of them belongs to love and is giving, creative and healing. The other contains all that is ego-centric in us – greed, envy, hatred, malice, all forms of lust – and is taking, exploitative and destructive. It is these that make a person receptive to evil: it is through them that evil enters into and takes roots in his soul. It is their unrestrained pursuit that constitutes evil. If you ask me what that, namely evil, is, I can only tell you if we agree on what goodness is. It is only in its light, only from the perspective of a morality of love in which goodness has its identity, that such pursuits constitute evil.

Now take love and the capacity for forgiveness which belongs to it and contrast it with the vindictiveness of someone who has received an offence which feeds on hatred. Forgiveness *releases* both the offending and the offended parties from being locked into an unproductive relationship in which their actions become more and more reactive and feed on each other. We have seen how these and their disastrous consequences have been portrayed by the literature of Early Greece. They thought of it as exemplifying the unfolding of natural laws which ruled the human soul with as much *necessity* as later in the dawn of the scientific age of Europe it has been thought that scientific laws hold sway in the physical world with *necessity*.

44

While the reactions of love and friendliness are equally natural and are part of the human soul, as Socrates makes clear in the way he represents the soul in the *Phaedrus*, they are subject to the influence of the other part of the soul – the ego and its appetites. The soul has to feed on beauty and truth, grow wings, and rise against the force of gravity, the natural laws to which it is subject (ascent of the soul in the *Symposium*, its purification in the *Phaedo*), before the love naturally present in most souls become a force for good there and overcomes and transforms those feelings and inclinations that are ego-centric in character and pull the soul down. This is, of course, a moral allegory, which means that it is a representation of human psychology and the human condition from the perspective of Plato's morality of love.

It is clear that Plato thought that the soul caught up in one of these two currents is pulled down and becomes subject to 'natural necessity'. The evil man lacks moral knowledge and autonomy: freedom. His soul is pulled downward in more than one sense. It is pulled downward in a *moral* sense, in the direction of what is 'low' or 'base' as opposed to 'elevated' and 'noble'. There is further the analogy with gravity, which is a force which on earth pulls all objects downwards. The idea is that one becomes evil by *yielding* to temptations and affective inclinations. Plato talks of *self-indulgence* which he contrasts with self-restraint. Indulgence is an expression of weakness. Here it is the ego that is indulged and allowed to have its way by a self which lacks conviction, coherence and strength.

Thus whether it is by imitation and conformity, through indifference to the consequences of pursuing one's self-interests, through malice, or even through 'love of evil', that one admits evil into one's life and becomes evil, it is by following a natural bent that one does so. In the case where we can speak of a love of evil, the pursuit of that love brings gratification and the ego thrives in it: it inflates the ego and gives the person a sense of power. Simone Weil speaks here of the tendency of the soul to expand:

> There is in the soul something like a phagocite. All those who are menaced by time secrete a lie in order to keep alive. That is why there is no love of truth without an unreserved consent to die.
>
> (Weil 1948, p. 64)

By 'those who are menaced by time' she means those who are caught up in affairs of this world which are vulnerable to changing alliances, changing interests, changing fashions on the one hand and are, in any case, of temporary interest to human beings, who grow old, lose their capacities and energies with age, and then have to face their own end and the loss of all the things they care for. The lie she has in mind is the illusion that they are immune from all this. We have seen how, she thinks, the ability to wield power gives them a sense of invulnerability. The 'love of truth' she speaks of is the knowledge which Plato speaks of in his various dialogues including the *Phaedo* and the *Phaedrus*.

So to fall into evil one has to allow the soul to follow its natural bent to *expand*. But goodness is not something one can fall into: one's soul has to be fed on truth and beauty to grow wings. As Simone Weil puts it, one has to make room for goodness to enter into one's soul by *contracting*. That means *renouncing* its tendency to expand. In the *Phaedo* Plato speaks of this as 'the purification of the soul' and 'dying to the self' – what I called 'the ego'. This is something that engages the person actively; it is something that takes inner work – e.g. forgiving one's enemies, renouncing one's grudges, giving up one's grievances.

Thus giving in to evil and receiving the good into one's soul are opposites: not merely in direction but in that in the one case one has to let oneself slide downhill, indulge the ego, whereas in the other one has to use restraint, to work, to renounce.

I asked what grounds Plato or Socrates has for thinking that the evil man is a slave to some natural necessity and so not free. We have seen that the natural necessities involved have to do with the responses of the ego and our ego-centric passions, the way in them the ego takes over the self and anchors it to repetitive patterns of conduct. It does so, Plato argues, because the person lacks knowledge of the good or wisdom. He also speaks of it as 'self-knowledge' in that to have it necessarily involves changing in oneself, coming to a new self, one in which one is oneself.

Simone Weil expresses Plato's 'determinism' – the determinism of belonging to evil, of living without the light of wisdom – in the following words:

> When a man turns away from God [from the good] he simply gives himself up to the law of moral gravity. He then believes that he is deciding and choosing, but he is only a thing, a falling stone. If we examine human society and souls closely and with real attention, we see that wherever the virtue of supernatural light is absent, everything is obedient to mechanical laws as blind and as exact as the laws of gravitation. To know this is profitable and necessary. Those whom we call criminals are only tiles blown off a roof by the wind and falling at random. Their only fault is the initial choice by which they become those tiles.
>
> (Weil 1968, pp. 176–7)

When Simone Weil speaks of the way a man who gives himself up to the laws of moral gravity becomes a thing there is a clear affinity between what she has in mind and what she says about force in her essay on the *Iliad*: the way force changes all it touches into a thing. What she finds in the *Iliad* is a particular case of the general point argued by Plato since, as

46

she argues and as Socrates argues in the *Gorgias*, force or power, which Callicles worships, is an evil. Indeed Simone Weil sees a close kinship between force and evil, as she does between weakness and goodness.

The evil person is worldly. If he is clever as well, he knows every trick in the book, pressure, deception, using people, and has no scruples about intimidating people, pressurizing them to do his dirty work. Even if he is not strong physically, he knows how to put himself in positions of power and take advantage of others. He has no scruples about doing so. A good person, on the other hand, is weak in the face of all this because of his scruples, because not every way is open to him. Fighting fire with fire, for instance, is not open to him. He is meek, the trappings of power are abhorrent to him.

Indeed, his inner strength itself and scruples may appear as forms of weakness to someone who has regard for power – as Socrates' appeared to Callicles. He is not afraid to stand his ground but, because he respects others as human beings even when he condemns their actions, he will not use force to impose his will or point of view on them. The fact that he supports punishment for the wicked does not contradict this. Socrates would have said that when punishment is just it does not constitute a use of force. He believed that punishment is legitimate only when it is administered by a legitimate authority. That makes it impersonal – or at any rate it makes it possible for it to be impersonal. He believed that the agent or the authority administering the punishment should have at heart the good of the person punished and let him learn the lesson it is meant to teach him. Just as one cannot fall into the good, one cannot be coerced into the good either: one can only come to it oneself. This is part of the asymmetry I have been commenting on, where 'learning goodness' is radically different from what is sometimes called 'learning evil' – in the way, for instance, young people who are sent to gaol are sometimes said to do.

4 Conclusion: moral knowledge and freedom

So is Plato a determinist? The answer is that while he is not one, he recognizes the sway that 'natural necessity' has in human life in the form of evil. We are all susceptible to what from Plato's moral perspective constitutes evil – envy, hatred, resentments, thirst for power, reactions of retaliation. To give in to these things is to give up one's freedom; it is to submit to the determination of one's will by evil. However much the evil man may be behind his actions, as is the case with Archelaus in the *Gorgias*, he is in bondage to evil since he has no knowledge of the good and so is ignorant of the evil in his actions. If he had this knowledge he could avoid evil, but as things are he cannot. So in doing what he wills he acts in bondage to evil. He has no alternative.

As I explained so has the good man no alternative – 'moral necessity'.

But that is not because he is unaware of an alternative, as is the case with an evil man, but because he is unwilling to consider it. This is the asymmetry between good and evil which I tried to elucidate. Thus if Archelaus has no reason for wanting to act differently from the way he does, it is, Plato argues, because he lacks wisdom, does not know the evil involved in what he does. In doing what he does he indulges in his love of power: it is not he who is in control of his destiny but something to which he sees no alternative. By contrast the man who is at one with the good has mastery over himself and, while no one is in control of his destiny, he is not subject to those desires and inclinations that have a hold on the evil person.

Since Plato holds that evil arises from tendencies that are natural to the soul, he thinks of freedom as something to be won and he believes that it can only be won by doing what it takes to let goodness into the soul. His view is that it is only the good man who is free.

4

ARISTOTLE

Moral knowledge and the problem of free will

1 Aristotle's treatment of voluntary action and moral responsibility

Aristotle's contribution to the problem of free will is measured and analytic.

At the outset of his *Nicomachean Ethics* he argues that just as a carpenter and cobbler have certain works and courses of action, so does 'man as man'. He adds that just as the eyes, hands and feet have each some special work to perform, so does 'the whole man'. He is not there just to live – like a vegetable. Nor just to pursue a life of nourishment, instinct and sensation – like most animals. Human beings pursue ends in accordance with reason, they form intentions, make choices, and act on them. As he puts it: 'the work of man is a working of the soul in accordance with reason' (p. 12).

Next he says that the work of a good man is 'to do these things well and nobly' (ibid.). A good carpenter or cabinet-maker makes the tables and other pieces of furniture he is making *well*. Here we can understand what 'well' means in terms of the function which what he makes are intended to serve. As Aristotle puts it: 'everything is finished off well in the way of the excellence which peculiarly belongs to it' (ibid.). 'If all this is so,' he says, 'then the good man comes to be "a working of the soul in the way of excellence"'. The trouble is this: if living a rational life, a life of reason, is putting into practice one's ability to deliberate, make choices and decisions, it is not clear what doing this well amounts to. We say of someone, 'you chose well'; but what this amounts to varies from case to case. There are no norms or criteria of excellence internal to rationality in this respect as there are in carpentry or cabinet-making.

For instance someone may be said to have chosen his holiday well, given what he wanted to have it for, what he wanted to get out of it. Someone may be said to have chosen his words to a friend well, given the nature of what he had to convey to him while not wanting to upset his friend. We can even describe the virtue he exercised as 'tact and discretion'. But I do not see how we could characterize all virtues in this way, least of

49

all what Plato has in mind when he talks of 'goodness'. I don't think we can come to understand it along these lines.

In Book II Aristotle says that 'there are principally three things moving us to choice and three to avoidance, the honourable, the expedient, the pleasant; and their three contraries, the dishonourable, the hurtful and the painful' and he adds that 'the good man is apt to go right, and the bad man wrong, with respect to all these' (p. 30). It would seem then that what Aristotle means by 'good' when he speaks of 'the good man' is not confined to moral goodness. He considers human beings to be pleasure-seeking, prudent, and also honour-seeking – in the sense of wanting to do the honourable thing. Consequently, he thinks of the soul as made up of *three* parts: appetite, rational wish as exercised in the pursuit of rational self-interest and in prudence, and thirdly concern for such things as honour and dignity, the exercise of moral virtues. We shall see later how Aristotle differs from Plato in his conception of the tri-partite nature of the soul and his understanding of self-mastery.

I now turn, briefly, to Book III where Aristotle discusses the distinction between what is done willingly and with one's eyes open ('voluntary' actions as Aristotle speaks of them) and what is done without the agent's willingness or with a willingness or consent that does not issue from knowledge but from ignorance ('involuntary' actions as Aristotle calls them). Thus when the agent is unwilling to do what he nevertheless does it must be that he is in some way compelled to do it – an action done on compulsion. If he is unwilling to do it because he is misinformed about what is involved, or has not thought sufficiently about it, then he is willing only because he is ignorant – an action done by virtue of ignorance. In the first kind of case, Aristotle says, the action has an origin external to the agent, and in the extreme case he contributes nothing to the action. His responsibility is at a minimum – although, depending on the action, he may feel terrible for having been the instrument of what happens, or indeed for having been the vehicle of the action, for the action having gone through him, for its having used him. In other cases he may feel responsible for not having been able to resist the compulsion. There are also cases, not mentioned or thought of by Aristotle, where the agent has not come together and is divided in himself, so that the origin of the compulsion lies within him. There are further cases where the agent submits to a compulsion not willingly but by choice under adverse circumstances – for instance he hands his wallet to a robber to avoid being shot and killed.

Aristotle distinguishes between actions that fall within his second category: (i) actions done *because* of ignorance and (ii) actions done *with* ignorance, as when the agent is drunk or in a rage. In the latter case ignorance is not the cause of the action, Aristotle says, but drunkenness or the anger. The agent acts 'with ignorance' (pp. 46–7). He is to blame for getting drunk or for losing his temper. So, a page later, Aristotle questions whether such actions should be classed as 'involuntary' (p. 48). In the former case, however, he is culpable only if his ignorance is culpable – if, for instance, it is due to neglect or irresponsibility. As we might say: 'he could and should have known better'.

These distinctions which Aristotle makes are appropriate and it is probably the first attempt in the history of philosophy to articulate them in general terms. Obviously they are susceptible of refinement and call for further discussion. But I am not interested here in engaging in such work. What is important for us to note is Aristotle's interest in conceptual analysis and its relevance to a discussion of the problem of the reality of free will. Aristotle does not question that reality; he is concerned to demonstrate its limits: when, under what conditions, can a man be said to act 'voluntarily', that is of his own free will and when, even though intentional, are his actions not free?

He comes near to the problems discussed by Plato in his (Plato's) view that 'every bad man is ignorant of what he ought to do and what to leave undone' and such ignorance makes men 'unjust and wholly evil' (p. 47). But ignorance, he says, is not the same thing as 'involuntariness': 'we do not usually apply the term involuntary when a man is ignorant of his own true interest'. 'Ignorance which affects moral choice,' he adds, 'constitutes depravity but not involuntariness' (ibid.). In other words, a man who does not know what is right and just and, let us say, cheats his brother of his inheritance, knows very well what he is doing, namely ensuring that the money or property left by his father to his brother goes to him: that is what he wants and that is what he works to achieve, and he delights in his success. Such a person has acted voluntarily: to obtain the money and property in question is what he wills and he is behind what it takes to obtain them.

'Moral choice,' he says, 'is plainly voluntary' (p. 49). He means, where a person makes a choice, whether moral or not, he is exercising his will. His point is that deliberation and decision are *par excellence* the exercise of the will – a 'grammatical' statement. But since moral choice is a species of choice it must be 'voluntary', and whether it is made by a good man or an evil person is immaterial to this point. It is on this last stage of his reasoning that he disagrees with Plato. I shall comment on this disagreement presently.

Aristotle further argues, somewhat like Hume, that moral deliberation and choice is directed to the means by which desired ends are to be achieved: 'we wish to be healthy, but we choose the means which will make us so' (ibid.). 'We deliberate not about ends, but means to ends. No physician, for instance, deliberates whether he will cure ... but having set before him a certain end [to which he has sworn allegiance in the Hypocratic oath] he looks how and through what means it may be accomplished' (p. 52). In this example the end is set by the physician's oath of allegiance; it is something to which he has committed himself. But is that an end whose worth is to be measured, assessed morally, or is it the measure of the worth and therefore moral acceptability of the decisions he makes and actions he takes in the course of his practice?

51

It is perfectly true that when he deliberates and takes decisions about what is open to questioning and decision there are certain matters that are not open to questioning and decision for him – in this case the sanctity of human life. But it is questionable that what is in question here is an end whose worth is constituted by what men desire independently of values to which they give their hearts. Certainly the desire for our life to continue when it is under threat of, say, some serious disease, is something we find in almost everyone. But that would never take us to a regard for human life in general unless we had regard for others and respected them in their independent existence. It is because of this care and concern in particular cases that when someone's life is under threat we want to do what is necessary, if we can, to help and save his life. Such concern is the expression of the value we place on life, of our conception of life as having sanctity; and that conception is tied up to a network of concepts and values which give us the particular perspective within which we naturally respond in certain ways in particular situations.

We come to such concern and care, no doubt, in the course of our development through the extension and transformation of certain 'primitive' affective reactions. But these are extended and transformed with what we learn within a particular culture and moral ethos as we, ourselves, are transformed in the course of such learning. The responses in which such care or concern finds expression are, after all, what comes from the agent and show where he stands as a person and what kind of person he is. No amount of instrumental, means to end reasoning, could get anyone there nor, for that matter, custom and habituation, as Aristotle holds: 'the intellectual springs … from teaching …; whereas the moral comes from custom' (p. 26). 'We learn how to make by making,' he writes, 'men come to be … harp-players by playing the harp: exactly so, by doing just actions we come to be just' (pp. 26–7). The idea is that a virtue is a settled way of acting.

What Aristotle leaves out is the change of heart and change of perspective that is involved in coming to justice. Doing the right thing merely by habit or imitation, following precepts which one has not made one's own, does not make a person good. He has to see what lies or is involved in goodness or justice – and he can only see this in particular instances or manifestations of it – and he has to love it for what it is, for what he sees there. The love he has is a love for what he sees; it is in the love he has for justice that the just man sees what is involved in justice. We can say, therefore, that the kind of love which the love of justice is sees, and in that sense appreciates, recognizes or knows justice. In other words, it is in coming to such love that a person comes to know what justice is; it is in such love that he knows justice. It is in this sense that Plato's claim that 'virtue is knowledge' should be understood. The love in question is a form of knowledge, and having it dwelling in one's heart is that mode of being which constitutes

52

virtue – that virtue, for Plato, in which all real virtues have their unity. Plato calls it 'goodness' or 'justice'.

Having claimed that 'we deliberate respecting such practical matters as are in our power' (p. 51) and that what we deliberate about are the means to ends that are determined ultimately by our desires – 'we deliberate not about ends, but means to ends' (p. 52) – Aristotle next argues that 'virtue is in our power; and so too is vice' (p. 55). He means it is in our power to do the virtuous or the wicked thing in particular circumstances or to forbear doing it. He plainly rejects Plato's claim that the evil person does not know what he is doing, since he does not know goodness or justice. Not knowing this, he is enslaved by or in bondage to evil, and so has no real choice in his wickedness. He acts, therefore, 'involuntarily'. As Plato's Socrates put it in the *Gorgias*: he does not do what he wills. In other words, what he does is not what he wills, for he is not a person who has come to himself, he has remained stunted in his wickedness. Though he may be behind his actions, his will is not his own – in the sense that it is not the will of a person who has come to himself, one who is in touch with both the good and the evil that enters into human affairs.

This is a form of bondage which Aristotle does not recognize. He rejects it. He argues (i) that we, as individuals and law-givers, chastise and punish those who do wrong (he adds, 'unless they do so on compulsion, or by reason of ignorance which is not self-caused' (p. 55). In other words, except for special circumstances, we do hold the wicked accountable for their deeds. (ii) Even when a man is of such a character that he cannot attend to those things in his care and concern, that a good person attends to, it is still true that he bears responsibility for being the way he is (p. 56).

This is how Aristotle puts it: 'It is wholly irrelevant to say that the man who acts unjustly or dissolutely does not *wish* to attain the habits of these vices: for if a man wittingly does those things whereby he must become unjust he is to all intents and purposes unjust voluntarily; but he cannot with a wish cease to be unjust and become just' (p. 56). He likens such a man to one who cannot help being ill and cannot get well, although he is in such a state because he has lived intemperately and disregarded his physician's advice: 'there was a time … when he might have helped being ill, but now … he cannot any longer; just as he who has let a stone out of his hand cannot recall it, and yet it rested with him to aim and throw it, because the origination was in his power' (ibid.).

On this last point Aristotle is right, and I doubt that Plato would have disagreed. A person may be in bondage, he may lack autonomy in the very form of character he has developed, and however much he may wish to change he cannot do so at will. Yet he may have participated in making such a fate for himself and so bear responsibility for it – though I do not think that we could say that he has done so 'voluntarily' or 'willingly', for he did not know where he was going, nor did he want to be where he is now. In one respect, however, I would go further than Aristotle and say not only that he is ultimately responsible for where he is now, even though he did not get there 'voluntarily', but that although he cannot return from it and be at a different place *at will*, the way that a sailor can change his course at will and reach a different destination, he can nevertheless *work* to free himself from the plight which is his prison. He can undo the web he has spun, without a thought or care for any consequences, a web in which he has hemmed himself in. He can undo it knot by knot and thus regain freedom. What he cannot do is walk out of it at will.

Where Plato differs from Aristotle here is in his attitude towards a man who is caught in a self-spun web, one who has sold his soul to the devil. Aristotle says to him: you have got yourself there, you have only got your-self to blame; and you cannot escape our blame when you do us harm. Plato, in contrast, distinguishes between the man and the evil in his soul, and feels compassion for the man in the identity he feels with him for his vulnerability to the temptations to which he has succumbed and for what he has done to himself in so succumbing to them. His view is, I think, that in blaming him one distances oneself from him and one shuts one's eyes to one's own vulnerability to what he has succumbed. One even risks partici-pating in that evil. But that is not to say he does not deserve punishment: for the good of his soul. For Plato punishment is not incompatible with compassions; on the contrary, it should come from compassion.

One could say that Aristotle's intellect is a great one, and in many ways he has been an innovator; but his 'common sense' approach prevents him from reaching the depth of Plato's moral perception. His conclusion is that 'if the virtues are voluntary ... the vices must be voluntary also' (p. 58).

Of the virtues he says, 'they are habits', and they and the actions that issue from them, actions performed by the agent possessing them, 'are not voluntary in the same sense'. The actions issue from our choices: 'we are masters [of them] from beginning to end', provided we have knowledge of the relevant circumstances (ibid.). But we are masters 'only of the origination of the habits', and that means of our piece-meal contributions to their forma-tion. Likewise in the case of vices what is 'voluntary' are each little step we take, without thought of consequences and without any vision of where they are taking us, which puts us on an ever more slippery slope. As for the actions which issue from our vices Aristotle's view is that they are 'voluntary' *in the same sense as* those actions that issue from a person's virtues are voluntary: the vicious man is the man he has become in going down the way of vice and his vicious actions issue from his will – the will of a vicious man. They are what he wills and so they are voluntary.

2 Are vices voluntary?

Plato holds that 'no man does evil voluntarily'. Of course the evil man's actions are intentional; in carrying out his evil deeds, in planning for their execution he deliberates and makes choices like any other man, and he uses his intelligence and powers of reasoning. Plato does not deny this. For Aristotle, we have seen, this is all that any man can do in acting; it is all that counts to make his actions voluntary. For him it is precisely what a man does in choosing between good and evil in particular circumstances. No doubt it is as the kind of man he is that he makes such choices in particular circumstances; but this is an unexceptionable truth and so, in this respect, there is no difference between the good man, the virtuous man, Aristotle would say, and the wicked, evil person. Each chooses and acts voluntarily *in his own lights* and *as the kind of person he is*.

Precisely, Plato would say, but here there are important distinctions to be made. The wicked man's 'lights' are illusory or, to put it differently, he lacks lights: he lacks moral knowledge. Plato, as we shall see in the following section, has a very different conception from Aristotle of the kind of knowledge the evil man lacks and the good man possesses. To act 'voluntarily', in the sense in question, is to act with intent and intent involves knowledge. While as far as the practical aspect of evil conduct goes, that is the putting into practice of his evil schemes, he may well have the relevant knowledge, the intelligence and the powers of reasoning needed to make the particular actions and choices involved in carrying out his schemes, that is to make them 'voluntary', this cannot be said of the schemes themselves. His relation to these is very different from the good man's relation to his pursuits.

Secondly, Plato would distinguish between different modes of being, different forms of character. He would say that the kind of knowledge that the evil man lacks and the good man has is *a state of soul* and as such, its presence and absence characterizes their modes of being. There are forms of character that are straight-jackets, forms of character in which a person lacks all abiding concerns and convictions and is vulnerable to the impulse of the moment, and so modes of being in which a person lacks self-mastery or autonomy, and has failed to come to himself. Such a man may 'please himself', as Plato's Socrates puts it in the *Gorgias*, but he 'does not do what he wills'. He may be a 'wilful' person and may have organized and settled desires, but he has no will of his own for it to be said that he does what he wills. The will we attribute to him in reality belongs to the devil – as it is sometimes put. It is the embodiment of the temptations which come from the devil and to which he is vulnerable in his ego. That is why in the *Phaedo* Plato argues that to come to moral knowledge one has to 'purify one's soul', to 'die to the self' – the self in the sense of the ego.

It is true that the conceptual connections in question are not morally neutral; they are connections between moral concepts and so belong to what comes to light within a particular moral perspective. To see what Plato is getting at one has to consider examples, and there is a whole range of examples one can consider. But let us take the instance of the difference between meanness and generosity. The mean man is certainly mean in a way in which the man whose politeness is false is not polite. Yet in his meanness the mean man is confined to repeating himself. For he is restricted to a tunnel vision of things, especially in his relation to other people, and he is held back from developing, that is from changing in the direction of a greater autonomy and a richer appreciation of things. I take the mean man to be someone ungiving, thoughtless of and nasty to other people. He is the slave of the ego in him: his judgements are coloured by it, his reactions are conditioned by it. It is his ego that blinkers his vision and so confines his actions to a pretty narrow track.

The generous person, in contrast, is giving and open to others, to the world. His conduct and responses are not repetitive in that his vision of things is not blinkered by his ego. He sees things in their variety and their individual differences and so each of his generous acts is directed to the individual person and situation that calls for or inspires it. There is nothing stereotyped about them. His givingness brings him in contact with people and situations in a way which meanness does not. For meanness, while it brings the worst in others, at the same time repels them, turns them away. But in any case in his givingness the generous person is open in himself and receptive. He is receptive not only to the good he brings out in others, but also to the evil he encounters in them – receptive to the latter in the hurt and the pain he feels. Unlike the mean man he does not return it, bounce it back, he takes it in and comes to know its taste in the pain he feels. Because of this he learns from his experiences and is enlarged by them. They change him without tethering him affectively; that is his experiences continue to contribute to his development. There is all the difference in the world between a settled personality and a rigidity of character. This is something Aristotle himself appreciated. In the latter case you know what to expect because you always expect the same thing. A settled personality comes from settled convictions and commitments, not from fixed inclinations and defences. There you know what to expect in the sense that you can trust the person, depend on his loyalties. What you depend on here is *the person himself*, not something he is bound to repeat.

One can bring out the same contrast between other forms of good and evil. Aristotle speaks of virtues and vices; Plato speaks of forms of good and evil. In seeing them as forms of the same thing he thinks of the virtues as having a significant unity. Furthermore what counts as a virtue and what as a vice varies with the morality in question and its moral perspective; whereas when Plato speaks of goodness and its many forms he is speaking from within a particular moral perspective. Elsewhere I characterized it as belonging to a morality of love – a spiritual morality: one in which spiritual love in its purity is contrasted with what belongs to the ego. It is precisely that which contaminates such love.

To return. Evil, in its variety of forms, as Plato sees it, is not so much a compulsion on the will as a 'determination of the will'. That is why it is natural to think, as Aristotle does, that a will for evil is the agent's own will, so that his actions are 'voluntary' exactly like the good man's actions, and therefore perfectly free. However in such a determination of will the person is *passive*. Here the person yields to the ego; there is no inner work involved in what he becomes. He 'learns' evil by copying what pleases him in his companions. He sees them getting on in the world, enforcing their will, getting a certain kudos which swells their head, and he follows them. When he succeeds, his success goes to his head. The acclaim of such success is all around him. He needs some conception of goodness and strength to resist wanting to participate in it. To find goodness he needs to empty himself of his ego, of everything in him which finds such success and its fruits attractive; and *that* takes both work and faith. This is very much at the heart of Plato's moral philosophy as I understand it.

They say 'revenge is sweet'. I would suggest that all evil is sweet in this sense to one whose contact with goodness has been severed. Once tasted it is also intoxicating. The person who gives way to it is captivated and enslaved by it. It feeds the ego. When a person feels himself diminished in his ego by a humiliation he receives he craves to return it to its original state; and when his ego expands this goes to his head and he wants it to expand further. He is thus caught up in evil and loses mastery of himself – however much mastery he may exercise in maintaining his success. For the mastery which a slavish employee exhibits in carrying out his boss's orders or in trying to please him is not what one would call self-mastery.

Goodness is never sweet in this way. When it is it ceases to be goodness; it loses its purity. Nor, strictly speaking, does a person have a motive in being good. He does not expect anything from it for himself. His goodness finds expression, for instance, when he puts himself out to help someone in difficulty. Why does he do so? To relieve the other's difficulty, to help him out of it. One can say: he has a motive for what he does, but not for being good. He is good in what he does, but that is not an object of his thoughts or awareness. He knows what goodness is, he is acquainted with it, in his life and actions; but he has no awareness of his own goodness.

The evil person, by contrast, does not know what goodness is, but he thinks of his evil actions as 'good' and of what he pursues in them as 'a good'. And he thinks of the qualities in himself as virtues which make him successful. There are many people around him who agree with him – who look up to him, admire and envy his success, and seek to emulate him. In evil he finds a power which the good man can never find in his goodness. Yet, for Plato, in that very power he is a slave. He is a slave in his need for it.

Aristotle's criteria for 'voluntary' action, we thus see, are too narrow. He recognizes a variety in what can constitute compulsions and constraints on the will, among them a person's own temper and his fears. But he does not recognize such cases wherein the will is determined from within so that a person does not own the will from which he acts but rather is himself owned by it. Here the person need not be false, but he cannot be said to have found himself. The will that is the expression of his character is not his will, since in that character he has not come to himself.

We find this in certain forms of character in which a person is vulnerable to the snares of evil, an easy prey to it. These are forms of character in which the ego is prominent – impulsive, narcissistic, or reactive characters – in which a person is disposed to becoming a vehicle for evil. His weaknesses and deficiencies make him an easy prey to evil. He ends up being used by evil. Such a person's soul is not his, his will is not his, even though in what he is, in the very character he possesses, he is at one with his actions.

It is thus in his very being that he lacks autonomy or self-mastery. This is where Plato says that even where he appears to have self-mastery this is really a form of indulgence – self-indulgence. As he puts it in the *Phaedo*, he refrains from one kind of pleasure because he cannot resist another kind (68B). One example would be the man who plans and executes a daring bank robbery with the kind of precision that takes self-discipline and endurance of hardship. As Plato puts it: it is because such a person cannot resist some pleasures that he succeeds in resisting others – he controls himself, in a sense, by self-indulgence. In the language of the Gorgias: he does what he pleases, not what he wills. The point is that he gives up what are possibilities for him by *yielding* – not through conviction.

It is, of course, not true that wherever we can say that a person pleases himself he is mastered by a certain form of pleasure. Indeed the colloquial use of this expression does not carry any such implication. On the contrary, it is often used to suggest that one has acted autonomously: 'I did it to please myself, not because I felt obliged.' But Plato uses it in connection with cases where a person acts in slavery to the pleasure he seeks. He also uses the term 'pleasure' in a broad sense to cover forms of 'self-gratification' – the kind which feeds the ego and for which the ego hungers. The idea is that the person has remained dependent on the ego, he has not outgrown such dependence and so has not developed a mature self independent of the ego and, in that sense, has not come to himself. Since, as I understand him, Plato rightly regards evil as ego-centric, it follows that the evil person is mastered by the gratification which the ego craves for (and so 'does what he – the ego – pleases'). Hence he lacks self-mastery, which is what Plato holds. This, I believe, is what lies in Plato's view that evil – what the evil man does – is involuntary. It is not what he wills, since it is done in subjection to the ego.

Aristotle asks: if evil is involuntary, as Plato claims, how come we hold the wicked accountable for his deeds? The short answer is that on Plato's view there is nothing unreasonable about holding the wicked accountable for his deeds. For if he acts in subjection to the ego, it is *he* who yields and *he does not have to*; however hard it may be not to do so. But though it is not unreasonable to hold him accountable for his wicked deeds Plato recognizes how much evil, when it is allowed to enter the soul and gets a hold on it, can turn the person into its instrument and, in that sense, into an 'object'. Plato's Socrates does in fact hold the wicked man responsible for his deeds, for in the *Gorgias* he argues that the wicked man ought to be punished – for the good of his soul, to reintegrate him with the good (see Dilman 1979, chapter 5). That is he does not stop feeling compassion for the wrong-doer for what he has done; on the contrary he feels greater compassion for him on account of just that – because he is himself a victim of evil and for what that does to his soul.

3 Self-mastery and weakness of will

In the previous section I have considered and tried to answer Aristotle's objection to the Platonic view that evil is not voluntary and hence that 'no one does what is wrong and embraces evil willingly'. For Plato, virtue and moral knowledge are one and the same thing and the virtuous man knows goodness in the way his will is at one with it. He cannot, therefore, do wrong knowingly. The evil man lacks such knowledge and so does wrong in ignorance. So, it would seem, for Plato 'no one does wrong knowingly'.

Aristotle says that there are people who are weak willed and though they know what is right and good, and so what they ought to do, they fail to do it or even do the opposite. They do what they themselves know to be wrong and condemn. So he distinguishes between (i) the wicked man who is indifferent to goodness and does not know it, (ii) 'the man of self-control', and (iii) the man of imperfect self-control (Bk VII, p. 153). What he lacks is not knowledge but strength of will. That is he denies the connection which Plato makes between moral knowledge and the will. Indeed, he takes a different conception of moral knowledge, regarding it as a species of 'practical wisdom'.

The man of self-control, he tells us, is one who is 'apt to abide by his resolutions'. 'Knowing his lusts to be wrong, he refuses, by the influence of reason, to follow their suggestions.' This is thus a case of reason's effectiveness, of its being able to guide the will successfully, or of its being able to restrain the person from yielding to his lust on a particular occasion. 'The man of perfect self-mastery,' he says, 'unites the qualities of self-control and endurance'. He endures pain, for instance, without complaining or trying to escape it when doing so involves doing something he is morally against. You can count on him to endure provocation without being provoked, to endure fear while he keeps his head and remains calm, to face temptations while remaining loyal to his convictions. That is he is not a man who is insensible to danger, desire and provocation. Without such sensibility he cannot be virtuous. As Aristotle tells us clearly, courage is not fearlessness but the mastery of one's fears. The courageous person is one who stands up to his fears (pp. 59–60). As for desire and provocation, we need to distinguish between different forms of their mastery, including the outgrowing of them in what Plato calls 'decent indifference', and sheer insensibility to them – which again is different from innocence. But at any rate my point is that strength of will presupposes sensibility or awareness of evil in temptation and provocation; self-mastery implies something mastered and 'decent indifference' to something overcome.

By contrast, Aristotle tells us, the man of imperfect self-control 'does things at the instigation of his passions, *knowing them to be wrong*' (p. 153 italics mine). What he lacks is not knowledge, but self-discipline and restraint. Referring to Plato's Socrates he says: 'it is sometimes said that the man of practical wisdom cannot be a man of imperfect self-control' (ibid.). He goes on: 'That he can so fail when *knowing* in the strict sense what is right some say is impossible: for it is a strange thing, as Socrates thought, that while knowledge is present in his mind something else should master him and drag him about like a slave' (p. 154). He adds that 'Socrates in fact contended that ... there is no such state as that of imperfect self-control', for his view was that 'no one acts contrary to what is best conceiving it to be best but by reason of ignorance of what is best' (ibid.).

Indeed, in the *Gorgias* we read the following words of Socrates:

> A man who has learnt about right will be righteous.
> A righteous man performs right actions.
> He will in fact of necessity will to perform right
> actions and will never will to do wrong (460).

Taken at face value these words certainly confirm Aristotle in the view he attributes to Socrates. So Aristotle says: 'with all due respect to Socrates, his account of the matter is at variance with plain facts'. He then raises the question whether failure in self-control is really the result of ignorance and, if so, what kind of ignorance. 'For,' he adds, 'that the man so failing does not suppose his acts to be right before he is under the influence of passion is quite plain' (ibid.). For instance, he *knows* that he must not lose his temper next time he is provoked – that is *before* he is provoked – but when he is provoked he loses his temper. So the question is: does he have it when he loses his temper? Do 'men of imperfect self-control act with a knowledge of what is right or not'? and 'if with such knowledge, in what sense'? what is it that they fail to resist and how are they related to it? (pp. 156–7).

Aristotle points out that a man may be 'possessed of knowledge' but on particular occasions 'not call it into operation' (p. 157). What allows for this may be that while the knowledge he has is general the man who has it may not recognize that it applies to the particular case. Aristotle's example is of the man who knows that dry food is good for every man but refuses to eat the dry food offered him because he wrongly thinks it is some other kind of food which is harmful (p. 158). But he may also fail to call it into operation because it becomes inaccessible to him. This happens when he is asleep or drunk. As Aristotle puts it: 'he has it in a sense and also has not'. A man who is in the grip of a passion such as anger or lust is in such a state. This, Aristotle says, is so in the case of the man of imperfect self-control: his knowledge is eclipsed by the emotion or desire that tempts him to act against his better judgement.

He may give in to his fear and act in a cowardly way for which he will later feel shame. He may be taken over by his anger, lose his temper, and do or say something he later regrets. He may yield to his lust and do something he otherwise knows to be wrong. But this knowledge at the time is simply an echo in his memory or reduced to a mere piece of intellectual cognition: it is simply 'in his mind'; he does not stand behind it in his affective commitments. It exists in a dislocated form.

Aristotle's view thus is that the man of imperfect self-control does have moral knowledge though at the time of action it is inaccessible to him. Secondly, he further thinks that such a man does not lack virtue either, although in particular actions he departs from it. As Aristotle put it: he *is* not unjust, but he *does* unjust acts (p. 170). I argued elsewhere (see Dilman 1979, chapters 3 and 8) that these two views are not at variance with what Plato holds. Aristotle is wrong in thinking that for Plato there is no such thing as imperfect self-control, that the good man has perfect self-control and the wicked person has no self-control.

For Plato, I argued, the knowledge which Socrates identifies with virtue is a love of the good. It is in that love that the good man is both at one with the good and knows goodness. The knowledge in question is not intellectual knowledge applied, and in that sense practical knowledge, but affective knowledge *lived* by the person who has it. Where a person has made his own the values of Plato's morality of love he knows goodness in the way he lives it: he is at one with it in his love and in his will. He is not dissociated from what he knows: he lives what he knows; it is not something confined to his mind or intellect. So too his reason is not dissociated from his emotions. His reasons for acting are affective in character, and the affects or feelings in question are shaped by his moral commitments, by what he sees in the values he makes his own. It is in such commitments that the good man comes to himself; that he grows together and finds inner unity. It is in coming to such unity in himself that he moves towards greater autonomy and, therefore, self-mastery.

Plato, however, does not deny that this admits of degrees. He recognizes, for instance in the case of Alcibiades as portrayed in the *Symposium*, that a person's moral knowledge may be tenuous. For he describes there, through Alcibiades' mouth, how when Alcibiades listens to Socrates his soul is thrown into confusion and dismay by the thought that his life is no better than a slave's, that he is still a mass of imperfections and persistently neglects his own true interests by engaging in public life. When in the presence of Socrates, whom he loves and has great regard for, all this is clear to him. Yet when he is immersed in public life he forgets him affectively. Consequently all that he has learned from Socrates deserts him. Unable to maintain contact with it he betrays Socrates as his teacher.

In fact Alcibiades is very much divided between his love of Socrates and his ambitions in public life. He stands somewhere between Socrates in his goodness, and Archelaus in his ruthlessness. He oscillates between the two, at least in what he wants. Aristotle's man of imperfect self-control, the weak-willed man, who cannot keep to his resolutions, perhaps stands nearer to goodness. As I put it in my book on the *Gorgias*:

> A man may love a woman deeply, steadily, and yet he may do things, perhaps through certain defects in his character, which *in another man* would constitute proof that he does not love the woman, or does not love her deeply, or thinks of himself more than he cares for her. Nevertheless this may not be true of him at all, as we may appreciate if we know him well, even though he hurts her and makes her wretched. In spite of this it may still be true that he loves her deeply and steadily – something which a great novelist may succeed in conveying to us ... Likewise it is possible to love the good deeply, steadily, yet unhappily, through some defect in one's character.
>
> (Dilman 1979, pp. 45–6)

After all, if Plato did not recognize weakness of will he would not have recognized a certain variety of cases of remorse; and that is unlikely to say the least.

It is true that Socrates' words in the *Gorgias*, 'and a righteous man performs right actions', seem to suggest that Plato does not allow for weakness of will. But as I explained 'this answer is not in tune, let alone required, by the idea of virtue as a state of soul' (ibid., p. 42). There is an internal relation, of course, between virtue and right actions: a man who never does the right thing cannot be said to possess virtue. But this relation is not such that if a man yields to temptation and does what is wrong we have to say that he no longer possesses virtue or cares for what is good. That he still does so may show itself in his struggle and in the remorse he feels for what he has done. The claim that one makes about a man's present state of soul logically involves a reference to his past actions, reactions and feelings. So there may be enough in a man's life and past actions to justify the claim that he cares for the good and is a virtuous man, despite the fact that on a particular occasion he has done wrong. If this is true and he is virtuous then he will repent what he has done and will try to make up for it.

> Caring for the good – this is not simply a matter of doing this rather than that, and it cannot be confined to any particular course of action. That is why ... an ethic, like that of Socrates, which locates virtue in the soul rather than in 'outward' action does not need to insist that 'a righteous man performs right actions; and that a man who performs a wrong action cannot have done so 'knowingly'.
>
> (ibid. p. 42)

To do something 'knowingly' obviously a man must have the knowledge in question. But he may have it and on a particular occasion do something 'unknowingly' – that is without exercising the knowledge he possesses. Here Aristotle is right; the knowledge he possesses may have become inaccessible to him at the time. Where Plato and Aristotle differ is in their conception of the knowledge in question – moral knowledge.

For Plato, evil, which excludes knowledge of the good, we have seen, determines the will from within. We now see that virtue, which for Plato is equivalent to goodness, and necessarily involves knowledge of the good, also determines the will from within, but differently. In the one case the person gives up what are possibilities for him by *yielding* to certain inclinations, in the other he gives up what are equally possibilities for him from *conviction*. He gives in, one could say, to 'natural necessity' in the one case and to what is or, at any rate, will become a 'moral necessity' for him in the other. 'Love of the good', in which what he gives up is subject for him to 'moral necessity', is not a mere inclination. It is something to which he has come by inner work and renunciation – and renunciation is the antithesis of indulgence. Because it dissolves the barriers which egocentricity erects around a person, such love enables the person to learn from his contacts with what exists independently of him, to grow and come together in what he thus learns and in the process to find himself. But this obviously admits of degrees.

So if a person who has come to goodness in such love does on certain occasions yield to temptation and thus fail the object of such love, fail that is in his loyalty to it, this must be because of some flaw in his character – a flaw which involves some form of self-division. Thus the impulsive person who, when tempted cannot sustain contact with what on other occasions he draws strength from in himself, namely his love of the good, is a weak willed person. He lacks self-mastery in the face of certain temptations. This is also true of the coward with respect of the fears he cannot stand up to. Aristotle mentions the fact that 'Socrates thought that courage was also knowledge' (p. 63). The knowledge in question is, of course, the brave man's knowledge of the good in his love of what needs to be defended and of what, therefore, he must not betray. It is in his allegiance to and faith in what he thus loves that he finds courage.

A person who loves nothing and cares for nothing outside himself, can exercise self-restraint only because obtaining what he desires demands it in the particular circumstances. Freud describes this as acting in accordance with 'the reality principle' and thinks of it as the most that a person can attain in his development. We have seen that Socrates characterizes such restraint as a form of self-indulgence. Here it is the ego that barters one form of pleasure for another, and so there is neither mastery of the ego nor any self to master it. For a person who loves nothing has nothing to be loyal to, to give himself to, nothing to find sustenance in, and so nothing from which to grow and come to himself – to a self in which he can *own* his actions, including the mastery of his inclinations.

Aristotle is right in likening the man of imperfect self-control to a man who is drunk or in a swoon. But what makes him vulnerable to certain temptations, defenceless in the face of certain provocations or fears, is something he lacks in himself to a degree: the love in which he is at one with goodness. In his development such love as he has come to is flawed; it is contaminated with what comes from and belongs to the ego. It is in this sense that Socrates would have said that the weak-willed person, the man of imperfect self-control, is a person of imperfect knowledge of the good. He is *like* a man drunk on alcohol; only what he is drunk on is not alcohol but the ego.

At the beginning of Book VII when enumerating certain common beliefs Aristotle points out that 'it is sometimes said that the man of practical wisdom cannot be a man of imperfect self-control' (p. 153). He explains later that the practical wisdom in question is not a form of knowledge but an aptitude: 'it is not possible for the same man to be at once a man of practical wisdom and of imperfect self-control: because the character of practical wisdom includes … goodness of moral character. And … it is not knowledge merely, but aptitude for action, which constitutes practical wisdom: and of this aptitude the man of imperfect self-control is destitute' (p. 173). Clearly for Aristotle anything that can be called 'knowledge' belongs to the intellect. No wonder he cannot agree with Plato or Socrates in the way they connect moral knowledge and the will. What Aristotle's reading of the above claim comes to can be put as follows: Practical wisdom or prudence is a moral virtue, and this is a matter of how a person is apt to behave. One who possesses such an aptitude is necessarily someone who is capable of self-control. For to be prudent is to be moderate and to have a sense of proportion, not to be easily carried away, to have one's feet on the ground; and these are the ingredients of self-control. To be sure 'to have one's feet on the ground' does involve 'knowing what is what', but it is not merely a matter of having knowledge; for part of what it means is 'not to be flighty and apt to be taken over by fantasy'.

In contrast, as we have seen, self-mastery for Plato does not belong to prudence but to the knowledge that is part of a love of the good that is pure, that is uncontaminated by what comes from the ego. One cannot come to such purity of love without a 'purification of the soul' as he calls it in the *Phaedo*; and this is a transformation in the person which I described as his 'finding himself', 'coming to himself'. It is this that necessarily includes self-mastery.

4 Conclusion

I have considered two aspects of Aristotle's contribution to the problem of free will, (i) his examination of the conditions under which we are said not to act of our own free will, and (ii) his contribution to the questions (a) whether the man who acts wickedly and does evil deeds acts 'voluntarily', that is of his own free will, and (b) whether a man can have moral knowledge and lack self-mastery, whether he can do what he himself knows to be wrong and condemn. I contrasted what Aristotle had to say on these two questions concerning the relation of moral knowledge and the will with what Plato had to say through Socrates as his mouthpiece in some of his dialogues.

We saw in our considerations of the *Iliad* and *Oedipus Rex* how much the early Greeks were impressed by the part that chance and the expressions of 'human nature' in the character of individuals play in determining the course of their lives and the fate which becomes theirs in their blindly following this course. There is a blind collusion here between the individual in his particular character and independent contingencies which are far greater than him – 'natural necessities' in the way things go: in the way they are ordered in nature, including human nature, and in human societies. What I found in the two pieces of literature I have examined – two pieces which rank among the greatest works of world literature – is a vision of the vulnerability of human beings to forces both within and outside them which turn them into puppets so long as they either remain unaware of these or set themselves to overcome them by force or trickery. But it is equally part of this vision that each individual bears a responsibility for either remaining blind to these forces or for their arrogance in thinking that they can overcome these. I find further, as part of the same vision, the hope of a different order in which the individual can find a freedom which he can never find by pitting his strength against any of these forces. This order does not exist in another place, but is to be found in the individual's relation to the world in which natural necessity reigns supreme.

It is this that I take Plato to articulate in his moral philosophy: human beings are blind or without light insofar as they are immersed in the world of the social, of pleasure, power and self-interest, and identify themselves with its values. They become slaves insofar as this identification leads to evil entering their soul.

In my estimate, however intelligent, perceptive and careful Aristotle may be in his approach, and the width of knowledge and experience he brings to it, the quality of his imagination and his rootedness in common sense are such as to deprive him from reaching the depth at which the vision I have articulated illuminates human existence and the plight of the individual.

Aristotle is right in taking the reality of human free will for granted, in seeing it as characterizing human existence, in radically distinguishing it from other forms of existence, and in concerning himself with the conditions which restrict and limit its exercise to vanishing point. But his articulation of them is too general and his examples are too restricted to cover the great variety of cases in which the exercise of human free will is tricked or is a mere appearance which hides a very different reality. And though he makes many good and useful distinctions, such as that between a person's responsibility for his character and his responsibility for what he does in acting within that character, in the way he talks about the virtues and moral knowledge, he does not show any appreciation of the asymmetry between good and evil, and so fails to see the way evil enslaves a person and goodness liberates him. This is lost in his replacement of Plato's duality of good and evil, and the radical difference between the two orders to which they belong, with a plurality of virtues which belong to the same world or order as the flaws and failures of those who have them or lack them altogether.

Aristotle agrees with Plato, of course, that human freedom takes self-discipline and requires self-mastery, and that it is to be found on the opposite side of licence. He is famous for having brought the existence of weakness of will into the limelight – where a person knows what is right, or what is in his own interest to do, sincerely wants to do it, and despite all this fails, leaving it undone or doing its opposite. This is puzzling and he asks how it is possible. We have seen that the gist of his answer is that his momentary lusts or other emotions eclipse his knowledge so that he loses contact with what he really wants – his enduring commitments and interests. I argued that this is correct as far as it goes and that Plato does not dissent from it: that it is not true that Socrates rejects the possibility of weakness of will or imperfect self-control as Aristotle calls it.

Aristotle distinguishes between weakness of will and ignorance. This is part of his claim that ignorance is not the same thing as involuntariness: 'ignorance which affects moral choice constitutes depravity but not involuntariness' (p. 47). Since for Socrates failure to do what is good and just is a failure of moral knowledge it seems to Aristotle that Socrates must reject the possibility of knowing what is right and failing to do it. What he does not appreciate, because his conception of moral knowledge is so different from that of Socrates or Plato, is that for Socrates or Plato moral knowledge is internally related to the will. The evil person lacks moral knowledge in his orientation of will; and the good man is someone who knows goodness in his allegiance to it, which allegiance finds expression in his commitments and, therefore, in the orientation of his will and soul. The weak-willed person is someone who is flawed in that very orientation as this finds expression in his character. The flaw, whatever form it takes, has its source in the tenuousness of his contact with goodness. In this tenuousness he lacks inner unity.

That is, the weak-willed person is the person who in his love of the good has not managed to attain wholeness. What he knows and wants to do, he does not know in his wholeness, he does not want whole-heartedly. For his love is not pure, he is not pure at heart. What contaminates his love and his heart's desire is what comes from the ego.

This is how I see the way Plato and Aristotle stand with regard to the problems of freedom and weakness of will.

Part II

THE COMING OF AGE OF CHRISTIANITY

Morality, theology and freedom of the will

5

ST AUGUSTINE

Free will, the reality of evil, and our dependence on God

1 Introduction

For Augustine there is no question that human beings have free will. Man is God's creation and free will is a gift of God. Human beings have been given free will so that they can do what is right. What this means is that a creature who has the capacity to choose can choose freely, and with that possibility we have the kind of life which has a moral dimension. But if man can, in particular circumstances, be presented with different options, and can choose to do the right thing, doing so freely, that is in the light of his moral convictions and, perhaps despite the pressure not to do it, or the temptation to do something else, he can also choose to do the wrong thing, to do something that is evil. So with the gift of free will God has given man the capacity not only to do good but also evil. In thinking of it as a gift of God Augustine is not taking free will for granted but is grateful for it and for everything which having it presupposes: indeed for human life.

So is God responsible for the evil that man does and hence for the evil in the world? The evil would not be there if God had not given men free will. Augustine in *De Libero Arbitrio – On Free Choice of the Will –* sets himself to answer this question. This is *one* of the questions he sets himself to answer in that book. It is a philosophical, conceptual problem for him because of the beliefs he holds within the Christian religion to which he is committed in his faith.

Augustine further holds that though men have the freedom to choose between good and evil, and so are responsible for their good deeds and wicked actions, so that their actions deserve praise and blame, reward and punishment, nevertheless they cannot do right, follow goodness, without God's grace. So another question that arises for him is whether this does not detract from men's freedom: are men's free will and God's grace compatible?

On the other side, the side of evil, he believes that it is men's lusts, greed and avarice, pride and hates which lead men to a life of evil deeds. But these are the kind of things that enslave the will. So how are they free in their choice of evil? He asks: how does that movement by which the will is turned from God come about? (Bk III §1).

Another question Augustine feels he must answer concerns God's foreknowledge. God is omniscient and so knows everything, and that includes not only all that is in people's hearts, all that they desire, covet, and their intentions, but also all that has happened, is happening and will happen. But if God knows all that will happen in the way that He knows all that has happened, that is directly, by memory, then the future is closed or foreclosed, which would leave no logical room for free will. So how is free will compatible with divine foreknowledge?

These are some of the questions that St Augustine takes up in his book *De Libero Arbitrio*. In the modern era, since the Renaissance, it is the assumptions of the sciences, in particular the general law of causality, that have posed problems for our 'belief' that as human beings we are capable of choosing, deciding and acting freely – in other words that we are the author of our own actions, that we determine our own actions in accordance with our own convictions and desires, taking into consideration the particularity of the circumstances in which we act, and that we have the capacity to withstand and resist outside 'interference'. This is what is usually meant by the attribution of *free will* to human beings. If we are subject to causality, if our very consciousness and will, our decisions and actions, are the consequences of antecedent causes, how can it be said that *we* are the author of our actions? How can what we take to be our decisions be decisions, that is conclusions that *we* have reached to take certain actions, intentions that we have formed *ourselves*? Indeed, would we be *intentional agents* in the sense we take ourselves to be?

Similarly, at the time of St Augustine, when Christianity was getting established and spreading within the Roman empire, theology raised problems for the reality of free will for those who embraced Christianity. Augustine in his youth had pursued a pagan life and also had given himself intellectually to certain philosophical movements. After his conversion at the age of thirty-three it became important for him to answer the philosophical difficulties raised by Christian theology for the believer, to resolve certain paradoxes which presented themselves to him, and to reject certain philosophical views which attempt such a resolution by tampering with theological doctrines.

In our day and age some of the philosophical problems about human freedom have been represented as arising at the frontier between science and 'common sense' where 'beliefs' central to each come into conflict: are these conflicts real or only apparent and, if real, what 'beliefs' do we need to give up or modify? It is the same with the conceptual conflicts with which Augustine attempts to come to terms in *De Libero Arbitrio*. Only in place of science we have Christian theology and in place of 'common sense' we have Christian morality: how are the demands of that morality to be reconciled with the conceptions of Christian theology? He wants to do justice to that theology of which he has seen dilutions personally in intellectual movements which captivated his mind in his earlier life; and he wants to proclaim and defend that morality which he ignored in his youth, at his own expense as he now recognizes with contrition.

I now turn to a discussion of what he has to say about some of these problems or conceptual conflicts.

2 The reality of free will

Augustine has no doubts about the reality of free will in human beings, that is about our *capacity* to act and choose freely, in other words according to our own lights as individual agents: 'When I willed or did not will something, I was wholly certain that it was not someone other than I who willed or did not will it.' 'Will' here means 'decide' or 'act with intention'. He is saying, in other words, that he had no doubt that he was the author of his decision and action, that he had himself formed the intention in his action. That is, his decisions, intentions, actions were 'his' in, what I call, the strong sense of the word – which they may not have been. For he could have acted the way he did, for instance because that was the way his comrades thought it was the way to do things. In other words he could have had no opinions or convictions on the matter and simply toed the line. He would then have been the instrument of a way of thinking and acting prevalent among his comrades and, perhaps being used by some of the less scrupulous among them. Augustine tells us, not in so many words, that this was *not* the case, though it could have been. The conceptual point is that even if that were the case, as it could have been, it *need not* have been so. That is precisely why I said that the reality of free will is our *capacity* to own our intentions, to be the author of our actions, to be responsible for what we do, so that we can be praised or blamed, rewarded or punished for what we do. Our having that capacity presupposes, of course, the logical space within which it can be exercised. It is what is distinctive of human life that provides that space.

Referring to the time before his conversion he tells us: 'I did not that which with an unequalled desire I longed to do, and which shortly when I should will I should have the power to do ... For in such things the power was one with the will, and to will was to do, and yet it was not done; and more readily did the body obey the slightest wish of the soul ... than the soul obeyed itself.' He means that the body obeyed the soul's lustful cravings more readily than the soul heeded its own moral scruples. Here the will, which Augustine identified with his scruples, failed; it was overcome by his lustful cravings and obeyed them. So he acted against his will and came to regret what he did. He knew even at the time that he ought not to do it and so, in that respect, would rather not do it. He might have said to himself: 'I *wish* I had the strength not to do it, to restrain myself.' He asks: 'Whence is this monstrous thing? and why is it? The mind commands the body, and is obeyed forthwith; and the mind commands itself, and is resisted.' Why? His answer is that the mind 'wills not entirely; therefore it commands not entirely. For were it entire, it would not even command it to be, because it would already be. It is, therefore, no monstrous thing partly to will, partly to be unwilling, but an infirmity of the mind.' 'I it was who willed, I it was who was unwilling ... I neither willed entirely, nor was I entirely unwilling. Therefore I was at war with myself.'

That is, he was unable to put himself wholly behind what he willed. For he was divided in himself. So in part of himself he remained unwilling. That is he could not gather that part of himself behind his will. He could not put his whole self behind his will – whole heartedly. He remained disunited in himself until his conversion. For him to come together that part of himself which existed in dissociation from where he wanted to stand, so as to be behind his will, would have to change. It would have to change so that what attracts it would no longer attract it under the same aspect. For instance, if it is women who attract him, living with a woman 'in sin' would no longer attract him. Or if it is money that attracts him, it would not attract him as a bribe or as an ill-gained recompense. Or if the attraction of women or money is still somewhat indiscriminate, he would have sufficient unity in himself to have the strength to resist it when succumbing to that attraction would mean committing adultery or accepting 'dirty money' for instance – not that the latter ever attracted Augustine.

Thus before his conversion to his mother's faith (his father was a pagan) Augustine was divided between his father's lights and his mother's precepts. He put his very considerable talents and qualities of heart in the life in which he followed his father's lights; but he dissipated himself. It was not until he was able to put them in the service of the life he found with his conversion to his mother's faith that he came to himself. He found the courage to reveal himself to God in all his faults and failings, to receive His forgiveness, and in that forgiveness he found healing and came together in himself. Where previously he failed to carry through what he willed he could now do without having to will it. For he had no doubts about what to do; he was in no conflict about it. In his clear conviction it presented itself to him as something he had to do. As Augustine puts it: were the mind entire, it would not even command itself, because it would already be. That is where one is clear and has no hesitation about what one is to do there is no effort of will to be made and so no 'willing' in that sense. There is then no question for one about what one must do. If anyone else questions it and suggests an alternative, the natural answer is: 'I have to do it.' It is in this sense that the action one is ready to embark on presents itself to one as a *necessity*. There is no division then between what one feels one ought to do and what one wants to do: one wants to do with one's whole being what one knows and feels one ought to do. That certainty is one paradigm of the freedom of the will for it overrides coercion, temptation and attempts at dissuasion.

So free will is the human capacity to act and choose freely within a life in which that freedom is threatened from many different quarters – as Augustine well appreciated. It is, further, at the heart of our capacity to do good and evil; the two are indissolubly linked. That is the ground for Augustine's interest in free will.

3 Good and evil: free will and God's grace

De Libero Arbitrio starts with a discussion of evil: how do we come to do evil? Is it something we *learn*? Augustine's answer is No. Evodius, his interlocutor, asks: so how is it that man does evil? Augustine answers: because he turns away from education. That is he turns away from moral knowledge, from the opportunity to acquire it. Evodius insists that there are two kinds of education: the kind by which we learn to do good and the kind by which we learn to do evil. Indeed, we do speak of someone having learned to lie, to cheat, to steal. But as Plato has pointed out, what we call learning here is imitation and copying: we learn such things by copying others, but good is not something one can copy. If you simply copy what a good man does you would not be doing what he does, for what makes what he does good is that it comes from him. That requirement is irrelevant to whether or not what a person does is evil. At the extreme, if you force someone to do evil against his will and he gives way under coercion, his soul will be soiled. The intelligibility of the remorse he may subsequently feel proves the point. By contrast, just as you can take a horse to water but cannot make him drink, you can take a man to the good but you cannot make him good. However much he copies what he sees that does not make him good. There is no goodness without inner transformation: it is the soul that has to turn to the good, in one's own soul that one has to turn to it.

Augustine refers to that as understanding. The second kind of learning that Evodius mentions, he says, does not involve gaining understanding. No one learns without coming to understand. One might argue that even where one learns a skill one comes to an understanding of what that skill is directed to – the skills of a metal worker for instance. The skills of an evil person at manipulating people do not involve understanding people. They are more what one would call 'knowing what makes people tick' – which Socrates would have described as a 'knack'. Thus his contrast in the *Gorgias* between 'argument' and 'persuasion'. It is like the difference between being wise and being 'street wise'. Of course goodness is not a matter of having any skills; it is a matter of the heart, of a disposition of the soul. But I wanted to point out that what Augustine says here is applicable even in the case of 'learning a skill'. The person from whom someone has 'learned evil', for instance, dishonesty – to lie and to cheat – is no teacher, he says: not worthy of being called a teacher. And if he is a teacher, that is someone from whom one can learn something, so that one's understanding is increased or deepened, then he is not evil. All this is closely related to Socrates' discussion of oratory in the *Gorgias*.

But if we do not learn to do evil, where does the evil we do come from? Are we born with it, and if not how do we come to it? Augustine tells Evodius that this is a question that greatly worried him in his youth, drove him into the heresy of Manichaeism, and indeed caused his downfall. As I understand it the heresy of Manichaeism in question is that evil belongs to a realm outside the jurisdiction of God, which implies the denial of God's omnipotence. But if God *is* omnipotent must He not be responsible for the existence of evil in the world, and so for the evil which a person might do?

'We believe,' Augustine says, 'that everything that exists is from God and yet that God is not the cause of sins. Yet it perplexes the mind how God should not be indirectly responsible for these sins, if they come from those very souls that God created and if, moreover, these souls are from God'. There follows a long and circuitous discussion. Evodius gives examples of various evils: adultery, homicide, sacrilege. Augustine asks what makes any of these things evil. In the case of adultery they come down to lust. What then of homicide? There are different cases of killing and some of them do not involve evil: the soldier who kills an enemy, the judge or official who puts a criminal to death. Augustine does not question Evodius' judgement that these do not involve evil. After some discussion they agree that what brings evil to the killing is lust – as in hatred or revenge, or the lust for what is to be gained.

This conclusion is then further refined when Evodius proposes a distinction between man-made law and eternal law which belongs to divine providence: 'How then, before divine providence, are these men free of sin when they are stained by human blood for the sake of things they ought to despise? I think, therefore, that the law that is written to rule the people is right to permit these acts, while divine providence punishes them. The law of the people deals with acts it must punish to keep peace among ignorant men, insofar as deeds are governed by men; these other sins have other suitable punishments, from which, I think, only wisdom can free us.' Augustine agrees. Here we may think of Antigone, in Sophocles' play of that name, who disobeys the law which Creon upholds as a necessity for the state's functioning. Augustine adds: 'The law which is made to govern states seems to you to make many concessions and to leave unpunished things which are avenged nonetheless by divine providence – and rightly so. But because it does not do all things, it does not thereby follow that what it does do is to be condemned.... It is helpful to men living in this life.'

Augustine then goes on to say that what is just in temporal law is derived from eternal law. In other words, eternal law is the measure of the temporal law's justice. What is temporal may change in accordance with the changing circumstances of men and their social arrangements while still remaining just by the measure of eternal law. He concludes that eternal law is 'that law by which it is just that everything be ordered in the highest degree'. Eternal law is unchanging because it is independent of the changing circumstances of men.

He then turns to 'how man himself may be most ordered within'. He clearly sees a close connection between goodness or justice and the order within the soul which underlies the possibility of what he called 'willing entirely' or, in other words, as one – that is where a person acts of his own free will. He argues that human beings possess the capacity of reasoning and when reason is master in human life men have mastery over themselves. When reason 'controls and commands whatever else man consists of, then man is ordered in the highest degree'. What is thus ordered includes what we share with beasts, though it includes much more than that – for instance the love of praise and glory and the desire for power. These cravings when not subject to reason make men wretched. 'When reason is master of these emotions, a man may be said to be well ordered. No order in which the better are subject to the worse can be called right, or can even be called order at all.' He concludes: 'When reason rules the irrational emotions, then there exists in man the very mastery which the law that we know to be eternal prescribes.'

I do not think that he is suggesting that emotions *as such* are irrational, thus suggesting a necessary schism between reason and the emotions. Nor is he suggesting that the light of reason is morally neutral. As I read him, when reason is *at one* with the emotions those emotions are no longer irrational, they are shaped by the person's moral convictions – as in the case of compassion, one's love of justice, one's moral revulsion when it is pure. It is only when reason is separated from the emotions that its rule becomes despotic. The order it imposes, if it succeeds, remains external. That is not real self-mastery, for the person remains divided in himself and where it obeys 'the dictate of reason' he does so unwillingly.

When there is genuine self-mastery a person is wise: 'when a man is so constituted and ordered,' Augustine says, we consider him wise. He has the understanding he was speaking of earlier: moral knowledge. Mind 'is present in men' – that is the capacity for judgement, reasoning, deliberation, acting on reasons, and self-awareness – 'for men do things that could not be done without mind'. That is their way of acting and living exhibit the exercise of these capacities. 'Yet [there are many cases where] the mind does not have control, for they are foolish. Rule by the human mind ... belongs only to wise men' (Bk I, §ix). 'Governance by the human mind is human wisdom.' In other words man needs wisdom to be able to use well the capacities that constitute his mind. When he does so he will not be overpowered by lust; he will have mastery over himself. Nor will he be over-powered by fear or pain, he will have courage and fortitude. These are expressions or aspects of self-mastery, and we count them as virtues.

The mind, thus, that has such wisdom is 'more powerful than desire' (Bk I, §x). 'Therefore, no vicious spirit overcomes the spiritual armed with virtue.' Like Plato, Augustine sees a very intimate connection between wisdom and virtue. (For Plato they are the two sides of the same coin.) Augustine then adds that 'no one can force the soul to be a slave to lust'; when it submits to lust it does so voluntarily. This follows for him from our capacity for free will and from what seems obvious to him, namely that such a soul 'merits punishment'.

Plato would agree that human beings have the capacity for free will and also that the wicked merit, and indeed he would say need, punishment. But he says that when the mind is overpowered by evil in the form of lust, meanness or hatred, the person in question does not act freely. He has yielded what Augustine calls 'the governance of his mind' to evil – to what constitutes the evil in question – without, however, recognizing it as evil. He would say, I think, that no one who knows evil and can recognize it for what it is – and he would have to have come to know goodness, and so to have found oneness with it, to be able to recognize evil for what it is – can choose to do evil. Hence a man who does evil does so unknowingly. So does Plato think that he does so unwillingly, involuntarily? I think he does, but not in the ordinary sense in which Augustine denies this.

The evil person is certainly behind his evil actions, and while he does not see what he does under the aspect in which the good person sees it, he certainly sees and seeks the pain and injury he inflicts on others. What he lacks is the perspective of compassion; he does not care – care about what he is injuring, destroying. He is blind to what makes what he is harming worthy of love, consideration, admiration, nurturing, protection.

One could say that he has something lacking in him, something that limits or impoverishes his life, that he has remained affectively and in appreciation stunted. He is acting in the dark in the sense that the world in which he is moving about and acting in does not fully coincide with the world of his victims. He has a superficial idea of the significance of what he injures or destroys. It is as if a thief, knowing the market value of a rare work of art, were to set out to steal it for gain, and then perhaps burn it to avoid being caught with it and going to prison. He is so distant to those who care for it, has so little idea of what they see in it, of what it means to them, and in that sense of what he subordinates to gain and destroys, that one could think of his act as little different from a storm which damages the work. If he knew, Plato would say, he could not do what he does: could not *will* to do so.

He is not unwilling to do what *he* does, *as he understands it*; but he does not *will* what he brings about – i.e. what his *victims* could describe him as doing. It is, therefore, open to them to describe what the evil person does in either one of the two ways: (i) he does what he does *willingly*, i.e. voluntarily, or (ii) he does *not will* what he brings about. Augustine prefers the first description, Plato prefers the second. The two descriptions are not incompatible, though they put the emphasis in different places. The second description invites an attitude of compassion towards the evil-doer without in any way excusing him.

Augustine who opens his soul to God in full consciousness of his sins puts the emphasis on the will: 'it is by will that we deserve and live a praiseworthy and happy life, and by will that we deserve and live a disgraceful and unhappy life' (Bk I, §13). But then, he asks, why are so few men happy when all want to be? (§14). 'How, by will, does anyone suffer an unhappy life when no one by any means wants to live unhappily?' His answer is that only those who will to live *rightly* are happy. If you do not will rightly, the happy life can neither be merited nor attained. 'Merit lies in the will, while happiness and unhappiness are a matter of reward and punishment.' He does not make it clear whether happiness or unhappiness *follows* willing to live rightly or *belongs* to it in the sense that virtue is its own reward.

What this emphasis on the will highlights is the evil-doer's responsibility, though we have seen that responsibility is divided. He is certainly responsible for the action that he wills, the one that is internal to his willing. That is he necessarily wills an action under a particular aspect, and he is certainly responsible for the action identified under that aspect. The action which the victim suffers brings in an aspect from which the evil-doer is alienated. Whether he can be held responsible for such alienation is at least debatable. Some would say that such alienation is an evasion for which the evil-doer is ultimately responsible. I have no doubt that sometimes this is so; but I am not sure that there are not cases where this is not so.

Plato's position is more complex. I think his view is that a person who is at one with evil is not himself. Therefore evil is always alien to a person. It takes hold of the evil-doer's will from the inside – somewhat as in the case of a post-hypnotic action. If there is a sense in which a person who has woken up from a hypnotic trance is responsible for the action he was commanded to do, then in that sense so is the evil-doer for his evil action. Augustine's position, I think, is that there is such a sense.

Next comes Augustine's claim that to do evil is 'to neglect eternal things – those things which the mind enjoys ... and which it cannot lose as long as it loves them' (§16). He has in mind spiritual goodness: to love it is already to possess it. By 'enjoy' he does not mean 'find pleasure in', in the sense of finding pleasure in one's own goodness, or in the good one does. That would sully it. He means that there is a part in the soul which is *drawn* to goodness. That does not mean – though Augustine does not say so – that it exists in every one, but that each individual soul can be awakened to the love of goodness, can be turned in its direction – in the direction of eternal things.

Many men, he knows, love riches, honours, pleasures, bodily beauty. These, he says, are temporal goods and they cannot be obtained by willing them – in contrast with eternal things or external goods – and they can be taken away from one who possesses them through no fault of his own. Consequently it has been said by some that one never truly possesses them: they are in one's possession temporally and accidentally. As we shall see Augustine says that eternal goods that one possesses in willing them, that is by turning the soul round in the direction of the eternal, are one's possession by the grace of God.

Towards the end of Book II he distinguishes between three classes of goods: great, intermediate and lowest (§19). The virtues by which men live rightly are great goods. The temporal goods, such as physical beauty, are the lowest goods, for men can live rightly without them. The will, which is among what Augustine calls 'powers of the spirit', is an intermediate good. One cannot live rightly without it but, like the lowest goods, one can misuse it and turn to evil. All these goods are God's gift to human beings – including, of course, the intermediate good of the will and its freedom. Free will, thus, is *necessary* for men to live rightly, though its possession does not guarantee that one who possesses it will not abuse it and so turn to evil.

He had said in Book I that we come to evil through a free choice of the will: 'What each man chooses to pursue and to love lies in his own will.' To do evil is 'to neglect eternal things', to give one's love wholly to temporal things. It is to make them one's sole good. In doing so one loses all sense of proportion; one becomes 'perverse and disordered' in spirit, and such a spirit is 'a slave to the pursuit of the things which divine order and law have prescribed should follow its bidding' (Bk I, §16).

So Augustine, while acknowledging Plato's claim that an evil person acts in slavery in loving temporal goods at the expense of goodness, or 'eternal goods' as Augustine puts it, nevertheless claims that he is responsible for giving himself to temporal goods. Plato would further say that those goods feed the ego in the person, which stands opposed to the spiritual and eternal part of the soul. So, at any rate, man falls by his own will even if he in the process is enslaved. The movement of will by which a man 'turns from an immutable good to a changeable one', that movement by which he falls into evil, is *not from God*. It is not from God for it is evil: it cannot be and it does not have to be. So God is not responsible for the bad use man makes of God's gift to him. As Augustine puts it, 'God is not the cause of sin' (Bk II, §20).

By contrast, Augustine says, 'a man cannot rise of his own will as he fell of his own will' (ibid.). The point is that Augustine sees the good in man's life as a gift of God, as something for which we must be grateful and, therefore, for which we cannot take credit. The moment we take credit for it we sully it and so fall. This does not mean, of course, that we have nothing to do with the goodness that comes into our life. One could put Augustine's point as follows: it comes through faith and not will; but it is up to us to keep our faith alive. We must neither take credit for it, nor just wait for it to fall into our lap. We have to put ourselves out for others, struggle with pride and temptation, and keep our souls turned towards God and open to Him. This is what I understand Augustine to be saying when he says that 'man cannot rise of his own will'. The conceptual relations which his statement takes for granted exists within the framework of his faith.

We have examined the two conclusions which Augustine reaches with regard to what he calls 'the origins' of good and evil and the role of the human will in their origination. 'The sole cause of evil lies in the free choice of the will.' This choice comes about in the will's turning away from goodness – from eternal things – as a result of which, in the perspective in which worldly things become goods it is captivated by the attraction they exercise as such and gives in to that attraction. In thus excluding any alternative perspective it becomes enslaved by that attraction. So God is not the cause of evil. It is the misuse by man of God's gift, free will, that is responsible for the existence of evil. Free will is a good, for without it there can be no goodness, no right action. It is not logically possible for God to have given man free will and at the same time to have prevented him from sinning, from doing evil. For to do that is to take away with one hand what He gives him with the other.

As he puts it in his 'Retractions': the discussion was undertaken with a view to reaching 'an understanding of what we already believed on the basis of divine authority'. In other words, philosophy here is given the role not of justifying the faith Augustine shared with others, but of *clarifying* it. He wanted to show the error of those who believed that since God is the Creator of everything he must be responsible for and so to be blamed for the existence of evil. That is he engaged in a philosophical debate with the Manichees.

Secondly, he engaged in a philosophical debate with 'recent Pelagian heretics' who maintained that 'free choice of the will is inconsistent with the Grace of God, since they argue that it is given in accordance with our merits'. This would be paradoxical, for in order for our merits to precede and so deserve God's grace God would already have had to have given us free will. On the other hand, if God's grace were to precede our merits, would that not make God's grace arbitrary. Augustine's answer, we have seen, is that God's grace is *available* to all those who struggle to turn to

God, including therefore to sinners. It is available to sinners in God's forgiveness. No one, however great his sins, is exempt from God's grace in forgiveness. God's grace, therefore, is not the same thing as 'predestination', which would make God's grace arbitrary. This is how Augustine puts it in his 'Retractions':

> Unless the will is freed by the grace of God from the bondage through which it has become a slave of sin, and unless it obtains aid in conquering its vices, mortal men cannot live rightly and piously. If this divine gift of freedom had not preceded grace, then it would have been given according to the merits of the will, not through grace, which is freely given.

Pelagius had insisted, like Kant, that 'ought' implies 'can'. So if, on this view, I ought to do something or to be good, then *I can*, which implies that I am not in need of God's grace. We have seen that Augustine thinks that this is a form of arrogance which denies our vulnerability. It is a form of individual independence which we have met in our consideration of Sophocles' play *Oedipus Rex*. It excludes gratitude for what one has, and the need for forgiveness when one does wrong. Indeed it betrays a state of soul which excludes goodness.

I now turn to a third question which Augustine is equally concerned with in *De Libero Arbitrio*, namely whether God's foreknowledge excludes free will, that is the possibility of free choice.

4   Free will and God's foreknowledge

In Bk III, §2 Augustine raises the question whether God's foreknowledge is inconsistent with man's freedom? He believes both that man has free will, as we have seen, and also that God knows everything, including everything that is going to take place in the future. He calls this foreknowledge: knowledge of what will happen before it has happened. The two at first sight seem incompatible. He wants to show that this incompatibility is only apparent and not real. Surely it rests on the way we understand what is meant by God's foreknowledge in Christianity. It is therefore the Christian conception of God's knowledge that needs clarification.

The problem is expressed through Evodius: 'How can it be that God has foreknowledge of all future events, and yet that we do not sin of necessity? ... Since God foreknew that the man would sin, the sin was committed of necessity, because God foreknew that it would happen. How can there be free will where there is such inevitable necessity?'

Augustine's answer is that not all things of which God has foreknowledge come about by necessity; some come about by will. For instance God knows that we are going to grow old, and who but a madman would deny that we grow old by necessity! God equally knows what we shall will, before we have willed it. Yet when what He foreknows comes to pass what comes to pass is my willing itself. His foreknowledge of what I shall do does not by-pass my willing it – my agency or authorship.

He is suggesting that what God knows in advance is what I shall freely choose. Thus, for instance, you may know in advance that someone you know well is going to sin. But this knowledge of yours does not of itself necessitate that sin. 'Your foreknowledge did not force him to sin even though he was, without doubt, going to sin' (§4).

Something here needs to be made clear. If I foreknew, or as it is more natural to put it 'foresaw', that someone was going to sin what I foresaw can be expressed as: '*given* the way he is going I would bet my last dollar that he is going to come to a bad end'. I am making a prediction about another person on an assumption – the assumption that he is going to hold on to a particular way of going. Even if what I foresee in such cases is that he *cannot but* come to a bad end, it always involves a third-person predictive assumption. That assumption can be of the form, 'unfortunately he cannot let go', 'he cannot give it up – it is an addiction' or of a very different form, 'he is resolved: he will stick to his decision, he won't give in to threats.' But, whichever form it takes, it is always, and inevitably, a third-person predictive assumption: inevitably so because the future can never be foreclosed.

A future time, we say, is a time to come; it refers to what is to come. We are tempted to picture it like a belt, ceaselessly running from an unseen region, coming into sight, and then disappearing into another unseen region, with objects prearranged on it coming into sight and then going out of sight. If only we could peer into that unseen region from which the moving belt brings to sight objects arranged before they come into sight we would know what we shall come to see before they come to sight for others. So even if we cannot peer behind the curtain of the present, God and the angels can, and perhaps some rare individuals with the gift of divination or clairvoyance.

But a time to come is a time when events that have not taken place – anywhere and in any sense – will take place. What is in the future does not exist and it is the 'is' in the expression 'is in the future' that misleads us. Nothing *is* in the future in the way that what has already happened *is* in the past. 'Is in the future' simply means 'will be', and 'will be' means 'is not yet'.

Augustine is right insofar as he is saying that if we predict that a person will do something this in no way implies that he is bound to do it, is forced to do it, that he has no choice in the matter. Some of our predictions do imply that – given his addiction to alcohol, he will accept the next drink that he is offered – and some do not. What Augustine is saying can be expressed as follows: God does *not* foreknow what I shall do *whether or not I will it*. He foreknows what I shall will – for instance what I shall decide. In that case it is still I who will what I will, decide what I decide. Here there is no suggestion that because God or another person knows what I shall decide I cannot decide otherwise. What is known in such a case is not that my decision is fixed, somehow taken before I take it. There are, of course, such cases and then though I may go through a process of deliberation, as it seems to me, and think that I reach a decision, I am in fact deluded, and the decision is a fake. But such fake decisions are parasitic on the possibility of genuine decisions, and Descartes' malicious demon can no more deceive us that there are genuine decisions when there are not any than he can deceive us that there are physical objects when all we have are hallucinations.

Augustine then goes on to compare foreknowledge with memory to reinforce the point that foreknowledge does not necessitate what is foreseen: 'Your recollection of events in the past does not compel them to occur. In the same way God's foreknowledge of future events does not compel them to take place.' What is now recollected or remembered has already occurred, however it has occurred, under compulsion or not. Your recollection now, after the event, cannot make a difference to it. For what is in the past has already occurred and so is fixed in that sense: it cannot be undone. The point is purely grammatical. We can express it in the form of a tautology: what has been has already been, it is over and done with. It is therefore now what it was. The truth of what I claim to know *now* is determined by what has already taken place. Memory thus gives me access to something that has already been, taken place. We can similarly say, 'what will be will be', which means that it is not yet. We cannot, therefore, have access to it in the way we have access to the past in memory. There is thus a radical, conceptual discontinuity between foresight and memory; foreknowledge can never be a form of clairvoyance – seeing in the crystal ball of our mind now shadows cast by what is in the future, in the way that I can see the shadow of someone standing behind me.

Augustine's comparison between foreknowledge and memory may thus court confusion but the point he makes is sound, namely that one's knowledge leaves what one knows as it is – as it *was* in the case of one's knowledge of the past, as it *is* in the case of one's knowledge of the present, and as it *will be* as in the case of one's knowledge of the future, where 'as it will be' means 'undetermined'. But the grammar of what one knows ('it was so-and-so', 'it is such-and-such', 'it will be thus and so') and the form of the knowledge in question are different. Thus my knowledge that you will keep your promise is inductive, though it may contain a large element of trust[1] in you. Your knowledge that you will meet me for tea, as you promised, on the other hand, is not inductive; for you know what you will do in your intention to do it. Here what you know is what you intend to do. But even here the future still remains open: what the future brings may cause you to change your mind, it may prevent you from doing what you now fully intend to do.

However all this still leaves open the question of what God's foreknowledge comes to and Augustine does not have much to say on this directly. Certainly it is part of God's knowledge: 'God knows everything.' Why is this said and what is meant by it? Certainly part of it is what is expressed in the words, 'God sees into your heart, you cannot deceive Him – as you can deceive your friends for instance'. But this does not mean that God possesses the power of telepathy, any more than 'God knows or sees what is in store for us' means that God possesses the power of clairvoyance. Surely at least part of what is meant by 'God knows what is in your heart' is that virtue is its own reward and vice its own punishment. Thus you may have evil thoughts towards people, but you may be able to hide them and get away with your hypocrisy. People may think you are a great fellow, a wonderful person. But you cannot escape the judgement that you deserve on account of your evil thoughts. No one may actually make that judgement since you hide what you are like from others. But it remains true that being the way you are, whether anyone knows it or not, you *deserve* a certain judgement. That judgement is automatic and timeless. That is what God knows: that you deserve such a judgement. This means that it is an illusion that all can be well when you harbour evil thoughts.

What about 'God sees what is in store for us'? Part of it refers to the consequences of our actions in their moral significance. As Socrates put it to Polus in the *Gorgias*: if Archelaus lives the way you say he does he cannot be happy, whatever he says, whatever he feels, whatever he may have. At the end of his life when he appears naked on judgement day, he cannot escape a certain judgement on the whole of his life.

As for what befalls us irrespective of how we act, independently of our actions, it too can be seen as falling under what God knows – since 'He knows everything' – in the sense that the believer accepts them as God's will. He does not ask 'why is this happening to me?': there is no why, it is God's will. 'God knows best' – in other words we should not question it, not ask what we have done to deserve what has befallen us. In this connection what God knows He knows as being what He has willed – that is what the believer is enjoined to take such an attitude to: an attitude which excludes ingratitude.

In none of these three cases is God's knowledge inductive. It is neither a form of clairvoyance, nor is it inductive knowledge. Rather attributing such knowledge to God is giving expression to certain eternal truths within Christianity – within the faith to which Augustine came in his conversion. Once we are clear about the meaning of those truths and see what it means to attribute 'foreknowledge' to God, it will be clear that such an attribution, far from excluding free will in human beings, on the contrary presupposes it.

5 Conclusion

This chapter has been confined to a discussion of the issues which exercised Augustine in his treatise *De Libero Arbitrio*. In it Augustine takes for granted that we have free will, which does not mean that we are always free in our choices, decisions and actions. Augustine thinks that it is when we are disunited in ourselves that we cannot be wholly behind what we will – that is behind our choices, decisions and actions. Thus, for instance, we may be tempted to do something which we know we should not do. As he puts it, 'the mind commands the body and is obeyed forthwith; and the mind commands itself and is resisted'. This is something Augustine knew from personal experience. In his youth he was torn between his mother's faith and his father's paganism. He came to an inner unity, a unity of self and will, with his conversion to his mother's faith: Christianity. This left him with the problem of resolving the conceptual conflicts which thinking within the framework of his faith posed for him.

At the heart of our capacity to own our intentions and be the author of our actions lies our capacity to do good and evil. So one question that exercised Augustine was how we come to evil, and how this differs from the way we come to goodness. He believed that we are free to choose between good and evil, but that we come to them in different ways. We come to evil by 'neglecting eternal things'. We fall a prey to temptations which cloud our understanding; we act without wisdom. The problem here is this: if temptation clouds our judgement and understanding are we not acting in slavery to our emotions and desires? Augustine argues that all the same we fall by our own will, and so are responsible for the state we are in and for what we do in such a state. *We* are the cause of our sins, *not* God.

Augustine holds that by contrast we cannot rise to goodness of our own will and that we need God's grace to do so. But if so, why does God give this grace to some and not to others? It cannot be because those who have this grace are already good and so deserve it since they need His grace to rise to goodness. And if it is not based on their desert then God acts purely arbitrarily. In any case, if it is by God's grace that they rise to goodness does this not make them a by-stander to what they come to, in which case how can what they come to be goodness?

Augustine's answer is that God's grace is not a form of predestination and that it is available to all those who struggle to turn to God, including to sinners. Sinners, for instance, turn to God in the remorse they feel for their sins. Their part consists in accepting the pain of remorse, not trying to evade it, and in waiting – in being patient without any ulterior motive. This is a turning away from the self, a mourning of the evil which constitutes their sins. The time it takes to wait is important and the patience it takes to wait, and also the waiting not being directed to obtaining anything for the self, but being purely sustained by the pain of the evil done in the experience of remorse. The flip side of this same coin is love of goodness, for without it there is no pain in evil. But the person who is steeped in the pain of remorse is unaware of it, the love is hidden from him. In the course of this work of remorse which necessarily takes time and patient, selfless endurance, the love gradually becomes visible, establishes itself, takes root in the person's life, and transforms it. This is God entering his life in the form of goodness. God's grace is this transformation welcomed by the person in the humility of gratitude: 'I owe it to God. God has been good to me.' What the person receives from God is thus a gift which comes to him from a God to which he stands in a *personal* relation of faith.

This is the way I spell out Augustine's 'answer' to the philosophical problem which God's grace raises for him in the way it challenges his belief in the reality of free will in human life, especially in its moral dimension. Let me point out in parenthesis that the form of predestination with which what Augustine calls the grace of God contrasts, is something which takes over a person's life if he takes the opposite attitude of patience and humility towards what befalls him in his life. This is in fact the attitude of *hubris* we have examined in the case of Oedipus in Sophocles' play. As Oedipus puts it in the play: 'Apollo … laid this agony upon me, Not by his hand; I did it.' This is an instance of what Augustine means by 'we fall by our own will' and do so by 'neglecting eternal things'.

Another problem for Augustine concerns God's foreknowledge: how is it compatible with man's free will? If I *know* that something is the case then what I know to be the case *must* be the case. And if it were possible to know that something will be the case in the future in the way I know that something is the case in the present or was the case in the past then it must *of necessity* be the case in the future. If what is the case is an action of mine, then I cannot avoid it, in which case it cannot be the case that when the time comes I act of my own free will. The die is cast before I act. But of course no one can know the future in this way.

However Christians believe that in His infinite wisdom God knows everything, sees everything. It is natural to take this 'everything' to include the future actions of men, as Augustine does, together with many other thinkers. Augustine's answer to the problem this poses for our 'belief' in the reality of free will in human life is this: 'God knows what we shall *will* before we have willed it. In that case what He thus knows in advance comes to pass by our *willing* it. Hence God's foreknowledge does not exclude human agency.' In other words he is suggesting that what God knows in advance in such cases is what we will freely choose.

I argue that this would be true only if God's foreknowledge in such cases is a *prediction*. But a prediction may not be fulfilled. That is if I know that p then p must be the case – of necessity, so that it cannot not be the case. Whereas, by contrast, a prediction that p does not entail its fulfilment. The future cannot be foreclosed; what is in the future is what has not yet taken place.

'A knows that p' entails 'p is true'. However that does not mean that A's knowing p *makes* it true, in the sense that p is true independently of anybody knowing that p. So, Augustine would say, the fact that God knows what I shall decide in advance of my decision does not make it happen. It is I who will decide when the time comes. I argue that this does not meet Augustine's problem with God's foreknowledge of what I shall decide. Because if it were possible for God or anybody else to foreknow what I shall decide, when the time comes I should only go through the moves of deciding it. My decision would not be a genuine decision.

The point is that the idea of such knowledge involves a contradiction and so even God cannot have it. It does not, however, follow from this that the Christian belief that 'God knows everything' is false or cannot be true. What follows is that Augustine's account of it is at fault. I take three different beliefs that may be seen to be covered by the claim that God knows everything, namely 'God sees what's in your heart', 'God sees what is in store for each one of us', and 'What befalls each one of us is God's will'. In the last case one could say that God knows it as part of his will. I argue that in none of these is a knowledge attributed to God that forecloses the future – as in the case of clairvoyance, such as is attributed to Mystic Meg before the lottery draw on television. But, in any case, the trouble with clairvoyance, even if it were intelligible, is that attributed to the God of Christianity it takes away some of His spiritual status and character. A belief in a God with the power of such clairvoyance would lack the spirituality of the belief in the Christian God as we find it in the Bible.

6

ST THOMAS AQUINAS
Reason, will and freedom of decision

1 Introduction

Augustine was writing in the second half of the fourth and the beginning of the fifth century. In his youth he lived a life of dissipation and had belonged to intellectual movements which he later came to see as heretical. After his conversion in 387 AD he confessed his sins to God and dedicated himself to mending his life and correcting both his spiritual and his intellectual errors. He saw these as closely intertwined. Hence he wrote his *Confessions* and also critiques of ideas to which he had himself subscribed in his youth. Philosophy thus had a strong personal dimension for him and in his philosophy he saw the *will* as playing a central role in the errors he wanted to combat. Here his chief inspiration came from Plato through Plotinus.

Aquinas was writing in thirteenth century Europe when Christianity had long had time to take a hold in people's minds. He was an academic and a university teacher, articulating and analysing settled thoughts. He wrote voluminously and set store by *reason*.

Medieval teaching on free choice had two sources: Christian teaching and Aristotle's *Nichomachean Ethics*. According to the former, God has given man the possibility of choosing between good and evil – that is free will. An individual's decisions, therefore, affect his ultimate fate or destiny; but salvation is impossible without God's grace. We have met these ideas in Augustine. The question of grace does not arise for Aristotle. But for him too man is a rational animal, and he considers that it is by virtue of his capacity to consider reasons that man can make choices and so can choose between right and wrong, good and evil. This distinguishes man from other animals and makes him more independent than they are from the nature he shares with them and also from his environment. Man also has a desire to do what he considers good and right.

In medieval thinking, apart from the dichotomy between reason and the will, which raises the question of their relation and the priority of the one over the other, there is also the dichotomy between matter and spirit. Freedom belongs to spirit and corporeal beings – in contrast with God and the angels – are seen as enslaved by the necessities of nature belonging to the matter of their bodies. They are subject to its laws and so they are seen to possess a 'lesser degree of freedom'. But among corporeal beings only human beings are seen as possessing free will.

Freedom of choice, it is considered, is not the licence to do anything one wants regardless of moral considerations – as Callicles thought it was in Plato's *Gorgias*. That would have meant that the damned are freer than the blessed. So the question whether a sinful or evil action is really free was one that was widely discussed.

A distinction was made between a superior and an inferior reason. The former is the bearer of wisdom and a man possessing such reason cannot choose evil; he can only choose between different goods. Inferior reason is the bearer of prudence and someone possessing only such reason can choose evil. For instance out of prudence he may decide not to tell the truth or to let an innocent person suffer persecution. Thus human beings were thought of as capable of making two kinds of free decisions – those responsible to prudence and those responsible to wisdom. Only the latter, some thought, are 'really' free.

It was thought that clearly the free exercise of our capacity for choice had to do with the ability of our reason to judge what is best for us – however that is to be understood – and the will's ability to heed the voice of reason. Hence Aquinas came to be concerned with the relationship between reason and the will in free choice.

2 The will as rational appetite and its freedom

The will, for Aquinas, is what moves us to action. It does so by its capacity to embody our desires. As such it is a form of appetite. For what moves human beings and animals to action is not something mechanical, but a form of seeking that originates in desire – on the analogy of hunger. Our desires constitute the affective and sensual part of our nature. So in our will we aim at something we desire and want to obtain. In obtaining it we find the satisfaction of our desire. Thus the will is directed to an end. That end is the object of the desire which it embodies.

That object becomes its end in particular circumstances by virtue of the agent's capacity for judgement. Thus animals and human beings act voluntarily in contrast with non-living things, as in the case of unsupported objects which fall down. As Aquinas puts it, a sheep, on seeing a wolf, judges that flight is appropriate. Presumably the judgement is implicit in the fear which the sight of the wolf inspires. That is it is the fear which, rightly or wrongly, takes the object which awakens fear as dangerous and to be avoided – rightly in this case. Aquinas speaks of this as 'natural judgement' in the case of animals (*De Veritate*, 'On Free Choice', Article I). Today we would speak of instinct. All sheep take to their heels at the sight of a wolf. 'Brutes,' Aquinas says, 'do not judge of their own judgements, but follow the judgement imprinted upon them by God.' He adds that 'since they do not cause their choice, they do not have freedom of choice'.

In human beings, by contrast, the judgement is one of reason. The shepherd too may take to his heels in much the same way at the sight of a wolf. We may call this an animal or instinctive reaction. But he can subsequently say why he was afraid and so why he ran away. Consequently it is possible for him on some occasions to check his initial reaction and consider whether he ought to be afraid: would it really harm me? can I not stop it harming me? He may thus consider whether or not to run away in the light of wider circumstances and the considerations they raise. He can decide that it would be prudent and in that sense best to run away and do so voluntarily in the full sense and not in panic. In another situation he may decide to stand up to danger – a danger that frightens him. So Aquinas says, 'man is his own cause, not only in moving but also in judging. Hence he has free choice, as one is speaking of free judgements as to whether to act or not.'

That is, a frightened animal has to run away, a frightened man does not have to. 'The whole nature of liberty,' Aquinas says, 'depends upon the mode of knowledge'. Sheep, upon the sight of the wolf, know they are in danger; they know it in their fear. The shepherd too knows it in this way; but he can put this to the test, he can if in doubt reason, and so Aquinas characterizes the human will as 'rational appetite'.

An animal can be wilful, obstinate; but not resolute. The dog may not do what his master asks him to do, resist giving up the stick which his master, perhaps as play, tries to pull out of his jaws. This is an expression of will; but we cannot characterize it as resoluteness. That would bring in the conviction of being right. In our resoluteness we stick to our convictions in the face of opposition. There is an obstinacy in human beings which is a reaction-formation: an inability to compromise, give up or give in because of the fear that one will be left with nothing and lose all autonomy in doing so. It is a form of slavery to one's fears to which there may be a basis in an inner sense of weakness. This is not the kind of obstinacy we have in the case of the dog, which is neither slavish nor free. Whereas resoluteness is an expression of freedom; a man stands behind it with his convictions.

This is, I think, the kind of thing that Aquinas is getting at in characterizing the will as 'rational appetite'. When the human will makes what a person desires its object through the guidance of reason, that is in its responsiveness to considerations of reason, it is of course the person who makes what he desires the object of his will by exercising judgement: is it prudent? is it right? what consequences will my pursuit of it have? do I want such consequences? within the circumstances can I attain the object of my desire? etc.

The will thus, Aquinas holds, is involved or finds expression in two forms of acts on our part: in our *commitments* to certain ends or values and in our *choices* in the light of these commitments in particular circumstances. I think under the influence of Aristotle, he fails to distinguish between ends and values and thinks of choices as being always concerned with means to ends we have adopted.

Our commitments involve our convictions – our moral convictions and our broader loves – and give direction to our will and create a whole range of desires which we would not have had in the absence of such convictions and the kind of life which makes them possible. So insofar as our will is determined by our moral convictions, by the values to which we give our hearts, our moral deliberations in particular circumstances do not concern means to settled ends. If I want to do the right thing by a person and deliberate whether, for instance, to tell him something or let him work it out for himself, these two alternatives are not a means to a goal or end, namely the right thing. The right thing here is not a goal to be realized by one of these means. It is one of these actions which, in the circumstances, of themselves *constitute* the right thing in the light of the values in which I believe. My values are not the goal of my actions but the measure by which I judge what I do.

Aquinas rightly allows reason a role in the determination of my will in its direction. But what he does not make clear is that the reasons that enter such a determination cannot be morally neutral. That is the foundations for the formation of my will are laid in the first place in my upbringing. It is *as such* that I meet the new values which attract me, *as such* that I may come to doubt some values which I have accepted. It is in such circumstances that I may come to reflect about my old values, scrutinize their content, *in the light of* new values that attract me, and even question what they mean to me, how I have taken them into my life, *in their own light*. Or again when new values I have come into contact with attract me, I may reflect on them *in the light* of those values of mine which they are putting into trial. More briefly, my values are my reasons and it is always one set of values that weighs another.

Here, as in my deliberations to choose between alternative actions, my value-laden reasons are *affective* in character. It is as such that they engage my will. They *weigh* with me because the values in question matter to me, because I attach importance to them. This means that I have given myself affectively to them, given them my heart. In other words I would respond to various eventualities, characterized in terms of relevant moral concepts, and so seen by me under certain moral aspects, with various feelings – indignation, concern, guilt, shame, remorse. These are expressions of my love for them, love for what I see in them. My love for them is my moral knowledge. So the reasons that weigh with me are 'affective reasons': they are assessments in the light of values into which I have invested my emotions – emotions shaped by those very values in terms of which I come to think and feel. The perspective of my assessments is the perspective of my emotions as shaped by my values. It is as such that they are reasons for me, as such that they demand that I act in certain ways in particular circumstances and so engage my will.

It is through those emotions that they engage my will; not through independent desires that come to be linked to my moral choices and actions externally as ends and means. The relation between what actions would lead to the attainment of an end I desire is an *objective* matter. In contrast, certain moral values are my reasons for actions, they count for me as reasons for the choices I make because I give myself to them. I stand in a *personal* relation to them; in the absence of such a relation, a relation in which I am who I am, they would not be reasons for me, they would not demand that I act in certain ways, they would not require me to choose. What makes my choice right here is *not* determined by the circumstances plus the external relation in which I stand to them, given my desires and objectives. Thus it could not be said that *anyone* so standing to them by virtue of the same desires must choose likewise. The choice, if it is to be right, must be *my* choice. I must engage with it. I do not enter into the deliberation which issues in the choice as a given in a complex equation. I am in the choice; I live by it, I am renewed by it – even if I do not come to myself in it, I keep to myself in it, remain true to myself, renew my contact with myself.

Aquinas has an inkling of this but his Aristotelian lineage does not permit him to articulate it properly. Thus he contrasts moral reasoning, conceived of as 'practical reasoning' along Aristotelian lines, with deductive reasoning. In deductive reasoning the conclusion is necessary and so *anyone* starting with the same premises has to draw the same conclusion. There is no such necessity about the conclusion a person draws in his practical reasoning about how he must act, what he must do, in particular circumstances. Different people with the same goal, in similar circumstances, may reach it in different ways, via different means, each by following a different course of action. He is not constrained and, therefore, Aquinas thinks, he is free.

This, however, will not do. In moral deliberation the choice presents itself to the agent as a *necessity* – it is true, not as a logical necessity but as a moral one. But a moral necessity is no more a constraint on the actions of a person for whom it is a necessity, since the values which make it so are *his* and so are *internal* to his will, than a logical necessity is a constraint on his thinking since logic is internal to thought. In ignoring it the thinker would not be free to think an alternative thought, reach a different conclusion. He would only depart into incoherence and unintelligibility. My values, of course, are internal to *my* will, whereas logic is internal to thought *as such* – the latter not being a personal matter.

My thoughts, my assessments are free when they are *mine*, that is when they are not subservient to fashions, trends, to norms of what is 'politically correct', when I am not a sheep in what I think – when I think for myself. Similarly, when I do what I find morally necessary I act for myself. Therefore acting under moral necessity is one of the paradigms of free action.

'Just as necessary truths constrain the intellect, so only necessary goals constrain the will.' But moral necessity is not a matter of having necessary goals. If a necessary goal is a goal imposed on the will by a need external to the will because, given one's values, one cannot endorse it, then indeed it is a constraint. If 'necessary' means here that one is unable to ignore it, then this means that it holds the will in bondage and that one is a slave to it. But one does *not have* to allow oneself to become a slave to one's needs. Some will say that we are, therefore, inalienably free: in other words we are responsible for our slavery to our needs.

'Man has free will' or 'free choice' of course, does not mean that individual human beings are always and inevitably free, that we always choose freely. 'We can posit free choice,' Aquinas writes, 'only in things that are the cause of their own motion' ('On Free Choice', Article I). He quotes Aristotle: 'that is free "which is its own cause'. For anything to be its own cause, to cause its own motion – in the sense of both voluntary movement and intentional action – Aquinas points out, it has to be capable apprehension and judgement – a judgement it makes as an individual. Putting God and the angels aside, it is human beings who fit the bill. Will and judgement obviously go together: you cannot have the kind of will that can be free – 'free will' – without individual judgement. On this point Aquinas is absolutely right. This is the foundation, as he points out, of the possibility of merit and demerit, of reward and punishment. Freedom of choice or free will and 'rational agency' are inseparably linked.

One could say that human will is necessarily free; in other words human beings *can* choose and act freely and so they can be held responsible for their actions and choices. But the will is free in its exercise – in our actions and decisions to the extent to which it escapes certain forms of necessity which Aquinas distinguishes: logical necessity, physical necessity, necessary conditions of a goal, coercion. He argues that it is coercion that excludes the free exercise of the will: 'coercion and voluntariness are incompatible.' For, he argues, a coerced act does not originate from the agent's will: if I do something because I am forced to do it, then I do it unwillingly or involuntarily. If I am condemned to a term of imprisonment because of a crime I committed I go to prison involuntarily: that is I am sent to prison, I do not go there of my own will – unless I feel remorse for what I did and want to pay for my crime. I said 'of my own will'; I could have said 'willingly' or 'of my own free will'. Aquinas suggests that if my will is coerced then the action does not issue from my will; in other words the will it issues from is not mine, but that of those who force me.

But it is my will that bends to the will of others in such a case. When I am forced at gunpoint to hit someone it is not my arm that is pushed or forced – an involuntary movement – but my will: an involuntary action. I give in to pressure and act against my will. The circumstances may be extenuating, but I bear some responsibility. There are however different cases here and some distinctions are in order. For instance it is one thing to be panicked into action or to collapse under pressure, allow one's will to be an instrument to a foreign will; it is another to choose to give in to external pressure, judging it prudent under the circumstances to do so. In the latter case is my choice a free one? It is not my will to give my purse to the highway robber; but under the circumstances I choose to give it to him rather than being shot. We normally describe this as an unfree choice; but there are transitions to cases in which a person compromises, tries to make the best of a bad job. No general formulae will do justice to the many possible differences we have in these cases.

As for a 'necessity imposed by need' Aquinas says that it is not incompatible with voluntariness. Thus, for instance, I want to make a voyage overseas and so I board a ship. The necessity of choosing this means it is a consequence of the choice to make the voyage. So it is a necessity imposed by the will itself: in willing the end I will the necessary means. This reasoning applies equally to my earlier example in which, under adverse circumstances, I choose to give up my purse to save my life. But as I said earlier these are cases where the necessity may be imposed on the will by a need – a need that may cloud my judgement or simply cause me to brush it aside. Thus I can do something I would regret against my better judgement; or under the pressure of a need I may persuade myself that it is all right.

These considerations apply to the freedom of the choices I make: I have to be the cause of what I will, what I choose; my actions and decisions must originate in me. Or to put it differently; I must act of my own will, I must be myself in what I will. But what makes me myself? What makes the will from or with which I act mine – as opposed to external to me? This question concerns what I earlier called the commitments which give direction to my will and define me in my identity as an individual – in who I am.

We make choices freely, in particular circumstances, as ourselves, given our commitments. But we have to have come a long way before we can make commitments. Surely it is not my choices and decisions that take me there, since I have to have come a long way before I can make choices and decisions. Does this mean that ultimately my choices and decisions, and indeed my commitments, do not come from me, but are determined by what gives me the make-up I have? Aquinas, rightly I think, denies that contingencies which go to make me who I am take away my freedom of choice.

He writes: 'our temperament inclines us to choose certain things and reject others. But such inclinations are subject to the judgement of reason, which controls the lower appetites. So this leaves the freedom of decision intact.' But where does the judgement of reason in accordance with which I decide come from? The values which give me my reasons exist independently of me – as the norms of mathematics in my calculations do. But, as we have seen, unlike the case of my calculations my values would not give me reasons for choice and decision unless they *weighed* with me. Their doing so has as much to do with what *I* am like in my relation to them as what *they* are like. For what I see in them, what they mean to me, cannot be divorced from my affective orientation. It is as much that which determines what they mean to me as the concepts of the morality to which these values belong which determine my affective orientation. In my identity as an individual I do not exist independently of my relation to those values, as this relation finds expression in my actions and in my relationships with people. Equally, conversely, the weight which the considerations of reasons they make possible have for me – apart from which they would not be reasons for me – cannot be abstracted from who I am. This is something which Aquinas does not appreciate.

The contingencies which enter into my formation include very much more than what gives me my 'lower appetites'. They include where I was born, to what parents, into what culture, and these set limits to what reasons can weigh with me, what can count as reasons for me in my choices and decisions. Yet they are not within the range of what is open to choice for me. Does this not mean that *ultimately* I am not the author of my judgements of reason and so of my choices, since I am what I am by virtue of contingencies about which I have no say? How can I be said to have free choice then on Aquinas' criteria?

The answer which Aquinas wants will emerge from considerations which will show that while much that is mine and makes me who I am is not mine by choice in the first place, and cannot be so, nevertheless in my growth and education it gradually comes within the range of what I can criticize, endorse and so make mine in a strong sense, or what I can reject or at least live with in myself without condoning or giving in to it. It is in this way that in the course of my growth as an individual I can come to participate in my own development, take greater responsibility for who I am and, in the process, move towards being myself in what I will – in other words autonomous. In this way my choices, decisions and actions will originate more and more in me. In Aquinas' words I shall come to be 'the cause of my actions – their voluntary and not their natural cause', and so they will issue from the free decisions of my will. That is my will – my commitments, choices, decisions and actions – will not be determined by what is external to it, even though I could not be who I am but for contingencies which, when they entered into my life, shaping me in my living of it, were logically outside the remit of my decisions and choices in the first place.

3 The will and the intellect: good and evil

Given the way Aquinas abstracts reason from what would give it a grip on the will, except as means to ends internal to the will, he gives the intellect, as a distinct faculty, a primary role in determining the will in our commitments as well as in our choices: 'the intellect is the final cause of the will's action'. In other words it is the intellect which presents the will with its ultimate aims or goals. The will as 'intellectual appetite' cannot help but desire what reason presents to it as good or as the better of two alternatives about which there is cause for some reservation: For 'good is the object of the will' (Article VII). What Aquinas thus seems to deny is that a person can be unreasonably wilful, that he can disregard the counsel of his reason in the choices he makes and in what he does. In other words while he certainly appreciates that there is an internal connection between the will and the intellect, he goes too far in thinking that a person can never be irrational in what he wills. When he seems to be so, Aquinas thinks, it must be because he has made a mistake in his reasonings or assessments: 'the will cannot desire evil, unless there pre-exists a defect in the cognitive power, through which the evil is proposed to the will as a good' (Article VIII).

Thus Aquinas thinks that to will evil is irrational and so he denies that a person can will evil, can freely choose to do what is evil, except by virtue of an error of judgement. In this he certainly differs from Augustine and also from Plato. Plato's conception of moral knowledge, knowledge of goodness, is very different from Aquinas' intellectualist conception of it. For Plato to know goodness is to love it; the knowledge in question belongs to the will, not to the intellect. Evil for him is thus a failure of love, not of the intellect. One cannot know evil if one does not love 'the good'. If one is indifferent to it one only knows 'what others call evil'. One knows evil only in suffering it, in the compassion one feels for those who suffer it, or in the remorse one feels in retrospect for the evil to which one has been a party oneself – and compassion and remorse are expressions of one's love for the good. That is why, on Plato's view, one cannot do evil knowingly and, therefore, willingly. That is one cannot will evil for what it is, appreciating in one's heart and sympathy what it means to its victim and what it means to its agent – however oblivious the agent is of it in the course of the evil he does.

Aquinas' view is very different and Aristotelian in its framework. The will is directed to an object only inasmuch as it takes it to be good – in the sense of desirable, that is able to satisfy a desire. Unless a person sees something as *desirable* and so thinks of it as good, that is valuable from the point of view of existing desires, he would not aim at it. It is its desirability, apprehended by the intellect, that makes it attractive to the will. This is the reason why Aquinas characterizes the will as 'intellectual 'appetite' – appetite guided by the intellect: 'appetite follows knowledge, since appetite seeks only the good which is proposed to it by a cognitive power' (Article II). It is true that the person may think of it as desirable when it is not so to him and so aim at it. But when he finds this out on obtaining or realizing his end he will be disappointed and regret having sought it.

Aquinas allows that we have moral desires and that we find moral goodness desirable and so seek it. Unlike Phillippa Foot, in her early writings, he does not take a reductionist view of moral goodness: he does not think that what makes moral goodness desirable is its instrumentality in the satisfaction of desires we have independently of our moral beliefs. So for Aquinas goodness is itself a good, something we find desirable as an end – not as a means to a further end. That is what makes it an object of our will.

On Aquinas' view, I said, we can will evil only because we mistakenly think it desirable. But what makes this thought mistaken? Why should not people, given their feelings of envy, hatred and jealousy, their resentments, their feelings of humiliation and insignificance, find evil attractive – genuinely so? Two different answers suggest themselves to one for Aquinas: (i) One who pursues evil will find ultimately that it will have undesirable consequences for one: one will end up being unhappy. But what guarantees that this will be the case? The answer is: nothing. As a matter of fact the wicked do often prosper; they do not always come to a sticky end. (ii) One who pursues it will eventually find that the pursuit of evil inevitably leads to the frustration of one's moral desires, one's desires for goodness, so that one will not be able to avoid ending up by being unhappy. But why should we assume that he has such moral desires that will be frustrated? The answer is that there is no good reason for assuming this in advance of the facts. There are, as a matter of fact, many wicked people who have no regard for moral goodness and no scruples or conscience about their wicked deeds. Aquinas has to answer one or the other of these two questions, and as I see it neither of them are answerable on his own terms.

We have considered Plato's very different answer which is that we will evil in *moral* error or ignorance, that is because either we lack a love of the good or because of a failure of the love we have – as when it is eclipsed by desire: by a desire for gain or power for instance. And if the evil person with no such love may be said to be unhappy, that is a *moral* expression of pity *on the part of the person who says so* – pity on account of the state of soul the evil person is in for lacking such love. It is from within the *moral* perspective of the person who speaks of the wicked person as unhappy that the latter's state of soul in its pitiable character comes to light. If the wicked person is blind to this it is only in the sense that he lacks a love of the good, is blind in his affective condition. It is not as if there is any remorse in his soul. How could there be in the absence of his love of the good? From his own point of view – that of Archelaus in the *Gorgias* for instance – he is *not* unhappy.

This line, however, is not open to Aquinas. Thus given the line he takes, he finds the possibility of human freedom to be founded on the intellect: 'the root of all liberty is found in reason' (Article II). This for Aquinas is certainly right, that is insofar as he draws attention to the internal inter-connection between free will and our capacity to judge and reason: 'according as something is related to reasons, so is it related to free choice. Reason is found fully and perfected only in man, and so free choice is found fully in him alone'. 'Man [in contrast with brutes] is not moved necessarily by things appearing to him or by aroused passions, since he can either accept or reject them. Therefore, man has free choice, but brutes do not' (ibid.). In short our intentions are a form of thought: what I intend to do or aim at doing is *in* my thoughts, in the sense that my thoughts are directed to it, so that intending to do it is a way of thinking about it. Hence it is subject to reasoning: I *form* my intentions and I can therefore evaluate and criticize them.

However, I think that Aquinas means more than this; he wishes to say not only that without the capacity for reason and judgement man could not be free, but that he can choose freely because the kind of reason that guides him in what he wills and chooses gives him the logical space for freedom.

More than this, one could say that insofar as we are free in our judge-ments and reasonings, in the sense that we think and judge for ourselves and our reasonings are not rationalizations, then we are free in our deci-sions and actions. For if we think and judge for ourselves and, in that sense, are ourselves in our thinking, judging and reasoning, then we shall equally be ourselves in our decisions and actions. But this carries no suggestion of any primacy of the intellect over the will. What it means – and Aquinas certainly will appreciate this – is that what underlies the possibility of thought and reasoning in human life also underlies the possi-bility of the kind of action that embodies intention and, therefore, also intention-forming decisions in situations of uncertainty. For our free will is the possibility we have of being ourselves in what we want, what we value, what we decide and what we do, and hence equally of our failing to be ourselves as individuals.

However, Aquinas sees the intellect as having primacy over the will and the will's freedom as depending on this primacy. A person's will, he thinks, is determined in general by his goals, and in particular circumstances by the means he chooses to those goals. As far as the means go, there may be more than one way of achieving his goals in the circumstances in which he finds himself. So his will is not confined to a particular course of actions; it is not so constrained by his reasons: it is free within the parameters of what is a reasonable action for him, given his goals, in those circumstances. As for his goals, Aquinas allows these to be amenable to considerations of reason and he regards these considerations to be unlike calculations in that they allow a certain leeway to the person adopting a goal. Consequently Aquinas thinks that in this respect too the will is free. The person's reasons thus incline him to adopt a goal without necessitating him to do so, and, having adopted one, they do not confine him to one particular course of action. It is in this way that, as I understand it, the will's freedom for Aquinas has its origin in the intellect.

If I am right in my reading of Aquinas here, I cannot go along with his conception of the primacy of the intellect over the will in making its freedom – our freedom of choice – possible. We deliberate before acting when we are uncertain about what to do, what we should do in a partic- ular situation. It is certainly true that those deliberations are unlike our mathematical and deductive reasonings. For the 'conclusions' we draw from our deliberations are 'decisions of the will', 'resolutions'; our reasons are 'affective' in character, they embody feelings shaped by our moral convictions, and they engage the will as such (see Dilman 1981, chapter 5).

A deductive conclusion is one which *anyone* can see must be drawn from the premises. One could say that the connection by-passes the person drawing the conclusion; the inference is an impersonal one: it is the same for everyone who understands the symbols, the language. A decision, certainly, is not an arbitrary matter, it is responsible to considerations of reason which presuppose values that exist independently of any particular agent. But reaching a decision, as opposed to drawing a deductive conclusion, is a *personal* matter. I *learn* both the norms of logic in terms of which I reason and the norms or values of morality in terms of which I come to judge and act. But while the relation in which I stand to the former is impersonal and purely intellectual, the relation in which I stand to the values which I have been taught is affective and personal: I can make them my own, reject them, merely conform to them or use them as when someone says 'honesty is the best policy'.

Where I have made them my own, they may come in conflict in a particular situation, or come in conflict with desires I have independently of my values. It may not be clear what I ought to do. You may put yourself in my place and on reflection say: 'this is what you must do; this is what I would do if I were you'. But even though we have the same values we may have different priorities. In any case, whether or not we do, each person finds out his own priorities in deciding. For in our particular decisions we fix our priorities, so that our decisions, unless we regret them, give direc- tion to our will and so delimit our future decisions. There is a two-way interaction between the direction of our will and our decisions: each shapes the other in a 'chicken and egg' fashion. This is how our will remains alive as opposed to fossilized. Thus evolving we put ourselves affectively into our decisions.

I am not denying that you can enter imaginatively into my situation, advise me and help me to see things clearly. But if on reflection you say 'this is what I would do if I were you', I still have to endorse your conclusion and your advice and turn it into a decision. You cannot make my mind up for me, decide in my place. It is not the reasons in question which make up my mind, but *I* who do so on their basis – those to which you draw my attention. Your conclusion remains *yours* unless and until I endorse it, make it mine. I am in the same predicament when the reasons I consider are second-hand. But normally this is not the case, and I am already in the reasons I muster in their affective character, and so considering them *is* making up my mind.

I can, of course, see what I must do without reasoning, and where I do not, and so am in doubt, I conclude what I must do as a result of reflection. But here, as Wittgenstein has pointed out, I speak on my own behalf ('Lecture on Ethics', *Philosophical Review*, 1965); and no one other than me can do so. The conclusion which my assessments and reflections lead me to is the expression of a resolution because of where I stand. This is not a matter of where I find myself standing – as in the case of a chair, building or monument. It is I who do the standing.

I am free in that *I* do the standing, that I am myself where I stand. I am myself *in* standing where I stand; but that is so because I stand there, stand there on my own behalf – as myself and for myself: in the way Luther did when he said: 'here I stand, I can do no other'. This is the purest expression of freedom or autonomy: no one can dictate where I am to stand, what I am to do. I do what I 'will' to do in my commitments, my convictions, in the ideals and causes to which I have devoted myself. Since I am myself in these, what they 'dictate', what appears to me as something I *must* do, is what *I* have embraced: the necessity which they impose is no other than my will. For they are not external to my will; my will is in them: in my devotion I have made them my own, I am myself in them.

I said that Aquinas gives precedence to the intellect over the will and as such abstracts our reasons for acting, as practical reasons, from what makes a person who he is in his actions, that is himself. He considers a person to be defined by his goals. I suggested, in contrast, that a person is who he is in his convictions and commitments, in his loves and loyalties, and that his reasons engage his will as affective reasons. In other words, when a person says, 'I cannot say that, for that would be dishonest' or 'I cannot do that, for it would be to betray his trust', these reasons he gives for refusing to do something embody feelings about honesty, dishonesty and trust. He refuses to do what is proposed to him in coming to see it from the perspective of these feelings. In the way he feels and the convictions which shape and direct them he enters these reasons as himself. He is himself in these feelings: he owns them, not they him. Their perspective is his perspective. It is thus that his reasons engage his will and that he is himself in what he wills. It is, further, thus that he is free in what he wills.

But that is what I take Aquinas to be working around and, at least in part, to miss. Yet this is how I understand we are free in our moral convictions and commitments; indeed the way they constitute a necessary condition of our freedom.

4 Free will, goodness and grace

Aquinas, we have seen, argues that our free will is bound up with what makes us human beings, and that a creature who cannot think before he acts, assesses the situation in which he finds himself, and makes judgements about his own actions as well as those of others cannot be said to have free will or free choice. He does not have to think before he acts, but he must be capable of doing so. He does so when he is unclear, unsure, in doubt, or in conflict about what to do and it matters to him what he does. If I may add, our free will is bound up with our living in a human world and act in circumstances which belong to such a world, characterized by the significances we find in them – significances constitutive of these situations and having their source in our cultures, of which our moralities form an important part.

Good and evil too belong to this world and are an integral part of the significances which characterize our actions and intentions and the situations we create for ourselves and others, and of course, through these our souls. There is pain, distress, aggression, competition and jealousy in the worlds in which different animals live; but not good and evil. The possibility of good and evil entering our lives comes from our being the kind of creature who can think, judge and choose, who know what they are doing in their intentions and, at a minimum, who can regret what they do in retrospect and so take responsibility for it. All this belongs together – indissolubly.

We choose good or evil, as it is sometimes put, *in* how we choose to live and what we choose to do in particular situations. Aquinas, we have seen, denies that we choose evil, knowing it to be evil in our own terms. Perhaps, in any case, we cannot always be said to choose the way we live; some people slip into a ready-made life or follow others into such a life. The more this is the case the less we can say that the person in question is living a life that is *his* in the strong sense and that he is *himself* in that life. But the fact remains that he could have asked questions and so can still endorse or repudiate it and so come to himself. Because, in this sense, we can take responsibility of the life we live and so are answerable for it, whether in fact we are prepared or willing to answer for it, we may be said to possess virtue or to have succumbed to one kind of vice or another according to how we live.

Aquinas holds that our virtues and vices are voluntary in the sense that it is ultimately up to us whether we acquire them or turn away from doing so. We have considered this question in connection with Aristotle: we are answerable for our virtues and vices. Answerable for our vices means that others can judge us adversely for our vices and we can take responsibility for them in the shame or remorse we feel for what we have done, seek to make restitution and in the process change in ourselves. No doubt we cannot change at will, the way we can change our clothes; but still this does not mean that we cannot change in what we give ourselves to in taking responsibility for the actions that issue from our vices. It was *I* who gave in to certain temptations, who agreed to take the easy way out in certain situations or to follow the example of others. It was I who gave my consent, even if only by default, to what led me to where I now find myself. So I can now regret it; and to do so is to take the first step in turning away from the direction my life took as a result. That, if I can sustain it in the regret I feel, would lead me to engage with different things which would bring something new into my life. It is in this way that I may change, genuinely turn into a new leaf.

Augustine, we have seen, said that we fall of our own will, but rise by God's grace. The gloss I put on this is that we can blame ourselves for our vices and others can praise us for our virtues; but we cannot rise to those virtues or keep them if we take credit for them or allow them to go to our heads. We have genuinely to feel remorseful for the way we have lived. It is in such remorse that we turn away from and so lose our ego, and at the same time may be said to turn to God. It is in thus turning to God in our remorse that we work through the envy and hatred in us that has so far anchored us in a life of vice. Christians thus describe what we come to in the process as coming from God. This is my philosophical gloss; to elaborate it further would take us too far afield.

Clearly to say that we rise to goodness by God's grace is not to abdicate responsibility and to take a passive attitude towards one's life. Both Augustine and Aquinas acknowledge this. Aquinas then asks how what comes from us and what comes from God are intertwined and how it is that God's grace does not exclude human freedom of choice. His view is a form of compatibilism: just as Hume argued that human freedom is compatible with causality, so Aquinas argues that divine grace does not exclude human freedom. But his argument is highly metaphysical and goes like this: 'By free decision a human being moves himself into action; but it is not essential to freedom that the free agent should be its own first cause, just as in general to be the cause of something one does not have to be its first cause. God is the first cause which activates both natural and voluntary causes. His action on natural causes does not prevent their activities from being natural; equally in activating voluntary causes He does not take away the voluntariness of their actions. On the contrary, it is He who makes their actions voluntary; for He works in each thing in accordance with its own characteristics.'

I see little connection between the *metaphysical* idea of God as the first cause which activates both natural and voluntary causes and the *religious* idea of divine grace. 'It is God who makes our actions voluntary' is simply an inference from 'God is the creator of everything.' If it has any sense of its own then what it says is that our free will is a gift of God which implies at least that we must use it well and not irresponsibly, mindful of God in how we act. Such claims which belong to orthodox Christian theology have their religious sense in their application to human life – that is in what they are meant to be made of in the living of one's life. It is in abstraction from *that* that they assume a *metaphysical* character. In Aquinas' attempt to reconcile human freedom with divine grace the reference to God as the first cause of our actions or as He who makes our actions voluntary I think assumes a metaphysical character. Or at any rate if something intelligible can be made of this in religious terms, this is not, to my knowledge, a path which Aquinas takes.

He is nearer to the religious sense of grace when he asks what we can achieve morally by ourselves and what we cannot achieve without God's grace. His view, briefly, is that we can resist temptation and so avoid sinning on a particular occasion by our own effort of will, but we need God's grace to become immune to temptation. Again he says that we can be generous, kind and loving by nature, but charity, of the kind we find in saints, which calls for total self-abnegation comes from God. As he puts it: 'free choice without grace remains incapable of accomplishing that good which is beyond human nature' (Article XIV).

This distinction of Aquinas seems to coincide with the one between what we can do at will and what we are by nature on the one hand and what we cannot come to without dying to ourselves and in the process turning to God on the other. The person himself, in the latter case, does not think of what he comes to as an achievement; he simply feels grateful for the change in his life – a gratitude which finds expression in what he makes of what he has come to in the change.

Thus properly understood, along the lines I have suggested, our dependence on God's grace does not exclude human freedom and responsible action. Indeed, if we were not free, if we did not possess free will, we could not depend on God's grace, and neither could we receive it.

5 Free will and God's foreknowledge

If God knows now that I shall commit a murder in the future must this not mean *either* that I cannot avoid committing a murder in the future *whatever I will now or willed then*, or at least that I cannot avoid *willing to commit a murder in the future*? In the first case my will does not engage what I do, in the second it is determined or fixed in advance so that what I *will* is not what *I* will, in other words my will is not free.

We have seen that Augustine's view is that if God knows now what I shall *will* in the future what He knows now is what I shall decide in the future and that this does not impugn my authorship of that decision and so my freedom of will in what I shall do. I argued that whether this is so or not depends on what we make of God's knowledge of the future.

Aquinas argues that God's knowledge of what I shall do in the future is not really a knowledge of the future. For God is not in time and so knows everything timelessly. We see and know the things we know from within time. So we can at best predict what will happen tomorrow on the basis of what we know today and remember in our experience of the past. God, on the other hand, sees it from a vantage point outside time. It is as if, Aquinas says, we were to be confronted with someone coming towards us from behind the hill. Someone viewing the scene from the top of the hill would already know what I would confront in the near future because he could see him now.

This is meant to be an analogy, but it limps. For what the man on the hill sees is a man walking towards me now. He knows now what I shall see five minutes later only on the assumption that the man in question will keep walking and won't change direction; and this is a predictive assumption.

Aquinas says that God did *not* know *in the past* what I do today. He knows it timelessly; not from within any particular time: 'God acts in the timelessness of his eternity.' What is to come, what lies in the future for us, does not lie in the future for God. Perhaps a different analogy would be appropriate here. What are the roots of a particular equation? The answer for me lies in the future; when I solve the equation I shall know. But the answer which I shall thus know is already timelessly present in mathematics. On this analogy what God knows is not contingent, but logically necessary, timelessly true.

How can this be? How can a future event be logically necessary in the scheme of things – even in God's scheme of things? Is this not as absurd as the suggestion that God's knowledge of the future may be like our knowledge of the past we can remember? As I argued in the previous chapter on Augustine what is necessary and timeless in Christian belief is God's judgement on our actions, past, present and future, and on our life when it is completed: that is what God sees. That is the sense in which He sees into the future. As for particular events in the future which affect our life for good or ill, when they are seen as God's will they are seen as unquestionable. Again in Christian belief God's will is eternal, what God wills is inescapable and for the believer it is therefore to be accepted. In other words in seeing what happens as what God has willed the believer sees it as willed not now, not in the present, but in eternity or outside time. That means that the believer sees it as to be accepted unconditionally: nothing that has happened or may happen in the future, nothing that *can* happen, can change that. The necessities in question belong to the connections in which things are seen and taken within the framework of Christian belief, within Christian theology.

6 Conclusion

Aquinas, like Aristotle, is nearer to what is called 'analytic philosophy' these days than many of the other thinkers I discuss in this book. Accordingly I give a fair amount of space in this chapter to his analysis of the relationship between reason and the will in free choice.

He thinks of human beings as having a material and a spiritual side. He thinks that if we were purely bodily beings we would have been enslaved by the necessities of nature belonging to the matter of our bodies. But we are not, and in what constitutes our spiritual side we have the source of our freedom. The will is what moves us into action by virtue of its capacity to embody our desires. As such it is a form of appetite; it is moved by needs presented to it by our desires – as it is in animals too. But these ends are presented to it in animals by instincts which belong to their species and not to the individual animal, whereas in human beings it is presented by a judgement of reason. As such he characterizes the human will as a 'rational appetite'. Thus a frightened animal runs away; but a frightened man does not have to. His convictions or loyalties in the particular circumstances can give him reason to stand his ground and in those reasons he has the possibility of resisting the urge to run away. This is not the outcome of the opposition between two conflicting urges or inclinations, one of which is the stronger of the two. It is not the urges to which he is subject which decide the outcome; it is *he* who decides what to do. He is not the plaything of inclinations to which he is subject, he does not have to be: he has free will. The first two sections of the chapter provide a critical discussion of the way Aquinas represents this. They contain comparisons and contrasts between Aquinas on the one hand and Plato and Aristotle and also Augustine on the other.

He differs from Plato and Augustine in thinking that to will evil is irrational and so denies that a person can will evil except by error of judgement. Plato's conception of moral knowledge is very different from Aquinas' intellectual conception of it. For Plato to know goodness is to love it. Thus turning to evil is for him a failure of love, not of the intellect.

For Aquinas the will is directed to an object only insofar as it takes it to be good in the sense of desirable. But he allows moral desires, so that goodness itself is a good, that is desirable to the will. On Aquinas' view, I pointed out, we can will evil only because we *mistakenly* think it desirable. But, I ask, what makes this thought mistaken? Why should not people, given their feelings of envy for instance, find evil attractive, desirable – genuinely so? I argue that only two answers are possible: (i) Because they will find ultimately that giving themselves to evil will have undesirable consequences.

This is what Aquinas calls an inferior reason and names prudence. (ii) Because they will find that eventually it will lead to the frustration of their *moral* desires. They will find this, Aquinas would say, if they are wise. In their wisdom they will have a superior reason for avoiding evil. In the case of the first answer I point out to Aquinas that the wicked may prosper, and indeed they often do. A wiley and clever person can get away with evil without paying any price measured in terms of non-moral criteria. In the second case we have the instance of Archelaus as referred to by Polus in the *Gorgias*. Archelaus does not care for Socrates' values and so has no moral desires to be frustrated and no moral scruples to restrain him. Socrates' response is that he stands condemned from the perspective of these values. But in his indifference to them this response means nothing to him. Aquinas has no answer to these objections. Thus I contrast Aquinas' intellectualist conception of the will according to which we will evil because we mistakenly think it desirable with Plato's view that we will evil in *moral* error or ignorance and that this is not a matter of the intellect but of the heart.

I point out that drawing a moral conclusion in the form of a moral judgement or decision from moral considerations is a *personal* matter and brings in the relation in which the individual stands to the values in which he believes and so is committed to – as an *individual*. Whereas, by contrast, a deductive conclusion, for instance, is one which *anyone* can see must be drawn from the premises. Here his relation to the logical norms or criteria is purely intellectual. He learns them as he learns to speak and so to reason. There is no question of where he stands with regard to them and whether or not he has made them his own. Intellectual reasons are *impersonal*, affective reasons are *personal*.

In the way Aquinas gives precedence to the intellect in its relation to the will and thinks of desire as providing it with goals which the intellect embraces he abstracts our reasons for acting, as practical reasons, from what makes a person who he is in his actions, that is himself. He considers a person to be defined by his goals. I suggest, in contrast, that a person is who he is in his convictions and commitments, in his loves and loyalties, and that his reasons engage his will as *affective reasons*.

Aquinas is in agreement with Augustine that to say that we rise to goodness by God's grace is *not* to abdicate responsibility and take a passive attitude towards one's life. In my discussion of Augustine on this question I spoke of 'waiting', 'time' and 'patience'. Patience is not the same as passivity. It is trust and self-abnegation. Aquinas asks how what comes from us and what comes from God are intertwined here and how it is that God's grace does not exclude human freedom of choice. His view is a form of compatibilism which is reminiscent of Hume's view that human freedom is compatible with causality. But his arguments are highly *metaphysical*. I see little connection between the metaphysical idea of God as the first cause which activates both natural and voluntary causes and the *religious* idea of divine grace. He is nearer to the religious sense of grace when he asks what we can achieve morally by ourselves and what we cannot achieve without God's grace. Properly understood, I believe, our dependence on God's grace does not exclude human freedom and responsible action, nor is it a form of childish dependence, a form of affective immaturity. Indeed, if we were not free, if we did not possess free will, we could not depend on God's grace, and neither could we receive it.

In the last section of the paper I consider what Aquinas has to say about the apparent incompatibility between God's foreknowledge and human free will. If God knows now that I shall commit a murder in the future it seems to follow *either* (i) that I cannot avoid committing a murder in the future *whatever I will now or willed in the past, or* at least (ii) that I *cannot avoid* willing to commit a murder in the future. In (i) my will does not engage what I do; in (ii) my will is determined in advance so that what I *will* is not what I will.

Aquinas takes a different line from the one Augustine takes. He starts by pointing out, rightly, that God's knowledge of what I shall do in the future is not really knowledge of the future. For God is not in time and so knows everything timelessly. All right; but the question is: what does this mean? Aquinas says, not being in time God, unlike us, does not predict what for us lies in the future. He sees it from a vantage point outside time. He tries to make sense of this in terms of a spatial analogy of a person not knowing that something is moving towards him because he cannot see it from where he is. Someone else, however, can know this because from where he is it is visible. I argue that this analogy fails to shed light on God's timeless knowledge.

I propose a different analogy of a timeless truth in mathematics: the roots of a quadratic equation. What are they? The answer for me awaits the solution of the equation and, therefore, lies in the future. But whatever the answer is, it is timelessly fixed in mathematics. On this analogy what God knows is not contingent, but logically necessary, and so timelessly true for the believer. But how can this be? How can a future event be logically necessary in God's scheme of things? Isn't it as absurd as Augustine's suggestion that God's knowledge of the future may be like our knowledge of the past we can remember?

As I argued in the chapter on Augustine, what is necessary and timeless is God's *judgement* on our actions, past, present and future, and on our life when it is completed. That is what God sees. This is the sense in which He sees into the future. In the following short passage in the *Gorgias* Callicles misunderstands this very thing and Socrates puts him right.

CALLICLES: You seem to me, Socrates, as confident that none of these
    things will happen to you as if you were living in another world and

were not liable to be dragged into court, possibly by some scoundrel of the vilest character.

SOCRATES: I should be a fool, Callicles, if I didn't realize that in this state anything may happen to anybody. But this at least I am sure of, that, if I am brought to trial on a charge involving any of the penalties you mention, my prosecutor will be a villain, for no honest man would prosecute an innocent party. And [since my prosecutor would have to be a villain] it would not be at all surprising if I were executed (521).

He is certain for this reason that whatever anybody does to him cannot harm him.

As for particular events in the future which affect our lives for good or ill, when they are seen as God's will they are seen as unquestionable. In Christian belief, God's will being eternal what God wills is inescapable and for the believer it is, therefore, to be accepted. That is in seeing what happens as what God has willed the believer sees it as willed not now, not in the present, but in eternity or outside time. That means that he sees it as to be accepted *unconditionally*: nothing that has happened or may happen in the future, nothing that *can* happen, can change that. The necessities in question belong to the connections in which things are seen and taken within the framework of Christian belief.

Part III

THE RISE OF SCIENCE
Universal causation and human agency

7

DESCARTES' DUALISM

Infinite freedom with limited power

1 The mind and the body

St Augustine said: what time is I know when I don't ask myself; but when I ask what it is I no longer know. Similarly, we have no problem with the concepts of mind and body in use; but when we turn our thoughts on them, ask ourselves 'what is mind?' and 'how is it related to our body?' they fall apart. Descartes gave a clear voice to the temptations which make themselves felt when we ask such questions and he gave in to them thus formulating his dualistic account of the mind and the body.

He separated the mind from the body. He divorced the identification of anything mental, which he conceived of as an act or state – say, for example, a bout of anger – from the identification of anything involving the body – say, for example, a scowl. He thought of the mind as something each person catches a glimpse of in himself when he thinks, feels pain or anger – as one may catch glimpses of an animal 'outside one', in a forest, as it moves in the undergrowth. What one thus catches glimpses of within, or in oneself, are modes or modifications of consciousness. Consciousness, thus for Descartes, is the defining property of the mind, the stuff which constitutes the mind.

Each person, he thought, *is* his mind; when he says 'I am angry', for instance, that 'I' refers to his mind. It is his mind that is the bearer of his anger; it is in his mind that he is angry – that is where his anger resides. The body, by contrast, is what he, as such, owns. Though very intimately related to it, much more so than a captain to his ship who has to use his eyes to see the damage caused when he hits a rock and also the direction in which it is moving, this body is still an external object to it. It is an object among others that constitute 'the external world'. It is depicted by the anatomy chart and its workings are studied by physiology.

We are thus made up of a particular mind with which each of us is identified as an individual and a body which we own and to which we are causally attached – like a lobster and its shell, except that in our lifetime we cannot shed our body and, perhaps, enter into and so come to own a

113

different one. The workings of each enter into the constitution of our being; as human beings: they determine the mode of our existence as human beings.

Having gone this far, it seemed clear to Descartes that the workings of the body influence the workings of the mind, and *vice versa*, that the mind and the body are in constant interaction. Thus the body needs food to produce the energy that keeps its processes going. When the stomach is empty one feels hungry; this is the mind's confused perception of the emptiness of the stomach of its body – the body it owns. When one thus craves for food one does whatever is necessary to eat. This involves various complex movements that are voluntary or made at will. The will is the mental component which moves one into action.

Similarly, if any part of the body is injured or damaged, cut, burnt, inflamed, bruised, or in decay, as in the case of a bad tooth, it hurts or aches: one feels pain there. The cut or inflammation is something physical, while the pain is something purely mental. The cut is visible to the eye and can be seen by anyone, whereas the pain felt is felt and thus 'cognised' only by the person in pain. Its existence is thus known only to him, and inevitably, by being present in, or forming part of, his consciousness. If anything is presented confusedly in his consciousness, his taking an inner focus on it so as to be clear is what Descartes called 'introspection'.

However naturally we may arrive at this dualistic view, it raises questions which cannot be met satisfactorily. Consequently throughout the history of Western philosophy thinkers have tried to develop alternative views which present equally unacceptable consequences, if not plain absurdities. They are 'reaction formations' to the Cartesian view; they remain rooted in its presuppositions and perpetuate its misunderstandings. These alternative 'theories of mind' are thus satellites of the Cartesian picture of the mind moving in its sphere of gravity. The problems and difficulties of Cartesian dualism thus cannot be resolved by putting forward any further theories of mind.

Let us consider the example of a sensation such as pain taken by philosophers in their abstract thinking as paradigmatic of the mental: a private occurrence. Is it not clearly an effect resulting from a physical stimulus, say an electric shock and the ensuing nerve impulse? Is this not, therefore, an instance of the body causally acting on the mind just in the way Descartes pictured it? Pain, here, is clearly thought of as the mental end-product of a chain of physical causes in the body, and as such as a self-contained occurrence, totally cut off from the public world in which we live – as a 'private' occurrence. We take the physiological story as a sequence of steps which lead to it, as in the case of any causal sequence of physical causes and effects. These two ways of thinking converge and complement each other.

It is perfectly true that we talk of the cause of pain. We say: the red-hot plate which he touched by mistake burnt his hand and caused him great pain. But what does this come to? The plate burnt his hand, he withdrew it with a shout while tears streamed from his eyes. This is a reaction to being burnt; it is a reaction of pain. What we need to recognize is that what we mean or understand by 'pain' cannot be cut off or isolated from all this. That is not to say, of course, that a person cannot be in pain without showing it in reactions of this kind. He can. Nevertheless when we say of him that he is in pain we are linking his case with others where people show their pain, do not hide it, and elicit reactions of recognition from others. It is in the light of such cases that we understand the person who exhibits no reaction of pain as being in pain but hiding it. For it is in connection with reactions of pain that, as children, we learn the meaning of the word 'pain' and come to understand what it means for a person to be in pain.

We may be inclined to think that pain exists in isolation from pain-behaviour and that communicating it to another person is reporting to others something that is open to view within one only to oneself. But the truth is the reverse of this. In the first place our pain flows into our reactions, very much as it does in animals – as in the case of a dog that howls with pain. It is as we learn to speak that we learn to restrain our reactions, to hide our pain, where the situation demands it of us. Indeed our life comes to contain such situations which it could not have contained at first. Only then does our pain become something we can keep to ourselves and, in that sense, something *in* us. Hiding it is not omitting to communicate it; it is a positive doing on our part: we suppress reactions which belong to being in pain – reactions reference to which would have to figure in explaining the meaning of the word.

These reactions are not external to what we understand by being in pain. They are not symptoms of something hidden, like the symptoms of an inflamed appendix. They are expressions of the pain: the pain itself shows its face to others in them. The pain is *in* these expressions of it for others to *see*. They are 'constitutive' of pain in the sense that for the child who comes running to his mother crying when he hurts himself, holding the hand he has hurt, this behaviour and the circumstances are an *insepa-rable part* of the whole situation in which he learns to use the word 'pain'. The mother does not take the behaviour as 'the outward signs of something hidden from her'.

We tend to forget that pain is not only *something* felt by the person in pain, but also something *seen* by others in the normal course of life – when the person in pain has no reason to want to hide it from others. It is the *same thing* – what we refer to as pain – that is both felt and seen, though not by the same person. In its everyday meaning the word 'pain' signifies something that is felt by the person in pain and, normally, also seen by those around him when it is intense. Hidden pain is what *remains* of what originally belonged together. I repeat, *originally* pain is not something hidden – as in young children and in animals. It takes much learning and the sophistication of culture for it, on some occasions, to come to be hidden. Hiding it is a voluntary action on the part of the person in pain.

So being in pain is not being in a state which is open to view only to the person in pain, one which is accidentally connected with pain-behaviour and, therefore, identifiable in separation from anything open to view by others. The question which has puzzled philosophers for a long time totally misconstrues this: how can physico-chemical processes in the body give rise to consciousness, to a mental content or state such as pain? and how can that, in turn, cause a bodily movement? Thus we think of what is in question as a chain of electro-chemical processes, causally linked, containing a maverick link in the middle – the maverick link being a non-physical private state. That is what puzzles us: how can *that* be produced by electrical impulses? and how can it, in turn, even if it leads to an act of will, bring about bodily movements?

This is the puzzle for Cartesian dualism: how can the mind and the body interact? What such dualism does is two-fold: on the one hand it abstracts our mental capacities – such as our capacity to feel pain, our capacity to think, to form intentions – from the life in the weave of which they are realized and exercised. On the other hand, as physical beings, it thinks of human beings as physiological organisms. That is what it is to start from the mind and the body in separation from each other, instead of flesh and blood human beings in the course of their lives, in interaction with each other.

To begin with it is not because the man who has burnt his hand is in pain that he reacts in ways we are familiar with in connection with pain. Rather his reacting in this way is part of what we mean by his being in pain. His reaction is a reaction or response to his hand having been burnt. In separation from such reactions one could not speak of pain, no matter what physico-chemical processes take place in an organism. What the burning *causes* is not something one can describe without referring to the man or animal. It is *he* who feels pain, who writhes, groans, or howls. This is the *effect* which his burning of his hand or paw has on him: it makes him cry or howl. The effect in question thus is not the kind of event that belongs with and forms a link in a chain that includes the secretion of acetyl-choline by nerve cells at synapses. Of course these processes take place, and if they did not – if the nerves were severed or anaesthetized – the man or animal who was burnt would not feel pain. These processes or changes are a necessary condition to the person's or animal's ability to feel pain; but they are not the *cause* of the pain he or it feels on a particular occasion.

Of course the body and the mind are intimately involved in pain and in other sensations, but very differently from the way pictured by Descartes when he talks about the causal interaction between the body and the mind. Very briefly, the body comes in for me, the person who feels pain, in that I feel the pain in some part of my body. That it has such a location is part of what makes us characterize it as 'physical pain' – as opposed to what has sometimes been called 'mental pain', for instance anguish, which is not a sensation at all. Yet it is related to the painful spot differently from the way the colour of the bruise I have received characterizes the place in my body that still hurts. It is not too difficult to articulate this difference – a difference 'in grammar'.

In connection with another person's pain the body comes in for me in that it is in the expression of his face, his bodily posture, tone of voice and reactions that I see his pain. But the body which Wittgenstein thus described as 'the best picture of the human soul' is not the one depicted on an anatomy chart. *As such* the body does not provide the logical space for any expression of the human soul – for instance a smile of recognition or gratitude.

"Smiling' (Wittgenstein writes) is our name for an expression in a normal play of expressions' (*Zettel*§527). Thus I would not be able to react to a fixed smile imprinted on a paralysed face as I do to the smile of someone who smiles at me in the ordinary course of affairs. A stranger in a bus drops his ticket. I pick it up and give it to him. He smiles as he thanks me. I smile back. 'No wonder,' says Wittgenstein, 'we have this concept [of a smile] in *these* circumstances' (ibid.). The significance of the smile, indeed its identity as a smile, is bound up with this background. Remove the background or alter it radically, freeze the smile so that it no longer varies with the circumstances, and you no longer have a smile.

The body to which the lips curled in a smile belong is not the body of anatomy. In fact the body of anatomy is invisible to us in our intercourse with people. We do not see it at all; what we see is a person greeting us with a wave of the hand and smiling. But try to see the greeting as a mere movement of the hand, the smile as merely a curling of the lips, and, as Wittgenstein says, 'you will produce in yourself some kind of uncanny feeling' (*PI*§420).

No wonder Descartes thought of the body as a screen which hides other people's souls from us: 'what you see are hats and coats that may cover automata'. For the body he has in mind is the body of anatomy: 'a machine fitted together in such a way that, even if there were no mind in it, it would carry out all the operations that do not depend on the command of the will, nor, therefore, on the mind' (*Sixth Meditation*). It is to *this* body, the body under *this* aspect, that Descartes wants to join the mind. (i) It is the instrument with which the mind acts in the world. Its arms are the levers by means of which it moves 'external' objects. Its eyes are the mind's periscopes, its ears the mind's sonar equipment. (ii) But it is also and inevitably a screen which makes the mind invisible to others.

On the first point the objection is that under this aspect the body is inevitably *external* to the mind – however much Descartes may say that it and the mind form a unity in the body's special accessibility to the mind. So, as such, the question of how the mind operates on or manipulates the body inevitably leads to an infinite regress. To pull a chair the mind has to move the arm and hand; to move those it has to operate the pineal gland, and so on. The gap can never be bridged: the gap between a self-contained mind, with a will the acts of which are purely internal, and parts of a body which stands to it as any other physical object. The intimate relation which Descartes sees between the mind as such and the body it happens to own is a purely causal, external relation. This gap, therefore, *cannot* be bridged. Thus it is not only the mind's knowledge of the 'external world' that is *indirect* on Descartes' view; so are its actions by means of the body.

This makes the same kind of scepticism as we have in the case of the mind's knowledge inescapable here too: if we cannot move the table by telekinesis, neither can we move our limbs 'by merely willing them to move' – by acts of the will. This is all that a mind that is logically distinct from the body can do: 'merely will' its movements. An inherently 'disembodied mind', one that is supposed to be identifiable in separation from the body, cannot be brought into causal interaction with the body which is to it one object in the physical world amongst others. Neither forms of scepticism can, therefore, be met head on: (i) How can we move our limbs and tongue, act in the world? (ii) How can we know anything outside of ourselves?

As for the second point, the body which Wittgenstein considers in contrast with Descartes, far from its being a screen which makes the soul invisible it is in reality 'the best picture of the soul'. As I explained in the case of pain, the mind finds expression in it and these expressions are not external to the mind – to the pain for instance. On the contrary it is the face which the mind or soul shows to other people, to the world. We show our pain, anger and other feelings to others *there*. That is where others come face to face with what we feel – in our behaviour and facial expressions. These are *not* movements and features of a purely physical organism. They are the behaviour and expressions of a flesh-and-blood human being. In our understanding – that is conceptually – neither pain nor anger can be divorced from its facial and behavioural expressions. On the other side of the coin, neither can a smile or a scowl, a wave of the hand or clenching of fists, in their significance in particular circumstances of human life, be divorced from the feelings and intentions they embody.

The body then – not the body of anatomy – is the possibility of our acting in the world, of the realization or execution of our intentions, of the expression of our feelings. Without this possibility there can be no actions, no intentions, no thought, no feelings, and so no mind. Just as without them there is no human behaviour and so no body in the being it has in human life – both for the person himself and for others. As Sartre puts it: 'my body comes into being through the tools I handle and use; it is at the end of the stick on which I lean, on the chair I sit, in the house through which I move' (Sartre 1943, p. 389). For oneself that is how one's body has being, that is what gives being to one's own body. As for other people's bodies they are like the glass of the window: we do not see it, we see the view on the other side – the body as 'the best picture of the human being'.

The intentions, feelings and thoughts I mentioned are what *I* have; not the mind. And I, contrary to what Descartes held, am not a mind or consciousness, I am a flesh and blood being. I have certain mental capacities: I am capable of thinking, capable of forming intentions and acting on them, capable of affective responses: words, for instance, can hurt me, upset me, anger me. It is in this sense that the intentions and feelings I have are mental.

It is what led Descartes, and leads us so easily, to split the mind from the body that put him, and puts us, where we face a dead-end. Once thus divorced it is impossible to rejoin them. With the various theories of mind we then develop to overcome our difficulties we are forever locked in a metaphysical dance. We are kept from starting at the right place: not with the mind and the body, but with flesh and blood beings in interaction with each other in the course of the life they share. That is where we are in our speech, thought and actions; that is where we find our being – are human beings. If we could find our way to starting there both the mind and the body would fall into place and there would be no hurdle in the way of our seeing them in their proper relationship.

2 Human action and the will

We have already seen that when the mind and the body are divorced from each other, in the way Descartes does, human action falls apart conceptually. It splits into 'acts of will' identifiable only in 'introspection', that is in separation from what the person does. And what is left over are movements of the person's body 'brought about' by these acts of will. In the notion of these being something we 'bring about' we treat these movements, as well as those parts of our body which we so move, as external to us. How we manage to do so then becomes a mystery. As William James puts it: 'I will to write and the act follows, I will to sneeze and it does not.'

Locke and Hume have tried to put a brave face on it, by pretending that what we have here is a casual relation like any other: 'we find *by experience* that *barely* by willing it, we can move parts of our bodies' (Locke – the word 'barely' is interesting); 'we learn the influence of our will from experience alone; and experience alone teaches us how one event constantly follows another' (Hume). On this view I can will *anything* that I wish or fancy. I then learn from experience what I can succeed in bringing about by so doing and what I cannot. As Descartes puts it: 'I am conscious of a will so extended as to be subject to no limits' (*Fourth Meditation*). And again: 'The will is so free in its nature, that it can never be constrained – the actions of the soul are absolutely in its power and can only be indirectly changed by the body' (*The Passions of the Soul*, Article 41).

But does this make sense? Do I, to take an example from William

James, know how to will the table to move towards me? Can I move it 'barely by willing it' to do so – that is as opposed to pulling it with my hands? For Hume, as for Descartes, the will has *an external thing* as its object: it happens to be my arm or tongue, but it could be a table or a mountain. In that case, however, the so-called act of will reduces to a mere wish or a magical command: 'Oh, yea table, please move towards me.' Similarly for the arm. The first time we wait to see whether the arm, my arm, will move. If it does, I am pleasantly surprised, and from then on I expect it to move when I will it. But this is to see the movement of my arm from another person's perspective; it is to treat it as an involuntary movement. The 'act of will' is voluntary for Descartes, but the movement it brings about is not.

I 'bring about' only what is not voluntary – for instance, the twitch of a muscle by tiring it, a spasm by taking a drug, the motion of the football by kicking it. But I do not bring about the kick; I do it – I kick the ball. That kicking a ball should set it into motion is intelligible to us. That a wish or a command should move a table is not intelligible. Hume's 'anything can be the cause of anything' removes the distinction between science and magic.

If somebody asked me to will the table to move towards me I should not understand him. I would not know what I am being asked to do, what I am supposed to do. It is not a question of doing something mental which is unproblematic and then waiting to see whether the physical effect I might expect takes place. Wittgenstein said: 'When someone learns to move his ears he thereby learns to will to move his ears. Similarly, when someone learns to speak he learns to think' (in an unpublished notebook). In other words just as the thought is not there before we have learned to speak and have the words to express a thought which is part of a life we live with language, similarly the will is not there, *ie* we cannot form an intention to make certain movements, before we have learned to make them. So we cannot, as Hume suggests, 'learn the influence of our will from experience'. Neither does the case of the man 'suddenly struck with a palsy in the leg or arm' support Hume's claim. For the man Hume is thinking of could walk and had learned to use his limits before he was paralysed.

So we learn to will, e.g. to form and carry out an intention, in learning to do various things – to coordinate our movements, to hold, catch, manipulate things. Indeed in a great many cases the will is *in* what we do, in the many things we have learned to do and now do without thinking. They embody the intention. The intention is not something that precedes the movement and brings it about. But because I have learned to do these things and am capable of visualising the future I can form an intention to do something in the future. Then, of course, the will – the intention, the resolution – exists before the action. But even then it is related to the future, and so to an as yet unexecuted action, *internally*. It cannot be identified or specified without reference to it – the action or the movement.

Similarly the arm that I move, as opposed to the table that I move by pulling or pushing it, is *my arm*; it is not something external to me: an arm attached to me which I manipulate by doing something or other – something other than simply moving my arm.

Yet that is how Descartes conceived of 'acts of will': I do something mental and that brings about the movement of my arm. If that were the case I could observe the movement of my arm like some third person: 'I wonder whether it will move; I hope it will.' This makes sense only in connection with something I *bring about*, not something I do. For what I bring about is something *distinct* from what I do to bring it about; they can be identified independently of each other.

Usually philosophers who think of our voluntary movements as brought about by an act of will think of the mental act which they thus postulate on the model of an effort of will and, as such, as something the person in question experiences. But, as both Sartre and Köhler have pointed out, 'we never have the sensation of our effort, we perceive the resistance of things' – for instance our arm getting heavier as we make an effort to hold it up. Making an effort here is simply continuing to hold my arm up as, with my increasing tiredness, it becomes more and more difficult to do so. It is not doing something additional to holding it up.

Likewise when I move my arm voluntarily, or at will, there are not two distinct things: an act of will and the physical movement I thus bring about. Equally just as my arm is not an object to me – the possessive pronoun here does not signify ownership – neither is an action a mere movement which I bring about. Consider a soldier's salute and all that must be in place in the life of the man who is a soldier for the way he moves and holds his arm to constitute a salute. Only in such particular surroundings of human life is the voluntary movement in question a salute. The soldier himself must be familiar with all this and appreciate it; otherwise he cannot be a soldier and nor can he form the intention – will – to salute his officer. Only then can what he does embody such an intention; only then can he form such an intention before his officer makes an appearance.

Such an intention which may thus precede the action ('I am going to salute my officer when he comes') is not a mental state, act or process, something that has any 'volume' so to speak, something that 'goes on', occupies a duration of time, or fills a mental space accessible to introspection conceived of as an 'inner observation'. As Wittgenstein puts it: it does not have 'genuine duration' (Z §§51–2). If at the beginning of the week I form the intention to do something at the end of the week then, unless I change my mind, I shall have that intention all week. But having that intention all week is not being in a particular state of mind all week. There is nothing that continues all week 'within me'. All we have are such things as the making of certain arrangements, perhaps, pertaining to doing what I intend to do – such as book a ticket, make a phone call, jot down an appointment in my diary. My having that intention continuously is not something continuing to occupy my mind all through this time or preying on it – such as a bout of depression.

When in the future I remember having had such an intention it is not some continuous mental occurrence that I remember, one which constitutes the intention in question during that time. No, I remember such things as the preparations that I made – washing a shirt, an appointment, the excitement at meeting someone as a result of carrying out that intention. It is equally possible for me not to be clear about my intention in having done or said something. I may then reflect on my action, on my reaction to the response it woke in the person to whom it was directed, on the circumstances and on past occasions when I may have done something similar. We call such *reflection* 'introspection' because it has the person reflecting as its object. It is not, as Descartes and so many philosophers and psychologists have thought, a species of observation directed to the landscape of one's mind consisting of private acts and states of consciousness and continuous modifications going on within it.

Indeed a third person can reflect on the same 'material', provided the person in question is willing to be open with him and answer his questions straight and without subterfuge. A man's *will*, thus, as it finds expression in his intentions and resolutions, for instance, can only be seen *from the outside* – as when one sees someone bent on carrying out a scheme. It is not something which the person himself sees from the inside. When he tells you what his intention is, he does so without observing anything – inner or outer. He can do so because the intention is *his*, because it is *he* who has made up his mind, formed the intention.

I said earlier that an intention can only be identified by mentioning the action it is an intention to do. There is no other way of identifying or referring to it. This is equally true, of course, of unexecuted intentions. An intention can thus exist without the action in particular cases; but without reference to the action it is nothing. Thus I cannot intend to do something I cannot think of and am incapable of doing – contrary to what Descartes claimed. I cannot intend to take off the roof and fly like a bird. Nor can I intend to carry out a delicate surgical operation to save someone's life. I can, of course, intend to do so in the future by doing whatever is necessary for me to learn to acquire the skills of a surgeon. If Descartes thought otherwise it is because he thought of an intention, an act of will, as something 'mental' and, as such, something divorced from anything 'physical'.

Both where a man forms an intention for the future and where he makes an effort of will, the expression of will in question presupposes the existence of the practice to which the action belongs and, furthermore, the agent's knowledge of it, and so his capacity to do the action. 'Willing,'

Wittgenstein said, 'is the action itself', and also 'trying, attempting, making an effort' (*PI* §615). It is, of course, deciding too, resolving, intending, for example to speak, to write, to lift a thing, to think about something. So, as Wittgenstein says, 'willing … cannot be allowed to stop anywhere short of the action' (ibid.). That would be to think of it as an inner process or a mental state which, we find by experience, brings about an 'outer action', conceived of as an event, or the movement of an external object which happens to be brought about by me.

Nothing of this kind can bring about a movement or an action. That would be bringing it about by telekinesis. Nor can what makes an action an action, or a movement voluntary, be understood in this way: as caused by an intention, brought about by an act of will.

Both Descartes and Hume went wrong because they started with a conception of willing in which willing had been 'allowed to stop short of the action'. They tried to graft the will, so conceived, onto a bodily movement to make it voluntary and then to turn it into an action. That is they began with the mind and the body conceived of as separate, divorced from each other. They then tried to figure out a way of bringing them together in human actions: human actions as bodily movements which issue from the mind's volitions. We have seen why this will not do. The whole idea of the will as something inward and self-contained, directing our outward, bodily movements, and to be grasped by inner observation, is a muddle. The will, we have seen, is what finds expression in the flesh-and-blood agent's resolutions, intentions, efforts and actions in the course of the kind of life in which the agent participates. This is where it can be seen and only there can its connection with human actions be understood. Indeed, it is also only there that human actions have their reality, their identity and their significance. The moment we start with the body and mind, as Descartes tried to understand them, all this will inevitably come out of focus and be lost.

3 Freedom of the will in Descartes

Descartes' conception of the will's freedom is tainted with this conceptual dissociation. He rightly wanted to distinguish human beings, their life and actions, from the rest of nature, including the animal kingdom. The need to emphasize this should be seen against the rise of the sciences which Descartes presided. As more and more came within the sphere of the sciences, more and more came to be seen as explicable in causal terms and to constitute deterministic systems. Descartes was impressed by how much the body was, in his own words, a machine, fitted together in such a way that for the most part it works by itself. As for animals, this is true of them without remainder: animals, though they have sight, hearing, etc, and can feel pain, are automata.

Descartes was wrong about animals being automata. But he was right in wanting to accord a unique status to human beings and in thinking that their life and actions cannot be explained or made intelligible in causal terms. What makes them unique, he thought, was their distinctive form of agency which involves the will and, intimately bound up with it, their sense of self, reflected in our use of personal pronouns – a sense of self connected with the fact that a person can tell others what he thinks, feels, wishes and intends to do, and can reflect on his actions and motives. Descartes is absolutely right of course, although what is in question was known to earlier philosophers as we have seen. But it threatened to be engulfed by science for which Descartes, himself, was enthusiastic. So he had to reassert it. Within the framework of his dualism, however, his account of the self, the will and its freedom was very unsatisfactory.

He thought of the unique agency of human beings in terms of the activity of the mind – an activity which Hume later abolished without, like Hobbes, resorting to materialism in the form of epiphenomenalism: the mind as merely a shadow or reflection of the body. This was not so in Hume: the mind as an independent realm of its own with its own laws of association. Thus, in Hume, though the mind acts on the body, causally as in Descartes, it is itself law governed, a deterministic system. In Descartes it acts through acts of will, as we have seen, and these acts of will are uncaused and represent the initiative of the self which constitute the mind's activity.

In these acts the will is totally or absolutely free. There is nothing outside the mind to restrict or limit it. What the mind wills is determined by the mind itself in accordance with its own wishes and judgements. It is in this sense that for Descartes the will is self-determined and, therefore, free. The person or self, in the sense of mind, can will whatever he wants to and judges can realize his objectives. Nothing can prevent him – or should I say it, the mind – from doing so. He may judge badly and fail to obtain what he wants, or otherwise come to grief; but that is only the result of his failing to judge correctly the course of events independent of him, external to the mind. It is in this sense that, for Descartes, the will is totally free in its own sphere – a sphere only causally and, therefore, externally related to the world in which the person, as an embodied being, acts.

> The whole action of the soul consists in this, that solely because it desires something, it causes the little gland to which it is closely united to move in the way requisite to produce the effect which relates to this desire.
>
> (*The Passions of the Soul*, Article 41)

As we have seen the mind's or soul's action on this gland is as problematic as any of its actions in the world in which the person acts.

The will is so free in its nature, that it can never be constrained –
the actions of the soul are absolutely in its power and can only be
indirectly changed by the body (ibid.).

I am conscious of a will so extended as to be subject to no limits.
(*Fourth Meditation*)

Descartes goes on to point out that when I have no special reason to act
one way or another I am free, of course, to do this or that. It has been
said, for instance by Freud, but also by others, that it is in such trivial
actions that we are inclined to think we are free. Descartes characterizes
this as 'the lowest grade of liberty'. It involves no decision. When I have to
decide, make a choice, 'then (he says) I should be entirely free without
being indifferent' (*Fourth Meditation*). He goes on:

The power of will ... is not *of itself* the source of my errors – for it
is very ample and very perfect of its kind – any more than is the
power of understanding. – Since the will is wider in its range and
compass than the understanding, I do not restrain it within the
same bounds, but extend it also to things which I do not understand; and as the will *of itself* is indifferent to these, it easily falls
into error and sin, and chooses the evil for the good, or the false
for the true (ibid., italics mine).

'The will *of itself* is not the source of my errors' – in other words, it is just
what moves but it cannot guide itself. It is the understanding that does so
with the judgements it makes. 'It is *of itself* indifferent to the consequences
of its acts' – again it is the understanding that informs it of these consequences in the circumstances in which the man acts. Its power is 'perfect':
there is nothing I cannot will. But what I actually do is what I bring about,
and that depends on factors outside my control, external to me. How well
I succeed in bringing about what I aim for depends on my understanding,
on the judgements with which I guide my choices and decisions.

As Sartre puts it in an essay on Cartesian liberty: 'a man's circumstances
and his powers can neither increase nor limit his freedom. Descartes, like
the Stoics, makes a central distinction between freedom and power. To be
free is not to have the power or the ability to do what one wants, but
wanting what is in one's power to do or achieve' (*Situations* I, p. 319). He
then quotes Descartes: 'The only thing that is wholly in our power are our
thoughts in the [wide] sense in which I use the word "thought". In that
sense all the functions of the soul, not only our meditations and acts of
will, but our visions and feelings too are thoughts. I am not, of course,
suggesting that our power does not extend to things external to us at all, but
that it does so only insofar as they are able to accord with our thoughts [that

is insofar as we are right in our assessments of them and in our predictions]. And so the power we have on things external to us is never absolute and total. For there are powers outside us which can prevent the effects of our aims and intentions.' Thus, Sartre adds, 'it is with a power, limited and varying from one individual to another, that man exercises a total liberty'. As we shall see, Sartre too holds that human liberty is absolute.

Thus, given the way Descartes conceives of the will as a form of thought only externally related to anything he regards as physical, there is no conception in him of the possibility of the will's freedom being limited *from within*. To act well all a man has to do is to judge well and to stick with determination to the decisions he takes in the light of his judgements: to will what he judges. This is the way his rationalism joins hands with his voluntarism. There is no conception in Descartes of any form of weakness of the will or of its bondage or servitude to anything external such as any fashion or trend or to an alien will, or of its slavery to fear or need. It was Spinoza after him who drew attention to all this.

8

SPINOZA

Human freedom in a world of strict determinism

1 Introduction

As far as I know all great thinkers concerned with the *sense* in which we attribute freedom to human beings and whether freedom, in that sense, is *possible* in a world in which human beings are so much part of nature, of the physical world and its causal order, have tried to make room for the intelligibility of that attribution without at the same time diminishing the force of everything that militates against it.

At one extreme are those like Sartre who see human beings as inevitably free, even when they are in chains or living under an oppressive regime. For they take freedom to be a distinguishing mark of human existence. Thus in a paper on 'Freewill', after having pointed out that 'we say of a mechanism that it is now running freely while before it was not', Professor Wisdom adds that nevertheless 'we think of human beings as having a freedom which machines have not' (Wisdom 1965, p. 26). Thus Sartre would have said that when we think of a human being as *unfree* in his actions in the way, for instance, he has sold out for financial gain, or in his slavishness to public opinion, his lack of freedom is very different from that of a mechanism whose movement is interfered with by a rogue magnetic field. The interference will continue until it is removed. But the person can turn around and stop caring about public opinion, or, in the other case, he may come to realize that there are more important priorities than financial gain. Sartre takes this difference to be a distinguishing mark of human existence.

Thus Sartre holds that human beings are *absolutely* free in the sense that they have the capacity to reflect on their situation, consider their priorities, make choices, engage in self-criticism, and bear responsibility for what they have done and where they stand. It is within this mode of existence that they may have or lack *relative* freedom.

At the opposite extreme are those like Spinoza and Simone Weil who are impressed by how much human beings are part of the causal order that constitutes nature. Through their physiological make-up human beings are subject to the causal laws which operate in the physical world. As flesh-and-blood beings they are part of the natural world to which animals belong, subject to hunger, thirst, sex and pain which, in certain circumstances, can exercise intolerable pressures on them. Thirdly, as part of the *human* world they are subject to ego-centric emotions, such as greed and envy, and individual cravings, such as the thirst for revenge when thwarted, hurt or humiliated, and the desire to acquire and exercise power. Human beings are vulnerable to slights and humiliation and do not take kindly to being thwarted. They generally only stomach these things when lack of strength leaves them no alternative But they do not like it and when they have the opportunity and the cunning, or the back-up of strength, they generally prey on each other. Hence they live with defences against exploitation. In any case, even among the more civilized, self-interest is a motive which can easily go into active mode when tempted by opportunity. Here, as we shall see, Simone Weil speaks of 'the laws of moral gravity' which rule in the human soul.

If, therefore, the world to which we belong is a deterministic world and subject to the rule of causality, as Spinoza claims, it is subject to determinism and causality in more than one sense of the word. Simone Weil uses the term 'necessity' to cover all this variety. She emphasizes how little human beings are in control of the big things that happen in their lives, the things which affect them most, and in the shadow of which they live their lives. Spinoza would agree; he represents human beings as merely a small part of a huge machine that grinds on relentlessly. The motion of the machine goes through each of us, transmitted through the motion of wheels within us, thus giving us the illusion that we do some of the moving, or at least contribute to the motion. But that is because we take a partial, as it were worm's eye view, of our situation when we act.

This worm's eye view, as we shall see, inevitably coincides with an ego-centric perspective on things. From that perspective a humiliation, for instance, calls for an almost automatic response. A person thus who can bounce an insult back to where it came from and has the satisfaction of having had his own back, feels he has restored the equilibrium which had shifted in his disfavour with the insult he received. He then feels potent and free. But Spinoza tells us that he has only been a party to a transaction in which his role has been purely reactive and, therefore, passive. His reaction is the expression of a necessity that works through him. In this respect he is like a puppet on a string. While he so reacts he is not himself.

Spinoza does not believe that there are any exceptions to such determinism or 'rule of necessity', as Simone Weil calls it. Does that mean that human beings are not free, full stop? In one sense Yes: we are a small part of a larger whole, subject to the movements that go through it, and we have no control over them. But there is a sense in which freedom is still possible for us. So how can we be free in a deterministic world, in the face of the kind of necessity which characterizes it? Spinoza's answer is again similar to Simone Weil's, so I shall put them side by side.

Spinoza's answer is that we shall be free by understanding and acceptance – understanding that we are part of a bigger whole and seeing that, as such, nothing that happens to any one of us could have fallen otherwise, given the state of the whole from which it arises. Once we see this clearly we shall stop fretting and we shall come free from the cycle of ego-centric, reactive transactions in which we are puppets on a string.

Simone Weil's answer is that we shall be free by 'obeying necessity', by making ourselves as docile as the waves in the sea are to the wind that blows them. To do so is to renounce the self, in the sense of the ego, and therefore to be so transformed in ourselves that our soul is opened to the grace of God. Thus when we are able to say 'Thy will be done' what we are subject to ceases to be something that thwarts or constrains us, or in any way stands opposed to us. Hence in willingly submitting to it we find ourselves and recover our autonomy. We make what is external to us our own.

The following example suggests some parallel that may throw light on what is in question. Sometimes people outside a strict religious order pity those who belong to it. They think of the many rules which those belonging to the order observe meticulously and these appear confining and even oppressive – as indeed they would be to the outsider. But what the outsider does not appreciate is that nobody has forced those who belong to the order to accept its life and, indeed, they are very much themselves in that life. It is there that they come to themselves. What they do they do willingly and what appears a burden to the outsider is no burden to them. For whether or not the rules are restrictive and the routines and chores of that life are a burden is a matter of how those who take part in that life are related to these rules and what they make of them.

In any case the outsider's own life has its own rules. If he is not even aware of them and does not find them restrictive it is because he is at one with the life of which they are a part. It is in being part of that life that he is someone, an individual, himself, has views of his own, something to say, and is capable of judgement.

Spinoza is recommending a particular way of living and facing life's tribulations – one in which one turns away from a worm's eye view of things to one in which they are seen as part of an infinite whole. Whatever one then suffers one will not feel it as directed to one, as singling one out, thus quickening the ego's reactions. Insofar, therefore, as one does not set oneself against it, it will not appear as in opposition to one in one's will. However hard or painful, it will be allowed to sink into the background against which one will carry on with what is still possible for one.

The parallel I suggested with the example I mentioned is this. As in that example here the person who follows Spinoza's precept takes the pains and tribulations that are his lot in life as a matter of course – much in the way that a poor man, used to being poor, takes his poverty. He sees it as his share, and he does not envy others who are better off. He knows that nothing is permanent in human life and that at any time things may change. Far from feeling envy he feels an affinity with all those creatures whose fate is out of their hands and in this affinity feels compassion for them. In this connection it is important to recognize the difference between envy and compassion and that the detachment which Spinoza advocates excludes envy and makes room for compassion.

So far I have merely wanted to point out that in both of the diametrically opposed views I have mentioned – the view that we are absolutely and unconditionally free and the view that we are only a cog in a deterministic world – room is made for a distinction between human freedom and human bondage. This is as true of Sartre as it is of Spinoza. In both views human freedom is seen as an achievement that is rare and precious, one that involves a change in one's perspective on things and so a change in oneself. Indeed, I can think of no deep and serious view on the possibility of human freedom which does not emphasize both how much human life is subject to forces beyond the control of any individual and how much, nevertheless, there is a difference between being a *mere* cog in the wheel and having the kind of autonomy that makes a human being an *individual*.

What such views on both sides thus wish to do justice to is, to my mind, different from Hume's easy compatibilism rightly criticized by Kant. Hume denied the conflict between the two strands of human life which divide determinism from those views which emphasize the kind of freedom that characterize human existence. Kant, on the other hand, perhaps one of the most abstract of philosophers, had a strong sense of this conflict. He was impressed by how much human beings partake of the natural world through many of their inclinations. He saw that if we are to be free, in the sense of 'autonomous', we have to transcend these inclinations in ourselves by giving ourselves to convictions which we cannot hold sincerely while we remain centred on ourselves – 'the dear self' or ego. Thus freedom, he argued, cannot be had in 'the phenomenal world' where causality is sovereign. But if we can enter 'the noumenal world' by renouncing the ego, which is the source of our inclinations and of our attachment to the phenomenal world, we shall escape the rule of causality to which our will is subject through our inclinations. We shall then find a freedom which is not to be had while we remain submerged in the phenomenal world.

In this context it is important not to read into Kant's conception of 'the phenomenal world' what he puts into it in his epistemology (see Dilman 1992, chapter 3). For what he is speaking of has close affinities to what in Christianity is referred to as 'this world' – the world of the worldly in contrast with the world of spirituality. And the 'causality' that reigns supreme in it is exemplified by such things as the pressure of public opinion, for instance, and the ego's need for approval or its fear of being disregarded or punished which makes it vulnerable to such pressure. I give this as *one* example of the causality that reigns supreme in Kant's phenomenal world *as understood in his moral philosophy*. It is important to recognize what is in question here, for it remains buried in Kant's abstract language.

There is thus a conception in Kant, lacking in Hume, of the way we have to turn away from much of what comes to us naturally if we are to grow up in our affective life and, in finding ourselves, become autonomous – capable of thinking for ourselves and acting on our own behalf. Only as such can we avoid being deceived into succumbing to pressures bearing on our will. What prevents a proper conception of all this in Kant's philosophy, however, is his *rationalism* – the way he divorces reason from man's affective life, as a result of which the freedom from what he calls 'inclination' now turns into another form of slavery: slavery to the tyranny of reason.

Spinoza who, though apparently himself a rationalist, has an altogether sounder conception of the emotions. Indeed for Spinoza the divide between reason and the emotions is not a conceptual one, but a purely contingent one which characterizes a divided self.

2 The most fundamental of Spinoza's conceptions of determinism

Spinoza develops what he has to say about human bondage and human freedom within the framework of a metaphysics in which he both labours under the weight of Descartes' metaphysical commitments and also tries to reject and replace them with alternative ones of his own. But he has something to say about human life which, though expressed in terms of these metaphysical ideas, can be expressed independently of them.

In him, Descartes' duality of two independent substances in causal interaction in the case of individual human beings is replaced by two, out of many, aspects of reality mirroring each other. The Cartesian activity of the mind through the exercise of a free will is replaced by 'active emotions' that are wedded to 'adequate ideas'. These are achieved by a passage from submersion to a life of fantasy in which our emotions separate us from the reality of the circumstances in which we live our life, so that on the whole we remain blindly reactive beings, to a life in which we are at one with our emotions and in them are in touch with the realities from which we had previously been separated. When Spinoza speaks of 'a life of reason' the kind of life he has in mind is to be contrasted with 'a life of fantasy'. Thus, for example, at an extreme, the life of a person who suffers from delusions of grandeur and persecution is a life of fantasy. A person who is quick to take offence, or one who in his love-life goes through a repetition of the same pattern again and again, or one who in his grown-up life goes on fighting his childhood battles – these are examples of people who on the whole remain immersed in a life of fantasy.

Take, for instance, the person who is quick to take offence. He may imagine he has been insulted when he has not. But he may equally be someone who takes offence at any insult in reality directed at him. Spinoza would say that he gets worked up into a state of anger and agitation because he has a partial and fragmented view of reality. Indeed, unless he broods over it, he may himself take a 'sober view' of the situation (as we say) and see little in it to get worked up about. Perhaps the man who insulted him was drunk, or perhaps he was in a bad mood. Even if the insult was cold-blooded and calculated, however, he may see the man who insulted him as a malicious person who is perhaps best avoided, and his insult certainly not worth losing sleep over. In his fantasy he has isolated him from everything that mattered to him in his life: he had allowed him to take over his affective life, to occupy the foreground of his affective apprehension of things and there, in the absence of what would cut him down to size, to assume gigantic proportions, dwarfing all else into insignificance. His anger thus was rooted in fantasy and in that sense exemplifies what Spinoza calls a 'passive' emotion – an emotion in which the person is passive in his acceptance of its perspective. Here the person, in Hume's words, is a slave to his passion and, in Kant's words, remains 'heteronomous' in his will.

In such a case the person who reacts in anger has not come to himself, however much to react in this way is part of his character. He is a slave to the anger; he has not made it *his* in what I call 'the strong sense'. Familiar and intimate as it may be to him, as something that comes from within him, it remains something external, not integrated into his life and so to who he is. It is an intruder and insofar as he gives in to it he lacks self-mastery. This is not to say that there is only one way to respond to an insult; but losing one's head is an expression of 'passivity', of being in a state of slavery to one's emotions, of one's lack of autonomy.

Thus self-control, for Spinoza, is not a matter of willing or the exercise of one's free will – as Descartes held. For in Spinoza the will is itself subject to causality; it is not a 'free cause'. 'Man,' he said, 'is ignorant of the causes by which he is led to wish and desire.' Consequently we think we are doing what *we* want and so it seems to us that we are free. If, as he said, a stone thrown and flying through the air had consciousness, it would imagine that it was flying of its own free will. For its consciousness, like ours, would represent the cause of its movement as the fulfilment of its own desire.

Schopenhauer agreed, but added that in that case the stone would be right in thinking it had free will (see Hamlyn 1980, p. 98). Schopenhauer's response seems to be: if you grant what Spinoza grants to the stone, then you have granted it free will; since that is what we mean when we say of a man that he acts of his own free will.

There is some truth in what Schopenhauer says, but it does not go very far. What one needs to be clear about is *how* one's aims and desires are determined. In one of the extreme cases of post-hypnotic suggestion they are imposed on one from outside and one complies without any recognition of this. So one thinks one is doing what one wants when, in fact, unbeknown to one, one's strings are being pulled. There are, however, more subtle and common cases of this as Freud pointed out. The example I mentioned of people who, in their love-life, go through a repetition of the same pattern again and again, with the same outcome every time, is a case in point. Such cases are well recognized by Schopenhauer himself, Freud and Dostoyevsky (see Dilman 1984a, chapter 5, §2). In them clearly people are not free; however much they may try, they cannot get out of the groove in which their life and actions have got stuck. Here Spinoza is right; they cannot free themselves *at will*.

Nevertheless this does not mean that there is nothing they can do. Proust once likened such 'willing' to what a man tries to do in wanting to learn to swim while insisting that he will keep one foot on the ground. The point is that an effort of will has a very narrow focus – what one may call tunnel vision. What the person needs in such a case is to turn around in himself, and that is not achieved by an effort of will, by pushing against what goes against the grain. He needs to shift his focus from what he is pushing to achieve – the will's focus – to the self which resists the pushing – the focus of self-knowledge. That would involve sorting out his priorities and working through his conflicts.

However we need to be clear that we cannot talk about 'the determination of the will' in any blanket fashion, the way Spinoza does. We have to distinguish between cases. It could be said for instance, that I would not have valued and wanted the things I value and want if I had had different parents, had been brought up in a different way, perhaps too in a different culture. Indeed I would not have been the same person. But this does not mean that what I do, go after, is not what I want, that I am not fully behind what I do. Being the person I am I do the things I want. The framework of values, for instance, which I have made my own is not a constraint on my life, a limitation on my actions. On the contrary in the absence of such a framework I could not come to myself; I could have no self to come to. I would be like a rudderless boat tossed about on the waves and drifting in the currents of the sea. That does not constitute freedom. It is by making my own what I learn, what comes to me from outside, that I come to myself, acquire a self to come to; and what is in question is the freedom of such a self.

We see that when Spinoza says that free will is an illusion he was not denying the possibility of human freedom. He was rejecting a confused conception of it. But he has a partly science-orientated, partly psychological and partly religious vision of how much individual human beings are part of a greater whole and how little they are aware of it. As flesh-and-

often one is unclear about or even unaware of one's contribution to a stormy relationship. As one becomes aware of it one is able to ask certain questions about it – for instance, why am I leading my friends on and then letting them down so often? Where am I failing them and how is that linked with my character? *If* I care about certain things, then the very asking of these questions will make a difference to my relationships, change them. In such changes I shall move towards coming to myself, that is find greater unity in myself. I shall thus be able to put into practice what I care for, stop undoing what I constantly attempt to move towards. For I shall become clear about my ulterior motives in what I pursue and in the light of such clarity and of my response to what thus becomes clear come closer to knowing my values and priorities and so find what I want. Here I should emphasize that coming to know one's values involves making commitments. It is in making such commitments that one finds what one wants. It is in this way that I come to know the self that I come to. I have emphasized elsewhere how much what we call 'knowing' in this kind of context merges with making and being. Thus I *know* myself in coming to *be* myself, and I come to be myself in working through my conflicts and so changing as I achieve greater unity in myself.

Spinoza expresses this in terms of coming to 'adequate ideas' about the objects of my emotions in my affective responses. That means seeing them not from the perspective of my passive, obsessive emotions, but in the light of a wide perspective, in the way I have tried to illustrate. As my emotions thus change into active emotions – for instance my hatred evaporates and seeing the person I hated as himself not knowing what he is doing I come to feel some compassion for him – I change. It is in this way that Spinoza thinks I come to myself, and in the process to self-knowledge, and thereby to greater autonomy. It is this autonomy that Spinoza calls 'freedom'.

'Free', he says, does not mean uncaused – taking 'cause' in a broad sense. It means 'self-caused', in other words 'autonomous'. Such a person is someone whose thoughts are his and whose actions come from him. But if he is thus part of a greater whole, as Spinoza conceives him, then how can his actions come from him?

4 Finding freedom through yielding to the inevitable

Being part of a greater whole is the antithesis of being centred in the ego, and a person so centred serves the ego. In doing so he is divided from others; his predominant emotions are those in which the vulnerabilities of the ego and its craving find expression. Such a person is at once oversensitive about how others treat him, quick to take umbridge or offence, and also unconcerned about what happens to them. He needs them for what he can get out of them by way of food for the ego. But he has no stake in their fate and feels little identity with the aims and activities he shares with them. He tends to blame his circumstances, to feel sorry for himself, and his actions often spring from his resentments. What we have here are *par excellence* instances of what Spinoza calls 'passivity'. As for his attitude towards nature he has as little feeling for what forms part of the natural world *for itself*, that is insofar as it does not in some way enhance or impede the ego.

Such a person lives in a permanent fog, surrounded by his ego, and does not see things in themselves. This is not a metaphysical notion; I mean things as they are when left to be themselves in one's apprehension of them, that is not seen in relation to the ego – *that is* the way they can serve or threaten it. The tussle here is between whether they are to be absorbed into the life of the ego or his own life enlarged in being given to them in their independent existence. In the first case he is cut off from their existence as such and the objects of his transactions become fantasy objects. His transactions are then with objects that are the product of his vulnerabilities, dreams, fears and wishful thinking, and in such transactions the ego's life is quickened. In the second case, by contrast, in the interest and concern he develops in giving himself to things in their independent existence he comes to *himself*. When that is the case the person is in touch with what his actions and responses are directed to and those actions come from *him*. In Spinoza's words, he is the cause of his actions; they are self-caused.

Such a person feels part of the existence of things and the life of others, he feels part of the world in which they exist. This obviously admits of degrees and Spinoza is thinking of an ideal extreme of this where the ego has completely dissolved and the person has found identity with nature and everything that forms part of it in his love for it – a love in which he both gives himself to it and is prepared to let it be whatever form that takes. Let me repeat, it is only in such love that the kind of detachment which Spinoza holds liberates us from a state of bondage is possible. Some readers of Spinoza have confused such detachment with scientific objectivity. That is a mistake.

I mentioned two closely related components in Spinoza's conception of detachment: (i) detachment from the ego and so contact with things in their independent existence and transaction with them as such, and (ii) turning away from the fantasy which belongs to passive emotions and the worm's eye view of things that goes with it to taking a view of things in which they are seen in their interrelations. Things are thus seen as part of a bigger whole in which their suitability or threat to oneself, in one's ego, stops being of concern to one. As one comes to oneself in the particular form of one's interest in and concern for *them*, one's life more and more shares and takes part in their existence. One is oneself in that life, but one is happy to let them be come what may.

In Wittgenstein's words from the *Tractatus*, one is in agreement with the world. One is no longer ensconced in one's ego, with all that this means for one's apprehension of and relations with what lies outside it; one is part of the world, in the sense of nature, in one's feelings. As for human beings, one sees them as part of nature, as part of the living world, and one respects them in their living of their life amidst all the hazards that are in store for them. In one's compassion for their vulnerability, like Plato, one sees them in the good that comes from them and as alienated from themselves in the evil they do. One is grateful for the former, like one is for the beauty one finds in things, and one is sorry for them for the evil that enslaves them.

This is not taking a passive attitude towards evil, nor a dismissal of its horror. One opposes it, one fights it, but one does not take it personally, any more than one takes personally the obstinacy of the mule who won't get out of one's way, delaying one in one's journey. The evil of which one becomes a victim will hurt and injure and even perhaps devastate one – I don't see how Spinoza could deny that – but one will not feel offended or sorry for oneself. One is free from those vulnerabilities to which one is exposed in one's ego.

I asked: if a person becomes part of a greater whole, in his feelings, as Spinoza conceives of it, then how can his actions come from him – how can he then be the cause of his own actions? How can the cause of what he does come to lie wholly within him so that he becomes active, autonomous, and, therefore, free? I have tried to explain. But the short answer to this question is that if in my feelings I am at one with Nature then everything that happens will be what I am in agreement with, not because of what it is, but regardless of what it is. Paradoxically in yielding myself, in the sense of giving up my ego and becoming part of nature, I stop yielding to something external to myself.

Let me again take a very limited analogy. If you do something in order to please someone and you are separated from him in your feelings of indifference or resentment, then even if you have reason to want to please him, you will not be doing what you want. You will not be acting autonomously. But if you want to please him because you like him, care for him, then what will please him will be what pleases you – that is you will want to please him. What he wants will be what you want. His will will be yours – but not as when it is imposed on you. You will sincerely be able to say: 'Your will is my command' – that is: 'whatever you wish I will do willingly.'

On Spinoza's view the will of Nature, as it were, is imposed on one because one separates oneself from it by rooting oneself in one's ego. If one embraces it, makes the will of Nature one's command, one will be set free. This is what I take Spinoza's conception of human freedom in a deterministic world to be.

There is one last question I would simply like to touch on: if we live in a deterministic world and are in a state of bondage to it, how can we come out of such a state, disengage from it? The same questions arises for Simone Weil. Her answer is that we cannot on our own or by our own devices. All we can do is to open our souls to God and wait: only by his grace can we be redeemed. I will not now try to elucidate what this comes to.

Spinoza's answer is in some ways similar: we have no free will and it is not by willing that we shall be liberated from our state of bondage: we cannot do so at will – which is the only way open to a Cartesian. But this does not exhaust all the possibilities. A person can grow, come to wisdom, change in his perspective on things, and so in himself, in the course of his life as a result of his experiences: he may come to see beauty in things, find love and gratitude in his heart and humbleness before the events of nature. He may gradually come to participate in the change that is coming about in him in this way. Ultimately he becomes the author of the change though he could neither have foreseen nor willed it. This is what I take Spinoza's conception to be of how we can move from a state of bondage to a state of freedom in a deterministic world where free-will is an illusion.

There is no one way in which this can happen. Here is how Edmund, a drug addict, a character in a play by Eugene O'Neill, *Long Day's Journey into Night*, describes his brief experiences of freedom:

When I was on the Squarehead square rigger, bound for Buenos Aires. Full moon was in the Trades. The old hooker driving fourteen knots. I lay on the bowsprit, facing astern, with water foaming into spume under me, the masts with every sail white in the moonlight, towering high above me. I became drunk with the beauty and singing rhythm of it, and for a moment I lost myself – actually lost my life. I was set free! I dissolved in the sea, became white sails and flying spray, became beauty and rhythm, became moonlight and the ship and the high dim-starred sky! I belonged, with a past and future, within peace and unity and a wild joy, within something greater than my own life or the life of Man, to Life itself! To God, if you want to put it that way. Then another time, on the American Line, when I was on the lookout on the crow's nest in the dawn watch. A calm sea, that time. Only a lazy ground swell and a slow drowsy roll of the ship. The passengers asleep and none of the crew in sight. No sound of man. Black smoke pouring from the funnels behind and beneath me. Dreaming, not keeping a lookout, feeling alone, and above, and apart, watching the dawn creep like a painted dream over the sky and sea which sleep together. Then the moment of ecstatic freedom came. The peace, the end of the quest, the last harbour, the joy of belonging to a fulfilment beyond men's lousy, pitiful, greedy fears and hopes and dreams! And several other times in my life, when I was swimming far out, or lying alone on a beach, I have had the same experience. Became the sun, the hot sand, green seaweed anchored to a rock, swaying in the tide. Like a saint's vision of beatitude. Like the veil of things as they seem drawn back by an unseen hand. For a second there is meaning! Then the hand lets the veil fall and you are alone, lost in the fog again, and you stumble on towards nowhere, for no good reason! (He grins wryly.) It was a great mistake, my being born a man, I would have been more successful as a sea-gull or a fish.

(O'Neill, 1973, pp. 134–5)

HUME AND KANT
Reason, passion and free will

1 'Passion and reason, self-division's cause'

Oh, wearisome condition of humanity!
Born under one law, to another bound;
Vainly begot, and yet forbidden vanity;
Created sick, commanded to be sound;
What meaneth Nature by these diverse laws?
Passion and Reason, self-division's cause.

Fulke Greville

    bless'd are those
Whose blood and judgment are so well commingled
That they are not a pipe for Fortune's finger
To sound what stop she please. Give me that man
That is not passion's slave, and I will wear him
In my heart's core

Shakespeare

Fulke Greville speaks of the will as inevitably divided between reason and passion. Shakespeare takes such a division seriously but, through Hamlet, he recognizes the possibility of reason and passion being united in a man's will and purpose.

Hume denies the possibility of such a conflict. He represents the will as inevitably determined by the passions, with reason as their slave. Kant allows this as a possibility, but claims that the will can and ought to be determined by reason, with the passions subordinated to its sovereign demand. Neither Hume nor Kant, however, can see the possibility of reason and passion being 'commingled'. The question which they pose is this: Is the will inevitably determined by the passions? Is it possible for reason to overcome the passions?

Behind Hume's and Kant's diametrically opposite answers to this question lies a dichotomy to which they both subscribe, namely the view that reason and passion are exclusive categories. Since for Hume reason is inevitably 'inert' there is no question of the will's conforming to reason in opposition to the passions. But for Kant 'conformity to reason' and 'subjection to passion' represent two exclusive and exhaustive conditions of the will, and indeed of humanity, and he favours the former as alone providing the condition necessary and sufficient for the autonomy of the will.

This question of the conflict between reason and passion over the control of the will is an old one. Plato was concerned with it when he asked whether pleasure and fear are the ultimate motives of human action and he tried to bring out the role which men's ideals and their conceptions of the worth of things play in their lives. He argued that when considerations of pleasure usurp the position of reason in a man's life they become destructive of the possibility of a man thinking for himself and acting on his own behalf. He was deeply interested in the question of what underlies the possibility of self-control, and he believed that it involves the use of thought and criticism.

The same preoccupations run through Spinoza's *Ethics*. There he is critical of Descartes' 'voluntarism', the view that self-control can be achieved by determining one's objectives through reason and pursuing them with resolve. He believes that such a view ignores the empire of the emotions in human life. Yet he does not subscribe to the dichotomy which drove Hume and Kant in opposite directions, and he differs from Hume in his account of emotions. He thinks of them as forms of thought which give rise to dispositions to respond to their internal objects in certain ways. Consequently there is no gap in Spinoza's view, as there is in Hume's, between thought and action. He holds, like Plato, that the passions can be controlled by thought, not, as Descartes claimed, through force, but through an understanding which transforms them. Indeed in his conception of 'active emotions' Spinoza recognizes the possibility of passions themselves being transformed into a form of reason. This transformation in men's emotional orientation from 'passivity' to 'activity' bears a close affinity to what Freud was searching for – as we shall see.

Hume too is opposed to Descartes' view:

> Nothing is more usual in philosophy, and even in common life, than to talk of the combat of passion and reason, to give preference to reason, and to assert that men are only so far virtuous as they conform themselves to its dictates ... On this method of thinking the greatest part of moral philosophy ... seems to be founded; nor is there an ampler field ... than this supposed pre-eminence of reason above passion.
>
> (Hume, 1967, p. 413)

Unlike Spinoza, however, Hume sees this 'supposed pre-eminence of reason' as a conceptual impossibility, and therefore the question of striving to achieve it cannot arise for him. So his endeavours are confined to exposing 'the fallacy of all this philosophy', and he sets out to demonstrate 'that reason alone can never be a motive to any action of the will, and secondly that it can never oppose passion in the direction of the will' (ibid.).

2 Hume and Kant: a conceptual dichotomy

Reason for Hume is a faculty we exercise in grasping connections between facts, in weighing evidence for and against propositions, and in assessing the validity of arguments. As such it is eminently suited to engage the understanding, which is our capacity to grasp facts and truths. But how can it engage the will which moves a man to action? Reason sees what there is to be seen, assesses what there is to be assessed. As such it is passive, inert. In order to move a man to action what is needed is an 'active principle', something that evokes desire or aversion. This Hume finds in the passions: 'Reason alone can never be a motive to any action of the will.'

So, on Hume's view, seeing something to be the case, understanding how things stand, is one thing; doing something about it is another. For a man to act he has to be affected by what he sees or understands; he has to have likes and dislikes, desires and aversions. What he sees or grasps would give him no reason to act unless he were already favourably or aversely disposed towards the kind of thing he comes to see or grasp. But that disposition is fixed by the passions, independently of reason. Therefore reason can guide the will and influence human actions only *indirectly* and in two ways: (i) By revealing or clarifying the features of the objects and situations that confront a man, features towards which he is affectively disposed and (ii) By pointing out the ways or means to ends determined by the passions.

Hume's view is that a man's likes and dislikes, desires and aversions are determined ultimately by the constitution of his mind, the nature of his passions, so that his ends are simply *given* in the end and as such unamenable to reason. Reason is an instrument, like a torch which a traveller with a set destination uses to make his way in the dark. It can never give him a destination or change his direction independently of his passions. It has, therefore, to serve and obey them, and can do nothing else.

Hume is certainly right on this point: it is through their connection with a person's likes and dislikes, desires and aversions, concerns, interests and fears, that reasons and considerations get a grip on his will, enable him to make up his mind, give him a motive for action. But is their connection with what may be called 'reasons for action' purely external, as Hume represents it? Hume's view is too narrow and monolithic; it excludes forms of connection which he should have been able to recognize had not his philosophical presuppositions shut his eyes to them.

Many of our likes and dislikes, desires and aversions, are not simply given to us, and they can change under the critical scrutiny of reason, as when we have cause to critically consider our values, the things we love, revere and loathe, those things that make us proud and ashamed. These desires and aversions are not given to us like our appetites, but formed in the course of a process of learning and education which involves a great deal of reasoning. Even our appetites, say our sexual desires, are not simply given and can change in character as we change – as our orientation to people changes, for instance, as our need to use them in various ways decreases. I said 'learning' and I am thinking of a great variety of things that we come to want in life, and the way this is bound up with the worth we come to see in things, the terms in which we learn to think of them, and our conception of what kind of life is worth living. Hume is wrong in the way he generalizes about the way our ends are fixed and in his view of their unamenability to reason. Here the defect comes largely from his account of the passions. He is also wrong in thinking that we always act for the sake of ends or goals. He does not appreciate how different the role which certain values and ideals play in human actions is from that of ends and goals. Here the defect comes from his account of morality.

He is right to connect moral values with sentiments, but wrong to divorce these from reason. Values that one has come to accept, and in which one has come to believe, like justice and honesty for instance, give one reasons to act in particular situations because one is affectively disposed towards them. In fact to say, for instance, that one believes in honesty surely implies that one is not indifferent towards dishonesty, deception and lying. To believe in honesty is to care for it, to see instances in which it is exemplified in a certain light. That is what makes certain considerations, reasons, weigh with one, engage one's will. But the values in which one believes are not ends which one is seeking to realize by means of one's actions. That is not how our values are connected with our emotions. Thus one may refuse to lie, even when tempted, because one finds it repugnant to do so, and not in order to be honest. One finds it repugnant because of the terms in which one thinks about lying and dishonesty, terms which give it various connections and a particular aspect. The values in question are our *norms*. But this does not mean that they cannot themselves be measured, be subjected to scrutiny, reason and reflection in certain situations (see Dilman 1981, chapter 5).

Hume was wrong to divorce judgement from the emotions in his account of the passions and to represent emotions as inevitably blind. Some emotions, for instance rage and terror, blind their subject to reason and cloud his thinking in a way which needs consideration. Others, through the forms of apprehension with which they provide him, enrich his contact with his environment. Thus think of a man who is incapable of feeling love, grief or gratitude. Hume was equally wrong to think of reason as inevitably cool. This is certainly not the case with moral reasons. Here the link between reason and emotion is an internal one. We could characterize the reasons in question as 'affective reasons' (see ibid., pp. 66–7).

Kant criticizes Hume's view that reason cannot engage the will directly but can only guide it by serving the passions. His view is that the will can be determined by passion and desire as Hume claims, but that this is only one possibility. When it is so determined the will is subservient. But it can also be 'self-ruled' or autonomous, and it is so only when it is determined by reason. Kant, however, takes over Hume's dichotomy between reason and passion, treating the passions, like Hume, as all of a piece; and he too thinks of passions, thus taken, as necessarily blind. Consequently, while correcting Hume's mistakes, he tends to err in the opposite direction. For the kind of reason which is seen by Kant as in charge of the will, when the will is at once free and virtuous, is represented by him as devoid of all warmth and antagonistic to the emotions. There is, I believe, a close affinity between Kant's conception of reason and Freud's concept of the super-ego.

Kant thinks, rightly, that where reason is subservient to appetite or desire, a slave of the passions, the will is determined by something external to it. He speaks of this subservient relation, which is the only one possible for Hume, as 'heteronomy of the will'. Here a man's reasons for doing what he does are relative to what he desires independently of his moral beliefs. Kant characterizes accounts of morality in which moral reasons are so represented as 'heteronomous conceptions of morality'. Hume's account belongs to this category. On any such conception, Kant points out, a person is represented as doing the right thing, not for its own sake, that is because he believes it to be the right thing, but for the sake of something else.

When the will is determined by reason, on the other hand, Kant argues, it is self-ruled, for reason – 'practical reason' – is not anything external to the will. A will that is so determined is at one with itself. Such a will, Kant argues, can override passion and desire. He has in mind such cases as where a man, despite dangers which frighten him, goes to someone's rescue, thus showing courage; or where he turns down a bribe, despite his poverty and need of money, thus showing rectitude.

Kant, like Plato and Kierkegaard, distinguishes between the man who faces danger because of his moral convictions and the man who does so for the sake of a reward or out of the fear of punishment – e.g. for fear of being branded a coward. The truly brave man's action is a response to the other man's plight. It comes from the desire to rescue the man from this plight and ignores considerations of safety. I mean it involves a willingness to put his own safety at risk, his own interests, where these are involved, in jeopardy. Given the way he feels about anyone in that plight (though Kant would not mention feeling in this connection and characteristically speaks of 'acting for the sake of duty') our brave man is behind his action. Kant speaks of him as having 'autonomy of will' and he says that only where this is the case does a man have a 'good will', in other words genuine moral commitment.[1] In other words, autonomy of will is a requirement of moral virtue. But Kant's claim is stronger than this, for he wants equally to make moral virtue a requirement of autonomy of will. This is also true of Plato (see Dilman 1979, chapters 4, 8 and 9). Thus, according to Kant, 'the good will', 'the autonomous will' and 'the rational will' are equivalent, they are one and the same thing.

We are interested only in the second part of this equation, namely in Kant's claim that the will is autonomous only when it is determined by reason. Since for Kant reason and 'inclination', in the sense in which he uses this term, are exhaustive categories and so exclude each other, as for Hume reason and passion do, this means that *either* the will is self-ruled *or* it is subservient to inclination – in Hume's terminology, 'a slave of the passions'. In the latter case Kant speaks of it as subject to natural causality; but we are not now interested in this claim.

Hume's 'philosophy of motivation', we have seen, is defective for its inability to allow for the autonomy of the will, for representing the will as inevitably determined in the end by passions that are blind. Kant is right to try and make room for it. All the same he is wrong in the way he separates reason and inclination in the abstract; though even then there is something right and important in the contrast he has in mind. Let me try to disentangle what is right from what is wrong in Kant's dichotomy.

Even when a man has settled habits and dispositions which form part of his character these need to be distinguished from and contrasted with his loyalties, allegiances and commitments. The way he is moved by the latter is different from the way he is moved by his dispositions, desires and fears. They are *his* in a stronger sense than his desires and fears are *his*. They constitute the centre of his identity. In contrast, he may find his own inclinations unacceptable, he may feel ashamed of his desires. Such a desire may be his though he does not endorse it. It is not simply in conflict with other desires he may have; it is incompatible with his moral beliefs. If he gives in he will not simply frustrate some other desire he has – like the man who takes a bribe, is caught, loses his job, and so regrets what he has done. No, if he gives in he will not be fully behind what he does, he will himself condemn what he has done. That is, his will is in his moral beliefs, and his desire to take the money, perhaps because he is greedy, is external to his will in the sense that he sees what he desires under the aspect of a bribe. Whereas the former man, even when he sees what he desires under such an aspect remains unmoved and unperturbed by it. He has nothing against accepting a bribe, and he would not have regretted what he has done if he had not been caught.

146

Let us imagine that he refuses to take it because he fears the consequences. Here we can speak of reason overriding a desire in a *conditional* sense. Hume allows this. He would say that here reason points to the undesirable consequences of acting on his desire in the given circumstances. He is averse to those consequences because of the way his passions and interests dispose him towards them, and so he resists taking the money which he wants. Were it not for reason pointing out these consequences he would have taken the money. So here reason guides the will only 'mediately' as Hume puts it – that is only because the will has the disposition given to it by the stronger emotion, the fear of losing his job. It informs him of the risk of this in the given circumstances.

Kant points out that there is another way in which reason can override such a desire; it can do so in an *absolute* sense. Here what is in question is not the undesirable consequences of taking the money in the particular circumstances, but the significance which the man's moral beliefs give to doing so irrespective of the consequences. In the former case, Kant argues, the man is acting for the sake of something else he desires or fears, to which desire or fear his reason is subservient in the way which Hume points out. But in the latter case he is not acting for the sake of any desire, or out of fear for any consequence; it is not inclination but reason as such which moves him. His will is determined not by any desire, but by reason. At least this is how Kant puts it.

As it stands, this account is not satisfactory; but it contains an important truth. To bring it out we have to ask two questions: (i) In what way is this man's will not determined by any desire? and (ii) In what sense is it determined by reason? Let me begin with the first question. Surely Kant does not mean that this man does not desire or want to do what he does do – though at times he comes close to suggesting this. The important point, as I understand it, is *not* that he does not desire it, but that his desire is determined by his moral convictions and commitments. Kant would say that here desire is subordinated to reason. He rightly wishes to find a contrast to cases where men act out of a desire for reward or a fear of punishment. But because he thinks that *all* passion is blind and *all* desire is self-interested he puts them on the side of 'inclination' and contrasts them with reason. So he holds that actions that are informed by a regard for moral values must be dispassionate.

Part of what misleads him is the fact that he runs together dispassionateness and disinterestedness or detachment. Yet passions can be disinterested, and a man may have strong feelings about certain things and still be detached from worldly concerns. Thus in the compassion he feels a man will be indifferent to his own interests relative to the plight of other people. At the level of abstraction in which he considers these matters Kant is not alive to this and his philosophical presuppositions prevent him from appreciating it. He regards the man who goes to someone's help out of pity or kindness as acting 'out of inclination', and not 'out of duty', and he questions the moral worth of his actions. But if such cases are excluded as morally suspect, so will be equally what we are left with on the other side. Professor Winch who points this out in his inaugural lecture on 'Moral Integrity' (Winch, 1972) mentions the case of Ibsen's Mrs Solness in *The Master Builder* to bring the point home. Mrs Solness is a character who fits Kant's prescription perfectly, for she does things for people without any feeling for them and 'because it is only her duty'. But she does not act out of any genuine moral concern and she is simply ruled by a conscience that is external to her will. Thus she acts in slavery to a tyrannical conscience, patterned on Freud's concept of the super-ego, and not autonomously (see Dilman, 1973, section IV).

If Kant had said that true charity is more than a mere spontaneous gesture or expression of kindness or pity, I would agree. For a compassionate man, one who possesses the virtue of charity, does not only act or react spontaneously in certain ways. He also checks some of his natural inclinations in particular situations. He uses his head, thinks of the best way to help someone in need, someone for whom he feels sorry. The exercise of charity thus combines feeling for other people with giving thought to their needs. Kant may not agree with what I say on the feeling side; but he would agree with my central point that the man who possesses the virtue of charity, or any other virtue, has a centre other than his inclinations, and he acts from that centre. Charity is not merely an expression of what a person is inclined to do, but an expression of his will, of his moral commitment. Thus if we reformulate Kant's dichotomy between 'reason and inclination' into one between 'commitment and mere desire' we would come nearer the truth which Kant was straining after without succeeding to focus on it.

Commitment is, indeed, an expression of 'will', in the sense in which Kierkegaard spoke of 'willing the good' (Kierkegaard, 1961) and Wittgenstein said that 'to love one's neighbour means to will' (Wittgenstein, 1961, p. 77) whereas what I have called 'mere desire' is not. Kant wanted to distinguish such a disposition from one that comes from the passions, appetites, and perhaps habits. It involves 'activity', in a sense that needs elucidation, while the latter are forms of 'passivity' (compare Spinoza). He did not see, however, that a disposition of the will does not have to and, indeed, cannot exclude passion – a point recognized by Hume. Kant too shows an obscure recognition of this when he distinguishes between two forms of love: 'a love seated in the will' and 'a love seated in the propensities of sense' (Kant, 1959, p. 18).

Kant says that a love seated in the will can be commanded, not one seated in the propensities of sense. The kind of love Kant has in mind informs the choices and decisions of a man who has it in his heart; but it is not something acquired by choice. It involves his responsibility in the sense that it is an expression of where he stands. The command to love one's neighbour is not obeyed in the sense in which the command to shut the door is. Such a love cannot be received through instruction; it is not something one can emulate by following precepts or copy from examples. It has to come from the self; yet it is something towards which the self can work when inspired by certain ideals. To find such a love involves a change in the self, a growth of the self in spirituality. Yet one cannot do so to command. My point is that while the love in question is an expression of will, it is not subject to the will: I cannot love my neighbour *at will*.

Kant is not alone in representing such a love as a form of reason. Plato does too. But Kant's suspicion of feeling prevented him from giving a satisfactory account of it.

I asked earlier (and this was my second question) why Kant speaks of the will as being determined by *reason* where a man's actions are an expression of his moral commitments. Kant has in mind the will's determination by values and ideals to which a man has given his heart – though Kant would not speak of the heart here. He identifies these with reason because they give him a new perspective on things and enable him to make sense of them; because they give him norms of conduct and standards of criticism which make it possible for him to have reasons for doing certain things or for refraining from pursuing certain objectives; norms which make it possible for him to reflect on and make judgements about actions – his own, past and future, and other people's. These values and ideals which determine the will, while a form of measure, have themselves a sense of significance which makes it possible for them to become an object of reflection[2] themselves in special circumstances. Hence there is some justification for thinking of what issues from them as the product of reason – for the values that weigh with a person are his reasons for acting the way he does in particular circumstances.

However Kant rarefies practical reason and moral ideals (which reduces into a single law – 'the moral law') into an abstraction: 'An action done *from duty* must wholly exclude the influence of inclination (p. 20). He does not recognize that not all passions are external to morality, that some passions are made possible by the moral beliefs that people hold. Contrast the fear of doing something wrong and the fear of losing other people's moral regard. The former, if it is genuine, presupposes a love of the good in the person who has such fear in particular circumstances. If he did not care for the good, hold certain moral convictions, he would not be afraid of injuring it. We could describe such fear as a 'moral passion'. There are many examples that could be mentioned – compassion, gratitude, indignation, remorse, etc. If Kant had recognized this the truth in Hume's view would not have posed a threat for him; he would have been able to accept that it is only through its connection with a person's desires and aversions, concerns, interests and fears that reason can engage the will. For where the connection is internal, as in the above example, the will is not 'heterono-mous' for being moved by a passion.

Hume could not see how this connection could be internal. Kant on the other hand could not turn it into an internal relation without emptying moral passion of its affective content. He held that reason engages the autonomous will through 'respect for the moral law'. This is an anaemic version of what Plato and Simone Weil after him call 'love of the good'. Under the aspect of 'respect' Kant is seeking an affective attitude which is determined by a person's values, and not the other way round. He is, further, seeking an affective attitude which has been transformed into a settled disposition of the will. He does not see that what he calls 'respect' is an affective attitude which finds expression in different feelings and is not a special feeling 'distinct from all feelings' (ibid., fn 2). He struggles valiantly, but his characterization remains too abstract. He speaks of the respect in question as the consciousness of the determination of the will by the moral values in which a person believes, though Kant refers to these in the singular as 'the moral law'. He describes it as 'the conception of a worth which thwarts my self-love' (ibid.). I take him to mean that it is a feeling evoked in me by what I see in the moral values in question. In being won over by them I transcend myself. Promoting them in my actions, posi-tive and negative, becomes my interest. But this new interest, although mine, does not have its centre of gravity in myself: 'All so-called moral *interests* consist simply in *respect* for the law (ibid.).

This is the best I can make of the affective content which Kant attributes to what he calls 'respect for the moral law'. It is the nearest Kant gets to a recognition of the way reason and passion are internally related in guiding the will to actions that are morally pure.

3 Kant and Hume on free will and determinism

In the *Critique of Pure Reason* Kant had argued that causality is necessary to the very possibility of experience. This means that everything that happens must be strictly determined by antecedent causes. In the latter part of that work he is torn in two between *this necessity of natural causality* (as he calls it) and *the possibility of human freedom*, because he finds them incompatible.

Kant's view, in his ethical discussions, is this: (i) For the will to be free means for it not to be subject to compulsion. (ii) But causality is a form of compulsion and the will is subject to it by virtue of our being a part of the natural order. (iii) What constitutes causal compulsion on the will is what Kant calls 'inclination', which has its source in our sensible nature (what Plato called 'the body' – 'the flesh' in Christian literature). Our sensible nature is what makes us part of what Kant calls 'the phenomenal world' where causality reigns supreme. (iv) We can be free by virtue of that aspect of ourselves which goes beyond or transcends that in us which partakes of the phenomenal world. That aspect is our *reason* or *rationality*.

This is highly abstract and contains many questionable assumptions; but it can nevertheless be shown to contain something true and important by connecting it with questions about the ordinary plight of human beings. That causality is a form of compulsion is one questionable assumption which I shall not question. However it leads him to search for the possibility of an alternative which he sometimes calls 'causality of reason' and identifies with 'practical reason'; and we shall see that there is something important behind this. Secondly the assumption that insofar as a man belongs to the natural world, that far he is not free, is not so much questionable as unclear. Thirdly, even if there is a sense in which what Kant calls 'inclination' is a cause, it is at least questionable whether it is a cause in the Newtonian sense, which is what Kant has in mind.

An avalanche is part of the natural world and its fall is subject to the laws of motion and to causality. Yet it may come down the mountainside unobstructed or unimpeded and, in that sense, *freely*. I do not know whether Kant would have denied this; but he would have regarded it as irrelevant to his problem about the freedom of the will. He would have said, rightly, that even if there is a sense in which an avalanche or any other physical body may move freely, this is not the sense in which we speak of human beings as acting freely. The possibility of their acting freely has to do with human beings having a *will*. This involves, primarily, the intelligibility of attributing *intentional action* to human beings and this, in turn, is bound up with *acting for a reason*. Having a will (a grammatical category) guarantees not freedom, but the *possibility* of it – the *possibility* of acting freely. That possibility is realized when a man's will is his own, that is when it is not subservient to anything external to it.

On Kant's view there is a certain *duality* about men: they inevitably belong to nature or the phenomenal world (Kant uses both expressions), and they are also rational creatures and by virtues of this possess the capacity to transcend what is 'natural' in them. Like Plato, Kant here runs together two claims which need to be distinguished. (i) The first one is that the *possibility* of free action, such as human beings are capable of, involves the *capacity to act for a reason*. Human beings are different from all other creatures with which we are familiar (animals) in possessing this capacity. A human being acts freely when his will is autonomous, and that means when it is determined by reason. (ii) The second claim relates to a timeless world in identity with which alone 'real' freedom is to be achieved – a view which is prominent in Plato's *Phaedo* and in Spinoza's *Ethics*. We are only concerned with the first of these two claims; but clearly achieving *autonomy* and achieving *spirituality* are by no means the same thing – even though there can be no spirituality in the absence of autonomy.

What does Kant mean by 'belonging to or being part of the natural world'? And how is this supposed to make acting freely impossible? Kant may mean, for instance, that human beings have to eat, sleep, keep warm, that they get tired, are subject to illness, to old age and death. It is true that all this involves causality and causal laws. But does it constitute an inevitable obstacle to human freedom? Does it not rather constitute part of the framework within which human beings have to exercise their freedom?

A man who is feverish, perhaps delirious with high temperature, cannot think straight. You cannot discuss things with him, seek his advice, while he is in that state. But is he subject to causality to a greater extent than when he is well? Is a car that breaks down more subject to causality than one which is in perfect working order? Is it not rather that *his body* is subject to causality both when he is well and when he is ill, and that what *he* is subject to as a person is what is involved in illness when he is ill – e.g. the delirium – namely *what interferes with the normal exercise of his capacities*? These are capacities the existence of which we presuppose when we speak of a human being as having acted freely or as having failed to do so.

Is there, then, another sense in which it would be true to say that insofar as a human being belongs to the natural world, that far he is not free? Perhaps there is such a sense which takes us nearer to Kant's problem. People do sometimes give way to their impulses, act without using their head. Later they may regret what they have done, and even be horrified by it. They may say: 'I wish I hadn't done what I did. If I had used my head I wouldn't have done it.' It looks as if they were rushed or panicked into doing something which they do not endorse and never did – except that at the time they did not stop to realize this, or if they did they dismissed the realization. Admittedly this is a special case, but Kant generalizes from it. He represents the conflict as between man's *appetitive nature* which has to do with the senses in the sense of sensuality (Kant refers to it as 'inclination') and reason or *man's rationality*, that is man's capacity to consider reasons and to be guided by such considerations in his decisions and actions. Kant defines 'practical reason' as 'reason insofar as it is itself the cause producing actions' (Kant 1961, A550/B578). By 'producing' Kant means that what reasons I have make a difference to what I do. So he talks of practical reason as one kind of cause and of 'inclination' as another kind of cause. That is he distinguishes between two broadly different ways in which human actions are determined – and in that sense caused.

It is, nevertheless, misleading to talk of reason as a kind of cause, in the sense that a cause is externally related to its effect; whereas, as Kant put it, when the will is at one with reason it is at one with itself. Secondly, it is also misleading to talk of everything that is lumped together under 'inclination' as another kind of cause – 'natural cause'. The word 'inclination', as it is normally used, covers many different things and to act in accordance with one's inclinations, or even one's impulses, is not always to give up one's autonomy. Thirdly, the term 'cause' or 'natural cause', as Kant uses it, is connected with 'causal laws' or 'laws of nature'; and yet there are no such laws (despite the faith to the contrary of many psychologists) as far as our impulses and desires go.

So while there is something important in Kant's dichotomy between 'reason and inclination', despite its defects (and I have represented what is important in it as the dichotomy between commitment and mere desire or inclination) it is not the same as the distinction many philosophers have drawn between reason and cause – for instance, Wittgenstein in *The Blue Book*.

The reason Kant regards 'inclination' (which he identifies with certain special cases of impulse and inclination) as 'natural cause' is because he thinks of causes as *necessitating* their effects, and of the necessity involved here as a form of *compulsion*. In some cases of 'inclination' this is so – such as when one is overwhelmed by fear or a desire which one finds difficult to resist. As for 'human beings belonging to the *natural* world by virtue of their "inclinations"', if 'inclination' is simply used here to signify man's 'appetitive nature', then 'man's belonging to the natural world' means his having an affinity with animals, that is with creatures who act from impulse and desire, without reason. But, then, the 'natural world' here does not mean 'the causal world', 'the world about which natural scientists formulate laws'. It means the world of impulse and appetite. There are, I believe, three different contrasts here which Kant runs together:

(i)   cause and reason
(ii) impulse and reason (or as I put it: mere desire or inclination and commitment)
(iii) appetite and spiritual aspiration (or sensuality and spirituality – in Plato: sense/reason)

It is the second contrast we have been concerned with so far. But it is the first contrast, namely the one between cause and reason, which will now move to the foreground of our concern.

Kant's problem in the context of his Third Antinomy in the *Critique*, insofar as it bears on the question of human freedom, relates to the contrast between reason and cause. Causality, he believes firmly, reigns supreme and there can be no exception to it. Yet it is equally evident that human beings consider reasons before acting, and these considerations make a difference to what they do. How can this be if their actions are subject to causality? Kant sees a conflict here and asks how it can be overcome, how it is possible for reasons and causes to govern the same action. He seeks a *reconciliation* between the conflicting claims (the thesis and antithesis of his antimony) because he cannot see his way to denying what is claimed on either side of the conflict, namely *the operation of causality* and *the efficacy of reason*. He expresses his problem thus: 'Whether freedom and natural necessity can exist without conflict in one and the same action' (Kant 1961, A557/B585).

The Libertarian resolves the problem by rejecting determinism, by making man and human actions an exception to the rule of causality. The Determinist does so by refusing to make man an exception and accepting the consequences. Freedom, he claims, is an illusion. There are those who accept this latter position, without qualms, in the name of science – for instance the behaviourist psychologist Skinner (see Dilman, 1988, chapter 6).

Hume, though he accepted determinism, did not deny the reality of free will. He sees no incompatibility between the claims of freedom and of determinism. So he is sometimes described as a 'compatibilist'. He holds that human actions are just as subject to causality as 'external objects': 'There is a general course of nature in human actions, as well as in the operations of the sun and the climate' (Hume 1967, pp. 402–3). He argues that causality is not only not excluded by freedom and accountability, but is positively required by it. His case is based on the way he identifies causality with order or regularity, and dissociates it from compulsion. Freedom stands opposed to compulsion, but requires order. 'Few (he says) are capable of distinguishing betwixt the liberty of *spontaneity* ... and the liberty of *indifference*; betwixt that which is opposed to violence, and that which means a negation of necessity and causes. The first is even the most common sense of the word; and as it is only that species of liberty, which it concerns us to preserve, our thoughts have been principally turned towards it, and have almost universally confounded it with the other' (ibid., pp. 407–8). What Hume calls 'the liberty of spontaneity' here is man's capacity to initiate actions unhindered. His negative argument is that the claim that we are subject to causality, to which he subscribes, does not entail that man does not, and cannot, possess this capacity. But the capacity in question is the capacity for intentional action, the capacity to act for a reason; and Hume's positive account of what this amounts to is unsatisfactory. For him the will and motives are causes of our actions ('the union betwixt motives and actions has the same constancy as that in any natural operations' – ibid., p. 404) and this rules out the possibility of a satisfactory account of intentional action. Be that as it may, Hume acknowledges man's liberty of spontaneity (men can initiate their own actions unhindered and are in that sense free), but claims that their supposed liberty of indifference is a chimera.

By 'liberty of indifference' he means man's alleged capacity to act without a cause. Since for Hume, 'motive' in its broadest sense is a cause, to claim that man can act without a cause is to claim that he can act without a motive. He thus makes it impossible to deny that there can be uncaused actions: 'Whatever capricious and irregular actions we may perform, as the desire of showing our liberty is the sole motive of our actions, we can never free ourselves from the bonds of necessity' (ibid., p. 408). He adds: 'We may imagine we feel a liberty within ourselves; but a spectator can commonly infer our actions from our motives and character; and even where he cannot, he concludes that he might, were he perfectly acquainted with every circumstance of our situation and temper, and the most secret springs of our complexion and disposition' (pp. 408–9). Hume is referring to two kinds of case which have figured in discussions of free-will *versus* determinism where 'freedom' has been equated with 'the liberty of indifference' which Hume claims is a chimera: (i) The so-called 'gratuitous act' where someone sets out to do an action which has so grave consequences or has in itself such a significance that no one would do it without reason, yet where all these possible reasons are absent. Thus in André Gide's novel *Les Caves du Vatican* the hero, Lafcadio, pushes a complete stranger out of a moving train in order to prove that he is free. Such a man seems to be saying two different things – (a) 'I do not know the man, I have nothing to gain, so I could not possibly have any reason for pushing him out of the train.' To which Hume replies: 'Oh yes you do! You wish to prove your opponent wrong.' (b) 'I can do what most men would balk at; I am not bound by their conventions. I can do what I want.' Sartre replies (the words are mine, not Sartre's): in his capricious act such a man acts in slavery to a misguided desire to be extravagant, original, independent or free. (ii) The second type of case to which Hume refers includes unimportant decisions and trivial actions. Thus (labouring under the confusion which Hume tries to point out) Freud says that the 'conviction that there is a free will ... does not manifest itself in weighty and important decisions'. And in the same vein Ernest Jones writes: 'Man's belief in free will seems to be stronger in proportion to the unimportance of the decision. Everyone is convinced that he is free to choose whether to stand or sit at a given moment, to cross his right leg over his left or *vice versa* "as he wishes".' Both Freud and Jones deny this in the way that Hume does. Thus Freud: 'It is impossible to think of a number, or even of a name, of one's own free will.' Freud means that if one were to associate to the name or number one would find out that there was some reason why one thought of it even though one is unaware of this reason. I am not now concerned with this claim.

I said that Hume holds that freedom stands opposed to compulsion not to causality, which presupposes order and regularity. More strongly Hume holds not merely that freedom and order are compatible, but that freedom requires order – and Hume is thinking of causal order. Where there is no regularity, what a man does is random and capricious, and so not free, and he cannot be held accountable for his actions: ''Tis commonly allowed (he writes) that madmen have no liberty. But were we to judge by their actions, these have less regularity and constancy than the actions of wise men ...' (Hume 1967, p. 404). Hume is right in thinking that unless a man's actions and words exhibit some order and regularity we could not hold them responsible for what they do; but he is wrong to identify the kind of order which they exhibit with casual order. He confuses the kind of consistency which presupposes the observance of rules with causal regularity.

Kant would agree with Hume that a man whose actions are random is not in charge of what he does and so not responsible for his actions. Such a man far from being free is really subject to the moment, subject to his changing whims. He says that the will when it is free is not lawless. He disagrees with Hume, however, on two major points as a result of which he cannot accept Hume's 'compatibilism' and has to seek a special kind of reconciliation. First, he differs from Hume on the nature of a causal connection in a way that makes it easy for him to think of a cause as a form of compulsion and second, he differs from Hume in his conception of the will and its relation to human action. While he, like Hume, sees that regularity may be essential to human freedom or the freedom of the will, he recognizes (unlike Hume) that the kind of regularity in question is not causal regularity. Thus the difference between the avalanche, I mentioned earlier, which comes down the mountainside *freely* and the man who gives money to a charity *freely*. Kant emphasizes that a causal order is not the only kind of order there is, that causal laws are not the only kind of laws there are. Thus a man shows consistency in his actions when his actions are governed by reason, by considerations. Kant points out that the sense in which considerations of reason govern the will is very different from the sense which laws of nature govern natural phenomena: 'Only a rational being (he says) has the power to act in accordance with his idea of laws – that is in accordance with principles – and only so has he a will.' A free will, he would say, is one not bound by the laws of nature; but this does not make it lawless. Willing, for Kant, is the exercise of practical reason (that is the reaching of decisions, the forming of intentions, the execution of these intentions, keeping to one's resolutions). It embodies acting on a rule of reason. It is not (as it is for Hume) a cause or a mental push.

Why, then, does Kant think that the reign of causality poses a threat to human freedom? He does so for two reasons. First because, in contrast with Hume, he identifies causality with natural necessity and he regards the latter as a form of compulsion. Secondly, because 'natural causality' suggests that an action issues from something external to the agent – as when, say, a lesion in the brain causes a man to twitch, or renders him incontinent, or makes him incapable of controlling certain impulses. But, as I said before, these are special cases where the normal exercise of certain capacities which a man has is impaired. So perhaps we ought to distinguish between causal conditions that are required for the normal exercise of certain human capacities and changes in these causal conditions which affect adversely and so interfere with the exercise of these capacities. It is only in the latter case that the operation of certain causes undermines the exercise of human freedom. In that sense we could accept that we are subject to the causal laws which govern our physiology. But it does not follow that those laws govern *us* and interfere with our freedom.

One big difference between Kant and Hume in their discussion of the problem of freedom and determinism is this. In Hume's account of freedom the emphasis falls on the absence of compulsion and constraint. While Kant appreciates this, his account is in terms of self-determination. Hence his contrast between 'natural causality' and 'causality of reason'. In the latter case the will is not governed by a law, in the way that the avalanche is governed by the laws of motion; it is governed by the idea of a law – at least that is how Kant puts it. That is, a person follows a rule that he has made his own and has identified his will with. He follows it *willingly*: following the law *is* what he wills. Indeed Kant is right in thinking that a man is free when he can think for himself and act on his own behalf. This, in turn, presupposes that he cares for things, has deeply held convictions, stands for something, has a centre from which he acts. Otherwise what could we mean by 'himself' when we say that he thinks 'for himself'? What could we mean by 'his own behalf' when we say that he acts 'on his own behalf'?

Kant's emphasis on reason, I have suggested, is a pale reflection of this idea. He is thinking of a man who knows what he is doing and is his own master, one who does not simply do what he happens to be inclined to do. If such a man does what he is inclined to do (in the everyday sense of this expression), his actions have his full backing and endorsement. In other words, he is not acting merely from inclination; he does not do what he is inclined to do simply because it is what he is inclined to do. In that case, Kant says, it is not his inclination that he obeys, but his reason which endorses his inclination. He could have said that while such a man acts 'in accordance with his inclination' he is not acting 'from inclination'. The important thing is that he has norms of conduct which he has made his own and that in conforming his actions to such norms he is in charge of these actions: he does what *he* wills.

Kant's main distinction here is between having such norms and being guided by them in what one does in particular situations, and doing what one is inclined to do without regard to any norms or values. One may act in the latter way either (i) because one is overcome by desire or passion (lust or fear for instance) which cloud's one's judgement, in which case one acts in slavery to passion or desire and not freely, or (ii) because one has no values and doesn't care for anything. In the latter case one will be the plaything of circumstances which evoke in one now this passion, now that desire. The case where one merely gives up short-term desires for long-term ones is a half-way house.

157

But 'to be the plaything of circumstances', 'to act in slavery to passion': is this to be subject to natural causality? I do not think so. There are, however, other questions relating to Kant's concern about causality in connection with the problem of freedom. Is man subject to causality in the sense that his desires and passions are causally determined? If the answer is in the affirmative, does it follow that he cannot act freely? Kant does not examine these questions.

I will venture this comment on them. The formation of our desires and character has many different sources. It would be very misleading to speak of causality here in any blanket fashion. However the fact that we do not choose our desires and passions, those that we act on, does not impugn our freedom of action. What does impugn it (as Kant knows) is if these desires and passions do not have our endorsement. The desire in accordance with which I may act on a particular occasion may be determined by my heredity or environment and upbringing. Nevertheless it may be *mine* in the sense of having my full backing. It is this latter fact that is relevant to the freedom of my actions.

Perhaps Kant's supposed reconciliation of Transcendental Freedom (as he calls it) with Empirical Causation evinces some recognition of this.

4 Kant's conception of psychology as an 'anthropological science'

Kant, like Hume, believed in general determinism, namely that all phenomena are subject to laws and have a cause. But unlike Hume, he did not believe that causal determinism is compatible with the possibility of free will. Yet he was equally convinced of the reality of free will which, he held, is necessary to the possibility of attributing moral responsibility to human individuals.

In *The Critique of Pure Reason* he discusses this antinomical conflict, but what he says remains highly abstract. As I see it, what emerges is his view that there is a certain *duality* about man: he is *both* part of the natural or phenomenal world where everything that happens is subject to causality and so governed by laws of nature, *and* he has the capacity to transcend what in him partakes of the natural world. This capacity is his ability to consider reasons for his action, before acting as well as in retrospect, and to be moved by such considerations. But it is not clear if, on Kant's view, he is still subject to causality when he acts from considerations of reason. For if he is, the question about the incompatibility between reason and cause remains unsolved, and if he does not remain subject to causality this means that Kant recognizes a limit to determinism.

In my reading of him Kant has two separate answers to this problem which are not incompatible with one another and are, in fact, connected. I have already touched on one of these. In his work on ethics Kant takes

the causality to which men's wills are subject to be what he calls 'inclination'. Men are part of the natural world through having a nature, 'human
nature', in which they have a certain continuity with animals: when
pushed their instinct for survival comes to the fore. They tend to forget the
things they care for, they think of themselves and put themselves first, they
become defensive, aggressive. When their needs are satisfied, they can
become greedy and want more, so that in themselves they remain unsatis-
fied. Within the surroundings of their life and culture they can develop
rivalries which fan their feelings of envy. It is the possibility of such inclinations that belongs to 'human nature'. Of course the expressions of these
inclinations presuppose the kind of life which takes the development of
capacities, such as speech, which are not found among animals. Yet in the
variety of forms which they take they bear a certain affinity to what we
find in animal life. Insofar as men give way to such inclinations and allow
themselves to be taken over by them, they come to be ruled by them.

Kant saw them as being expressions of what he called 'the dear self'.
The more a person feeds it and becomes one with it the more he is imprisoned in it – imprisoned in thinking of himself. So Kant holds that it is by
turning away from 'the dear self' that a person transcends the natural
world and is freed from the causation of 'inclination'. Such inclinations are
a form of compulsion because though they are part of the nature a person
shares with others they have not been endorsed and so are not owned by
the individual. To endorse anything a person has to come to his moral self;
but these inclinations are antithetical to the moral self. Since a person can
only find himself in coming to his moral self, it follows that what Kant
calls 'inclination' is inevitably alien to the self – to the self a person has to
come in becoming an individual, autonomous. It is in this sense, as I
understand Kant, that he holds that freedom is to be found not in the
natural world but in the noumenal world which is subject to reason and
not causation. It is in this sense that the person transcends the phenomenal
world and finds freedom in becoming autonomous.

As I said, though human beings belong to the natural world of which
animals are a part, human nature has reality in human life – the kind of
life to which animals have no access. As such, whether or not they have
found a moral self in which to be themselves and as such become
autonomous, they have the capacity to do so: such autonomy is a possibility for them. In this they differ radically from animals and, indeed, from
everything else in nature. Descartes, we have seen, was aware of this and
tried to articulate it, unsatisfactorily, in his notion of the activity which he
attributed to the human mind. Here was a limit to the causal determinism
that reigns supreme in nature.

But after Descartes in Hobbes, Hume and Mill this idea gave way to the
idea that human life and behaviour is susceptible of scientific study, like any
other object. Hume who was a dualist, though he rejected the Cartesian

idea of the mind as a substance, thought of mental phenomena as subject to laws of its kind as are physical phenomena subject to material laws. He prided himself in being a Newton of the mind. Mill developed Hume's ideas and laid the foundation for a scientific psychology which led to the conception of psychology as an experimental study. Kant's was a lone voice which opposed this development at its very origin. As we have seen, he distinguished between causality and reason, between laws of nature and norms of reason. He recognized that we have the capacity to act for a reason and that this distinguishes us not only from physical things but from animals as well. He thus brought into focus man's capacity for intentional action and his ability to think about things at will.

In Descartes acts of will are the mental counterpart of a push. Human actions are physical phenomena brought about by such mental acts. The relation between these mental acts and the actions is causal and as such 'external'. These acts are free in that they are uncaused – a view which Hume was to reject though, not surprisingly, he erred in the opposite direction and turned acts of will into phenomena. In Kant, in contrast, willing is the capacity to act for a reason, and an intention, the formation of which is an exercise of the will, is *internally* connected to the intended action – whether the intention is executed or not.

Actions in most cases involve bodily movements, but they cannot be identified with these. The bodily movements have causal, physiological explanations. But treated as such, that is as bodily movements, desires and intentions do not belong to their explanations. On the other hand, taken as actions done at will, such as moving an arm by way of greeting someone, their explanation is not in causal terms. It simply takes for granted certain background causal conditions – e.g. the nerves being in good working order. When I move my arm thus at will certain physiological processes are set into motion which are causally necessary to such a movement. But these processes are not what I set into motion: they are not the object of my intention, they do not enter my thought or mind. The agent does not have to know anything about them and in the majority of cases does not. Though causally necessary, however, these physiological processes do not explain the voluntary movement, as they do where my arm moves when I have a fit. In the latter case the movement is involuntary; it is not something I do, but something that happens to me. It is in this way that we are subject to causality – I cannot move my arm if my arm is paralysed – though we have the capacity to act for a reason.

Where an involuntary movement is a movement of a part of *my* body I have, of course, a way of telling that it is happening – e.g. that my eyelid is twitching – which no one else can have without being me. But as far as explaining the twitch goes I am not differently placed from anyone else. The explanation, like many other causal explanations, waits on research. This is not the case, however, with a voluntary movement. I have a way of telling why I have moved my arm which no one else can have without being me. For the question is not about the cause of the movement but about me – about the reason for my volition. Equally, of course, I can know that I am going to move my arm, when I intend to do so, without evidence. I have thus a way of answering questions about what I intend to do which no one else can have without being me. Other people can at best predict what I am going to do; I simply tell them what my intention is.

No one can do what I do by simply imitating what I do, that is by copying my movements where this is possible. It is possible for a chimpanzee or someone from a totally alien culture to do this; but in the absence of any notion of what I am doing what he does cannot add up to the same action. At an extreme, robots in a car assembly line are not building cars; it is we who are using them to do so. Equally, tribesmen from a village belonging to a country with no democratic traditions can be made to put a cross on a ballot paper during an election arranged for or imposed on the people for the first time; but they can hardly be said to be voting. That is the agent's own view of what he is doing or is going to do, his view of the situation in which he acts, goes into determining the identity of his action. Kant's recognition of this is at the centre of his distinction between a natural and an anthropological science.

Indeed the actions and behaviour which are the concern of what Kant calls an 'anthropological science', such as psychology, cannot only not be described, but they cannot also be explained without using terms that belong to the agent's vocabulary, terms whose significance belongs to his understanding and so can be used to articulate what he is able to think and be aware of. They must be terms which belong to a language embedded in a life and culture in which the agent participates.

This point that the explanations of human actions must be in terms that belong to his grasp of the significance of his actions and their circumstances is directly connected with Kant's conception of the connection between the will and human action. For Kant in contrast with Hume, we have seen, this connection is not an external one; the will is not a cause. For the will, as it may find expression in the agent's intentions, necessarily involves the thought of what he is doing or is going to do, and this in turn contains the terms in which he sees or thinks about his present situation and formulates his objectives. The intention, one could say, is a form of thought and it already contains or visualizes the action intended. Furthermore, the way that an agent is guided by this thought in what he does is in some ways like the way he is guided by a rule he is following. So, as Kant puts it, the will is not governed by laws when a person acts, but by the idea of laws or rules which enter into the constitution of the action willed.

Thus, for Kant, desires and passions are linked to human behaviour not as blind mechanical pushes or impulses, but through the will. He describes that (the will) as 'the faculty of taking a rule of reason for the motive of an action'. The will then is determined not by antecedent causes but by considerations which take the role of reason for what we do. What a man does on a particular occasion depends on what he makes of his particular situation in terms of the concepts he employs. His experience of it is not a passive reception of stimuli through his sense organs. It is centred on an assessment of its significance through the way he thinks of it.

I shall conclude this chapter by quoting from an article in *The Monist*, vol 51, 1967, where Theodore Mischel sums up the difference between the Humean scientific conception of psychology and the Kantian 'pragmatic' conception:

> Many writers, before and after Kant, attempted to provide 'scientific' explanations of human behaviour by treating external events and situations as causes of internal events which, in turn, cause bodily behaviour. Explanations of human 'responses' were thus fitted to the model of the physical sciences by interpolating 'mental events' in the causal series that runs from the 'stimulus' situation to the behaviour it elicits. As a result, the relation between agent and patient presupposed in our ordinary, teleological explanation of human actions was reversed ... The person [is conceived of] as passive, being merely caused to move by the stimulus situation.

> On Kant's view [by contrast] the relation between inner states and outer objects cannot be causal in the Humean sense; it cannot be a correlation between two separately identifiable events because the mental and the physical are logically connected aspects of one and the same experience. This interpretation also suggests that the explanation of human actions must differ in type from the causal explanations of the physical sciences.

> On Kant's view an 'Anthropology from a Pragmatic Point of View' aims to discover not 'what nature makes out of man' but 'what he, as a freely acting being makes or can and should make, of himself'.

> What is relevant to the development of such a science [according to Kant] is travel, history, biography, novels, etc ... Introspection of inner states, far from being stressed, is repeatedly held to be misleading.

> (*The Monist*, vol. 51, 1967, pp. 617-21)

Part IV

THE AGE OF PSYCHOLOGY
Reason and feeling, causality and
free will

10

SCHOPENHAUER

Free will and determinism

1 Schopenhauer's arguments for determinism

In his prize winning essay, published as a book, *On the Freedom of the Will* Schopenhauer raises the question of whether the will is free – whether we have a free will. He rightly points out that we say of a person that he acted freely when he can do what he wills, that is when he is not hindered or restrained by something external to his will. That is he is free in what he does when what he does is what he wills. If what he does is against his will, he must have been forced to do it.

But if 'free' thus means 'in accordance with one's will', what could 'free will' mean? He denies that a person can be divided in what he wills. When restrained a person can be deflected from doing what he wills, he can fail to do what he wills. How, Schopenhauer asks, can he fail to will what he wills? That would be a contradiction in terms. 'I can will what I will,' he says, is a tautology. He concludes that in the sense in which we speak of a person's actions as free we cannot establish a direct connection between the concept of freedom and that of willing. We have, therefore, to modify this concept of freedom by making it signify the absence of any necessity (p. 6).

A thing is necessary, he argues, when it cannot be otherwise, and so when it follows from a given sufficient ground. The ground can be logical, mathematical or physical, and when physical it is a *cause*. The ground is compelling and the consequence is necessary. The antithesis of necessary is accidental; but what is accidental is only relatively so. 'I did not drop the vase deliberately,' we say, 'it was an accident' – that is relative to my intention. But that does not mean that it did not have a cause. As Schopenhauer puts it: 'in the world of reality [as opposed to e.g. in mathematics], where alone accidents can be encountered, every event is necessary in relation to its cause' (pp. 7–8).

So, in connection with the will, 'free' would have to signify 'absence of necessity'. A free will thus is one that is absolutely independent of any cause, not dependent on any ground. Schopenhauer calls it *liberum arbitrium indifferentiae* and finds it inconceivable. Hume called it 'freedom of

everything else in nature, take place in any given case as an effect which follows necessarily' (p. 24, italics mine).

Schopenhauer's argument and conclusion contains presuppositions which need criticism and I shall return to them. All the same in the distinction he makes between human beings and animals he finds room for what he calls a 'relative freedom'. Human beings, he says, are capable of speech, reflectiveness, retrospection, concern for the future, making plans and forming intentions for the future, joint action with others. They are creative and have developed the arts and the sciences. The situations in which they act and to which they respond impinge into their lives through their significance which they have the capacity to grasp, to question, to reject. They can step back from these situations, hold their actions in abeyance, consider what is at stake as well as future consequences of possible actions.

Animals too, he says, at any rate the higher animals, pass through cognition, and have enough to become aware of motive, to be moved by those things that confront them perceptually. But they are not capable of stepping back from and considering the situation in which they find themselves. The range of significances which these situations can have for them is very restricted; they are at least in the main biological. Since they cannot step back and consider, they live in the present and their actions are primarily reactions. In the case of the lower animals he writes:

> Small insects are drawn by the shining light into the very flame; flies alight trustfully on the head of a lizard that has just now consumed their fellows before their very eyes. Who will dream of freedom here? (p. 40).

'In the higher, more intelligent animals,' he points out, 'the action of motives becomes more and more indirect, that is, the motive separates itself more distinctly from the action to which it gives rise; so that one could even use this difference of distance between the motive and the action as the standard of animal intelligence. In man this difference becomes immeasurable' (ibid.). In higher animals such as dogs, I think wrongly but significantly, Schopenhauer speaks of choice: 'in animals where a choice is already possible, it can take place only from among those things which are perceptually present' (p. 41). He mentions the case of a dog who catches the sight of a she-dog while he is being called by his master. He stands hesitatingly between the two. He adds, 'the stronger motive will determine his motion' (ibid.). Perhaps; but then this is not what we understand by choosing.

Indeed, Schopenhauer compares it with a mechanical case: 'a body which is thrown out of equilibrium oscillates for a time alternatively from one side to another until it is finally determined on which side lies its centre of gravity – and then falls to that side' (ibid.). It is very much in these terms that Schopenhauer thinks of choice and decision in human beings too: where there is a conflict of motives, the person may hesitate and struggle with the conflict; but 'finally the strongest motive drives the others from the field and determines the will' (p. 37). 'The outcome,' he adds, 'is called resolve, and it takes place with complete necessity as the result of the struggle' (p. 37). But on this view 'struggle' is a metaphor and the person in question is a by-stander to the oscillation as well as to its outcome. Furthermore what Schopenhauer calls 'resolve' is no choice or decision, but what in physics is called a resolution of forces.

On this point however Schopenhauer oscillates between free will and determinism:

> By means of his capacity to think, man can present to himself the motives whose influence on his will he feels in any order, alternatively and repeatedly, in order to hold them up to his will. This is called deliberation. Man is capable of deliberation, and thanks to this capacity he has far greater choice than is possible for the animals. Because of this he is, of course, relatively free. He is free of the immediate compulsion of the perceptually present objects which act as motives on his will. To this the animal is subject absolutely. Man, on the other hand, determines himself independently of the present object, namely by thoughts, which are his motives. It is this relative freedom which is popularly called 'free will' (p. 36).

So far so good – except for the innuendo in 'this is what is popularly called free will', the innuendo being that in reality this is no freedom of the will at all. Having said this Schopenhauer comes down on the side of determinism: 'by its means only the type of motivation is altered, while the necessity of the effect of motives is not in the least obliterated, or even diminished' (ibid.).

The essay ends with a section entitled 'Conclusion and a Higher View'. He refers approvingly to Kant's distinction between the empirical necessity of action and its transcendental freedom. I have discussed what Kant makes of it in the previous chapter. But what Schopenhauer says here is brief and highly abstract and I do not know what to make of it; so I shall not comment on it. He concludes:

> Consequently, my exposition does not eliminate freedom. It merely moves it out ... of the area of simple actions, where it demonstrably cannot be found, up to a region which lies higher, but it is not so easily accessible to our knowledge. In other words, freedom is transcendental (p. 99).

169

2 Flaws in Schopenhauer's arguments

Schopenhauer's principal argument for claiming that free will is an illusion is that our actions issue from our will and that our will needs a motive to issue into action. That is to make up our mind to do something we need what he calls a motive. What provides us with a motive are particular circumstances in the significance they have for us as we understand it, that is grasp it by thought – in our intellect. Given that significance and our grasp of it, *ie* our contact with it in thought, whether we do anything and, indeed, what in particular we do, depends on what we are like in ourselves, in other words on our character. So far so good.

He thinks of this as the determination of the will and contrasts it with what, like Hume, he calls the freedom of indifference. 'If freedom of the will were presupposed (he says) every human action would be an inexplicable miracle – an effect without a cause' (p. 62). Clearly if we were indifferent to everything, if we felt nothing, wanted nothing, if we were still alive, our life would have become purely vegetative and we would not be capable of any action: our active life would be at an end. It is because we engage with the life around us, take part in its various activities, have interests, desires, needs, care for things that we act. Acting as we do is living as human beings do. Each of us, of course, takes part in the life around us and makes his own life or, at any rate, comes to the life he lives as the person he is. Just as his personality or character shapes the life that he lives, equally what he finds in the life in which he takes part, what he meets there, shapes him, or at any rate constitutes the framework within which he develops. To describe the matter the way Schopenhauer describes it is an oversimplification – an oversimplification resulting from the kind of abstract thinking that flourishes in philosophy.

Within what I have just sketched there are many different possibilities. To speak of the determination of the will by motive through character, the way Schopenhauer does, is a big jump. Such a jump is conditioned by presuppositions which need to be criticized and, indeed, rejected. Primarily among these is the assimilation of motives to causes and the acceptance of the analogy from mechanics – that of the clock, the spinning top and the billiard ball:

> As natural beings become more and more complicated in the process of rising to a higher and higher level and as their receptivity rises and becomes more refined – from the merely mechanical to the chemical, electrical, irritable, sensible, intellectual, and finally, rational – the nature of the activating causes must also proceed *pari passu* and correspond on each level to the beings which are to be activated. Consequently the causes must also present themselves as less and less palpable and material, so that

in the end they are no longer visible to the eye but can indeed be reached by the understanding ... For here the acting causes are raised to the level of mere thoughts struggling with other thoughts, until the most powerful of them becomes decisive and sets the man in motion. All of this takes place with just such a strict causality as when purely mechanical causes work on one another in a complicated combination and the calculated effect occurs without fail (pp. 46–7).

No doubt at the physical and physiological level of the evolution which Schopenhauer describes here there is a continuity which can be expressed in terms of degrees of complexity. But in terms of the different forms of life that the 'organisms' in question develop, thanks to the rising degrees of complexity, the differences that come to be exhibited are no longer differences of degree but differences in kind. They can no longer be understood in terms of the concepts applicable at the lower levels. Schopenhauer appreciates this; but wedded to the scientific analogy he rejects the implications of what he does appreciate.

He speaks of choice, but thinks of the action chosen as 'decided' by the balance of forces represented by the conflicting motives. It is not the person who decides but the stronger motive or force that tips the balance: 'the stronger motive asserts its power over the will, and the choice often turns out quite differently from what we initially supposed' (p. 50). Clearly the person is thought of as a spectator to this resolution by Schopenhauer. In other words, he takes no decision, makes no choice; the resolution is quasi-mechanical, it by-passes him. He is no agent. No wonder Schopenhauer says that 'as little as a ball on a billiard table can move before receiving an impact, so little can a man get up from his chair before being drawn or driven by a motive' (pp. 45–6). The language is more appropriate to a paralysed man being shoved out of the chair on which he is sitting.

It is in a similar vein that Schopenhauer speaks of Buridan's ass who is said to have starved because he could not choose between two bales of straw. The ass is supposed to represent a person who cannot make up his mind between two equally attractive options. As we say, such a man is spoiled for choice and has no initiative. But Schopenhauer likens the ass to an object which cannot move, until some third force is introduced, because two equal forces are acting on it, one from each of two opposite sides. They cancel each other out (p. 61). Later he quotes early Spinoza who in 1665 wrote: 'were a man instead of the ass placed in such a condition of equilibrium, he would be regarded as not a thinking being but as a most stupid ass if he perished of thirst or hunger' (p. 78). Indeed a man in this position would think, 'I am hungry, there is no difference between the two plates of food offered me. I like them both – equally – so it makes little difference which I choose to eat', and he would choose one at random. It is pure prejudice that in such a situation chance could not play a part on which option he goes for.

Schopenhauer quotes from a later letter by Spinoza:

> A stone receives from the impulsion of an external cause a certain quantity of motion, by virtue of which it continues to move after the impulsion given by the external cause has ceased ... Conceive of that stone, while continuing in motion, should be capable of thinking and knowing that it is endeavouring as far as it can, to continue to move. Such a stone, being conscious merely of its own endeavour ... would believe itself to be completely free, and would think that it continued in motion, solely because of its own wish. This is that human freedom ... which consists solely in the fact that men are conscious of their own desire, but are ignorant of the causes whereby that desire has been determined.
>
> (Schopenhauer 1960, p.78)

Schopenhauer says that 'Spinoza came to this insight only in his last years'. He contrasts it with Spinoza's earlier comment on Buridan's ass and blames that earlier comment on Descartes' influence on Spinoza.

We have seen that Schopenhauer characterizes 'I can will what I will' as a *tautology* in contrast with 'I can do what I will'. Indeed, here the will and the self are indistinguishable, as Schopenhauer points out. This means that 'what I will depends on me': I am the author of my action, it is I who make up my mind – not with a flip of the coin, that goes without saying, but in accordance with my desires, concerns and values in the light of considerations of the circumstances and of consequences of what I do for the future. That I can do so is a truism: it is a possibility embedded in the character of human life. To spell out how human life underlies such a possibility is a task of philosophy. Schopenhauer speaks of 'I can will what I will' as a tautology in the sense that what I will must be something I can will, but he misses out the sense in which what I will comes from me – the sense in which I am *active* here as a human agent.

To say that we have free will is to say that we are intentional agents, and as such capable of being moved by considerations of choice and decision. Schopenhauer recognizes that we are such agents but denies what that implies. To say that we have free will does not mean that we inevitably act freely; it means that we *can* act freely – in the sense in which only human beings can so act. To say that free will is an illusion is to say that the will is inevitably in the service of something other than itself. While that can some-times be the case, so that a man is in bondage, a will that can never be free is no will. To deny free will is to deny the kind of agency which characterizes human beings and their life or mode of existence.

We need to be clear that if, as Schopenhauer himself emphasizes, my will is an expression of the way I am, of my character, this does not mean that it is determined in the circumstances in which I act. In other words, being what I am like I could not will otherwise than I will. I am neither a manufactured product nor is my character inborn, the product of the genes I inherit. Much that comes into my life to shape my character is what I learn. It is in what I make my own from what comes to me from outside – my values, my interests, my forms of thought and assessments, my habits, etc – that I become the person I am and come to have a will of my own. As long as my will is truly my own, that is insofar as in what I will I am not subservient to something external, something I have not made my own, it is not determined by something external and is therefore free. This is very different from *liberum arbitrium indifferentiae*. That is a philosophical fiction. But to point that out, to deny the possibility of what Hume called 'the freedom of indifference' is not to deny the freedom of the will.

To deny that I can will anything whatsoever is not to deny free will. I can only will what I have learned to do and can do, as I pointed out in my discussion of Descartes. I cannot will to fly like a bird, but that does not mean that in that respect my will is not free. Schopenhauer writes: '"I can will this" is in reality hypothetical and carries with it the additional clause, "if I did not prefer the other". But this addition annuls the ability to will' (p. 44). I do or choose what I prefer, what I want; whatever I do or choose is what I prefer under the circumstances, being the man I am. This is not determinism. I cannot, of course, just will anything. What I will depends on my values, interests, etc. But this does not mean that I am not free.

This idea that to be free I must be able to will just anything, regardless of motive, has led to the idea of the gratuitous act – Gide's Lafcadio who to prove to himself that he is free throws a total stranger out of the window of a moving train. He is, of course, confused and his motive is to prove that he is free. No doubt there are other reasons for this action of his of which he is not aware.

On the opposite side of the coin we have 'moral necessity'. Schopenhauer quotes what Vallerius Paterculus writes about Cato: 'He never did a right action for the sake of seeming to do the right, but he could not do otherwise' (p. 56). Schopenhauer takes this to support his view that 'if one assumes the freedom of the will, it is absolutely impossible to say what is the source both of virtue and of vice' (p. 57). It does no such thing. What is said about Cato is that he had no purpose in doing what was right; he acted out of compassion or because he could not tolerate injustice. Given his commitment to the values he cared for what the sight of another person's suffering or victimisation inspired in him left him with no choice but to go to the sufferer's or the victim's rescue. There was no 'calculation' behind his action and it came from him, he was fully behind it. This is one paradigm of a free action. Such commitment gives the will direction, indeed it enters into the formation of the will; it does

173

not restrict its freedom. It is as such that the will is free, is owned by the person. It is one antithesis of the indifference of the will, or of its apathy.

There is a sense in which the thought that I can do something if I will it is a form of self-deception. Schopenhauer gives the following as an example: 'I can, if I will, give everything I have to the poor and thus become poor myself – if I will.' Tolstoy's Kitty Scherbatsky in *Anna Karenina* comes to mind, who thought she could be like Varenka, just because she 'willed' it. She finds out that she had deceived herself in thinking it. As Schopenhauer puts it astutely in 'Free Will and Fatalism':

> A man's conduct, taken as a whole, and in all essential particulars, is not governed by his reason or by any of the resolutions which he may make in virtue of it. No man becomes this or that by wishing to be it, however earnestly.
>
> (Schopenhauer 1951, p.52)

Again he writes:

> Conscience accompanies every act with the command, 'You could act differently', although its true sense is, 'You could be other than you are' (p. 56)

However, he goes on to deny that a person can change: 'a man does not alter', 'his moral character remains absolutely the same all through his life', 'he must play out the part which he has received, without the least deviation from character', 'neither experience, nor philosophy, nor religion can effect any improvement in him', 'everything that is essential [in the course of a man's life] is irrevocably fixed and determined'. All this comes from his essay on 'Character'. In his essay *On the Freedom of the Will* he speaks of the constancy of character: 'it remains the same throughout the whole of life' (p. 51). In a passage worth quoting, he writes:

> Under the changeable shell of his years, relationships, and even his store of knowledge and opinions, there hides, like a crab under its shell, the identical and real man, quite unchangeable and always the same. Only in respect to direction and content does his character undergo apparent modifications, which are the result of differences in one's age in life and its needs. Man never changes; as he has acted in one case, so he will always act again – given completely equal circumstances which, however, includes also the correct knowledge of those circumstances (p. 52).

I now turn to this claim: what is wrong with it? Yet what truth does it contain?

3 Character and change

I can see no justification for Schopenhauer's claim that character is constant and unchangeable as an *a priori* contention. Schopenhauer's claim is that a man learns many things in the course of his life, his intellect develops. He meets new people and new situations and his opinions change. As a result his ways of doing things, of coping with situations and of adjusting to things change. But he remains the same man, not in the sense of what he remains true or loyal to – his identity – but in the sense of his character. If for instance he is selfish, he remains selfish. He may for instance learn he would get on better with people by making concessions from his selfishness. But his motive for doing so remains selfish, and when the going is rough his selfishness surfaces in, say, his marital relationship: 'on looking back over our past we see at once that our life consists of mere variations on one and the same theme, namely our character, and that the same fundamental bass sounds through it all' (Schopenhauer 1951, p. 63).

No doubt this is true more often that we are willing to admit. But why *must* it be so? Why is it not possible for a person to change in what he wills, for a person to acquire genuine humility, to learn generosity, to turn his back on his meanness? This may be rare, often such changes may be more apparent than real, but why should not the experience of suffering, contact with an extraordinary person, or a deep relationship make such a change possible? Why should it be ruled out *a priori*? Again, it may be true that the influence of reason and resolution on the course of one's life is very limited, much more limited than 'rationalist' thinkers are willing to admit. But why should this be the only way in which change is possible?

Surely from the fact, if it is a fact, that 'no man becomes this or that by wishing to be it, however earnestly' it does not follow that 'a man's conduct is the necessary product of both character and motive like a planet' (p. 32). Such a man must be prepared to pay the price for changing, to give up things he wants, to do emotional work. Such a change, where it is possible within the context of a man's age and commitments, does not come cheap. Realistically it may not be possible for him, but that does not mean it is never possible for someone else.

For Schopenhauer only the education of the intellect is possible, not of the emotions or of the will: a man cannot learn to will other than what he wills. As Konstantin Kolende points out in his Introduction to Schopenhauer's long essay: 'although Schopenhauer insisted that virtue, like genius, cannot be taught, he left no doubt that enlightenment of the will is morally desirable and effective'. However, given the way Schopenhauer separates the will and the intellect – and on this point Schopenhauer bears comparison with Hume – such enlightenment does not add up to any sort of moral enlightenment. Here is what Schopenhauer says:

What can be corrected is only his knowledge, from which he can come to see that this or that means which he used before does not lead to his goal, or brings more loss than gain; then he changes the means, not the ends. ... It is in cognition alone that the sphere and realm of improvement and ennobling is found. The character is unchangeable, and motives operate of necessity; however they must pass through cognition, which is the medium of the motives. ... The cognition [its enlargement] is the goal of all education (pp. 53–4).

This is no enlightenment of the will; obviously Schopenhauer does not accept that the will can be enlightened. Let us imagine that experience of life teaches a habitual liar that honesty is the best policy since lying, as he sees it, never pays in the long term. If, as a result, he stops lying, has he become an honest man? I think, rightly, Schopenhauer would say no. But in that case how has he been ennobled? Schopenhauer is thus forced to the conclusion that like all forms of characters 'virtues and vices are inborn'. 'If they come from reflection ... they will be inauthentic,' he says, 'and then we could not count at all on their permanence' (p. 55). He is right about the last points; that is no way to come to virtue. Where such a person sees his chance of getting away with, say, lying and cheating his old vices will come to the fore – as Socrates tried to bring out by offering such a man the ring of Gyges which makes him invisible so that the wrongs and crimes he can then commit with impunity cannot be attributed to him by others.

Certainly 'being virtuous or vicious is not a matter of choice' – words which Schopenhauer quotes from Socrates with approval. Indeed if a person adopted virtue by choice he would only be seemingly virtuous – which Paterculus says Cato was not in the words quoted by Schopenhauer: 'he did the right thing because he could not do otherwise'. But, as I pointed out, this does not mean he lacked free will; and neither does it follow that virtues and vices are inborn. We acquire them in the course of our life – though we acquire virtues in an altogether different way than we acquire vices.

In the Appendix to the first chapter of his essay *On the Freedom of the Will* Schopenhauer writes:

When the intellect provides an undistorted knowledge of the circumstances which constitute the motive to action it can express itself unconstrained, in accordance with its own essence. The man is then *intellectually* free, that is, his actions are the pure result of the reaction of his will to motives which are present to him in the external world as they are to others. Accordingly, actions must be charged up to him both morally and legally (p. 100).

What Schopenhauer is saying or trying to say here, as I understand him, is

that when a person is free to think clearly and so can assess his circumstances and what they mean to him personally without bias then he can be
held accountable for what he does, for he is acting in character.

But, and this is something I add by way of criticism, to act in character
is not the same thing as *being oneself* in what one does. For there are
different forms of character. There are forms of character, as Wilhelm
Reich has pointed out in his book *Character Analysis*, which are forms of
evasion: evasive adjustments to what one finds painful which restrict one's
freedom of choice. Excessive envy, reactive politeness, avarice, defensive
propriety and certain extreme forms of conventionality are forms of character or features of character in which a person is trapped or, at any rate,
in which he has failed to come to himself. In being true to character such a
person is caught up in patterns of adjustment and behaviour which he
repeats whenever circumstances bate or threaten him. These are the forms
of character by which Schopenhauer is impressed and his determinism is in
part a generalization from them: a man behaves in a way he recognizes he
ought not, regrets it and resolves to avoid such behaviour.

> He recognizes what it is that he ought to have done; and sincerely
> repenting of his incorrect behaviour, he thinks to himself, if the
> opportunity were offered to me again, I should act differently. It is
> offered once more; the same occasion recurs, and to his great
> astonishment he does precisely the same thing over again.
>
> (Schopenhauer 1951, p. 54)

I think it is in this sense that Schopenhauer says that to a certain extent
'every man is the architect of his own fortune' ('Character'). We shall see
in the next chapter that Freud has pointed out, very much as
Schopenhauer did, that there are fatalities in life which can be attributed to
unconscious design rooted in certain forms of character. Schopenhauer's
determinism thus contains much insight into human psychology.

However there are other forms of character in which acting in character
is a mark of authenticity. The kind of consistency which a person of such
character exhibits is not a 'repetition of the same' but an expression of
stability. This is true of a genuinely honest person, one who is trustworthy
and has integrity. Schopenhauer is surely wrong when he says that 'in
general we treat a person whom we know well like any other thing with
whose properties we have already become familiar, and we know in
advance what can be expected of him and what cannot' (p. 50).

We refrain from riling a person we know to be nasty, we avoid coming
near a dangerous dog lest it bites us, we do not tie a parcel with a rotten
string, we do not offer alcohol to a person we know has a weakness for
alcohol. But it is not in this spirit that we trust someone we know to be
trustworthy. In the former cases we rely, if this is the right word, on some-

thing which, in the case of a person, he cannot help, or something which he cannot resist. It is, as Schopenhauer points out, on inductive grounds that we know that in such-and-such circumstances his reaction will be such-and-such. He is himself the passive recipient of his reaction: it is elicited from him much in the way that one releases a spring. His envy or malice, for instance, is a coil in him from which his reaction is sure to spring if you parade your goods in front of his eyes.

When, on the other hand, one trusts a person to help one or to keep a promise it is the person one relies on – not some habit, proclivity or weakness in him. 'Only after the test has been passed,' Schopenhauer says, without making such a distinction, 'is one sure of the other' (p. 50). But 'test' means something different in the two kinds of case. Where the other has been 'tested' in one's relationship with him one comes to trust him in coming to know *him* – not simply what he is like. Trust here is something one gives from oneself; it is one's response to him. It forms part of a human relationship; it is an engagement. The French expression 'faire confiance' expresses this clearly: what is in question is not what an inductive inference dictates; it is something one *does*: it is putting oneself in someone else's hands. Just as a person commits himself for the future in giving one his word, so does a person in trusting him. Trusting someone is a form of commitment.

Here one's knowledge of the other and one's trust are different in character from Schopenhauer's estimation of these. Indeed one can only trust in this way a being who is free, a being who has free will.

4 Conclusion

Schopenhauer has an eye for human failure in freedom. Here he shows psychological insight. But he assimilates such failures to the causal determinism central in the physical sciences. This clouds his vision of the human capacity which attributing free will to human beings signifies. His arguments are ingenious but they mask this capacity which characterizes human existence.

11

FREUD

Freedom and self-knowledge

1 Freud on the psychological limitations of human freedom

In his determinism Freud is close to Schopenhauer. He was acutely conscious of that aspect of human bondage rooted in the individual's psychology and of the way the individual himself contributes to his own bondage. Like Schopenhauer he thought of it as an instance of the causal determinism which holds sway in human life: 'are you asking me, gentlemen, to believe that there is anything which happens without a cause?' (Freud 1949a, p. 21). Like Schopenhauer and Hume he thought that to deny this is to turn human thinking and behaviour into something accidental, random and unpredictable: 'there is within you a deeply rooted belief in psychic freedom and choice ... [But] this belief is quite unscientific and ... must give ground before the claims of a determinism which governs even mental life' (ibid., pp. 87–8).

Freud, like Hume, thought that we identify free will with indifference and so are most inclined to believe in its reality where very little hangs on what we do – e.g. whether we stand or sit, sit on this chair or that. So he thought that if it can be shown that even here what we do is strictly determined little doubt will be left that 'determinism reaches farther than we suppose' (Freud 1954, p. 193). Even a person's 'free associations', he endeavours to demonstrate, are not really free: 'it is impossible to think of a number, or even of a name, of one's own free will' (ibid.). His reason for thinking this is that what comes to a person's mind or to his tongue in unguarded moments reveals his real thoughts. But this has nothing to do with causality and determinism. It is a matter of connections which Freud is able to make between what comes of the person's mind and his various preoccupations.

Indeed Freud himself speaks here of the *sense* that he is thus able to bring out by means of such connections and determinism interchangeably: 'the thorough-going meaningfulness and determinism of even the apparently most obscure and arbitrary mental phenomena'. He means that aspects of a person's character, with what it embodies of the person's conflicts, his adjustments to these, his anxieties, defences, reaction-formations, find expression in his thoughts and behaviour, particularly when he is most off his guard. But this has little bearing on the question about the reality of free will. After all a person's character is normally apparent in his voluntary actions and choices. How free he is in those actions and choices depends on his character – on the kind of character he has. If, for instance, he is the kind of person who has reacted to his inclination to show off by keeping his head down this will find expression in the choices he makes. His quiet taste will thus be inauthentic and the choices he makes will be determined by this 'reactive' trend in this character. To that extent his choice of dark and unostentatious colours in his clothes and curtains, let us say, will not be free. We could say: 'though he would like to choose bright colours he is afraid to do so; something in him won't let him do so'. Freud is able to spell out this 'something in him' by analysis.

By contrast a person who is himself in his character, one whose character embodies relatively few defensive measures, will be free in the choices he makes. Nothing in him will stand in the way of his pleasing himself in the choices he makes. The choices in which his character finds expression will be *his*, he will be more fully in them, more fully in what he says and does. Thus what, in the words I quoted, Freud takes to be an expression of determinism will, on the contrary, be an expression of the person's freedom. Clearly, then, it is not the 'meaningfulness ... of apparently arbitrary mental phenomena' *as such* which constitutes 'determinism', that is the kind of psychological determination that by-passes the self and thus excludes freedom of choice, but only *certain kinds* of meaningfulness.

Freud's denial of the freedom of the will, however, has a life independent of the confusions embodied in these ideas. Wedded to certain presuppositions Freud represented the psychological determinism which he detected in so much of human life as inescapable. Character, for instance, which he claimed is formed in the first four to six years of life, never changes afterwards. The divisions of personality which he conceptualized in terms of the ego, id and super-ego, he often thought, are immutable structures – on the model of the structure of the atoms of the chemical elements. The ego, he said, is the servant of its three harsh task masters and is never master in its own house. Human nature, he said, is in irreconcilable conflict with culture, implying that civilized man is bound to be divided in himself and, therefore, unfree.

Freed from his scientism and other philosophical presuppositions, however, Freud's determinism is a conception of certain forms of slavery or bondage to which the individual becomes subject in the course of his early development and for which he is ultimately responsible. Thus divided in himself he cannot put himself whole into what he does. Taken up in attempts to defend himself from what he finds painful, to compensate for what he feels he lacks, to make amends for feelings of guilt which persist in his unconscious, to fight his childhood battles in his present life, he cannot respond freely to what he meets in his current life. His contact with others in his relationships is impaired, coloured by phantasy, restricted. He cannot be himself in them. He is haunted by his past, he lives his past in his present behaviour. He is thus caught up in patterns of behaviour which he keeps repeating. Even when he wants and tries to turn away from such patterns he is unable to do so. In *Beyond the Pleasure Principle*, giving examples of such cases, he said that such men's lives seem to be plagued by 'a pursuing fate, a demonic trait in their destiny' and added that such a fate is 'in a large measure self-imposed' (1948, p. 22). His examples and what he says about them are very close to those of Schopenhauer. What is in question is determined by such a person unconsciously, or in his unconscious. It can be called 'unconscious determination'.

Freud's determinism, then, purged from its metaphysical underpinning, including his scientism, is an attempt to articulate the role of the unconscious in human life. This expression 'the unconscious' is used to refer to those aspects of a person which he disowns though he is active in them without being aware of it. In his unconscious activity he is a loose cannon; he pursues aims or purposes without regard to his overall interests and values. He has no say in such activity; he is only aware of its consequences for him. He may not like these, he may indeed be harmed by them, but he is unable to do anything about this state of affairs. Given such dissociation in both his will and consciousness we can say that he stands in his own way. This description involves no self-contradiction.

Given Freud's view that no person comes fully together in his development and that with varying degrees 'the unconscious' plays a part in some aspect of every person's life, in intention at any rate, Freud's determinism is that no man is fully free: let no man boast that he has self-mastery. For the course of a man's life, where it runs counter to his conscious purposes and desires, is not amenable to alteration through a rationalistic approach. This is, of course, the antithesis of Descartes' rationalistic and voluntaristic view. No amount of reasoning which confined to a person's conscious purposes and desires can alter the course of his actions. This is no *a priori* philosophical thesis; one can call it 'psychological determinism'. Also purged of its philosophical presuppositions it coincides with Schopenhauer's view. We find in Freud a detailed working out of it – except that in his various conceptualizations philosophical presuppositions and prejudices intervene and turn his vision into an *a priori* thesis.

The big difference from Schopenhauer is that Freud devoted a great deal of his energy into finding a way of liberating man from his inner shackles and helping him to enlarge the sphere of his autonomy and gain greater self-mastery. Obviously if Freud was really a strict determinist *a priori*, if the divisions he attributed to personality and mind were immutable structures, there would be no question of such psychological liberation. Indeed the kind of liberation he developed centres around the healing of divisions and dissociations within the person and engages the person in his will. What the psycho-analyst does is no more than to enlighten him through 'interpretations'. Indeed the psycho-analyst treats him as a responsible being and makes him understand that the outcome of such 'treatment' is up to him.

Thus Freud, far from being a philosophical determinist, has devised a 'therapy' which in every way assumes the capacity for free will and responsibility in individual human beings. The therapist's immediate concern is confined to enlightening the analysand with a view to helping him to come to greater self-knowledge. I now turn to the question of how such self-knowledge brings the kind of change which liberates a person: brings him greater autonomy and self mastery.

2 Self-knowledge and change in psycho-analytic therapy

Psycho-analytic therapy is a method for helping individuals who seek it to change in themselves, individuals whose problems stem from having been stuck in the way they are. It does so primarily by helping them to come to know themselves. It is a method which engages the patient as agent. It can only work through his participation. It leaves any change in the patient to come from him; it leaves the patient to heal himself. What it does is to put him in touch with 'healing processes' within him. It is the patient who is responsible ultimately for the outcome of his analysis, the receiving of which is a form of learning – learning to be oneself.

But why should self-knowledge make change possible in the person who has got stuck in the course of his development so that it begins to move again? Why should such movement be in the direction of greater wholeness and autonomy? But first, what is the self which the patient comes to know in the course of his analysis?

It is not, as Hume put it, a bundle of impressions and ideas. Indeed, it is not a bundle of anything. It is not a thing, not even, as Descartes will have us believe, a thinking thing. So what is it? It is what a person is searching for when he asks 'who am I?'; it is what the person is who is himself. This is not a common-or-garden question like 'who is he?' or 'who are you?' asked of a stranger standing at the door. It is a question which a person may ask of himself who has lost his way in life, one who finds himself doing things he can no longer make sense of, or worse, things that are repugnant to him, or someone whose life has become flat and who in it no longer knows what he wants. Such a person can be said to be lost and no longer know who he is. It is true that he has to look *within* to get clear about where he has gone wrong: what has he turned away from or neglected? Why? What consequence did that have in his life? This is where analysis helps. It remains true, however, that he will find himself in his engagements with what lies *outside* him. It is only there that he can acquire a self to which he comes.

This is true of a person's development from childhood to adulthood: it is in what he learns in his engagements with others, in the first place with his parents, that in time he comes to himself. There are, of course, hazards, pitfalls. He may hide from what he finds overwhelming, develop defensive postures in which he becomes false. He may evade, shelve difficulties which need to be dealt with. Consequently he will be unable to be fully himself in his engagements and his contact with the world around him will be curtailed. He will start running on the same spot and little that is new will enter into his life: he will stop growing affectively.

Freud spoke of what such a person thus fails to come to as his *true self*. He used a metaphor of Michaelangelo to explain what he meant. He said that the psycho-analyst, like the sculptor, helps the patient to find himself, his true self, *per via di levare*, that is by chipping away at his, the patient's, defences and resistances. The sculptor comes to the sculpture he creates by chipping away at the block of marble. But clearly the sculpture is not in the block of marble in the way that later it is in the crate on its way to an exhibition. Nevertheless there is a perfectly good sense in which the sculptor *finds* it in the block of marble. This is the sense in which we speak of the artist finding the right blue for the sky he is painting, or the poet finding the right word or line for the poem he is writing. What they find does not exist in the way that the continent of America existed before Columbus discovered it. It exists, nevertheless, in the sense that it is what the individual person or artist comes to when he moves in the right direction – the right direction for him, personally, given his experiences, his past, the artistic tradition within which he works. It lies at the end of a path he has to forge for himself on a terrain that is shaped by the tradition to which he belongs, in the case of the artist, and by his past, in the case of the analytic patient.

In his *Introductory Lectures on Psycho-Analysis* Freud speaks of this as the patient's 'best self'. He describes it as 'what he would have been under the most favourable conditions' (1949a, p. 364). Compare with: what the artist or sculptor comes to when he moves in the right direction. The artist too has to be himself if he is to move in the right direction, if what he comes to is not to be a mere imitation or copy. He has to be creative. He must not merely repeat himself. The sculpture which the sculptor 'finds' in the block of marble is his creation. There is a sense in which this applies to the patient in analysis: he too has to be creative in dealing with the old conflicts that come up for revision in the course of analysis. For he has to find his own solutions to them. These must come from him; they must not be imposed on him, they must not be copied from others. Otherwise the patient will be constrained within an alien pattern of conduct and he will not be himself in it. As Freud puts it: 'we want nothing better than that the patient should find his own solutions for himself' (ibid. p. 362). Thus in a paper, 'Turnings in the Ways of Psycho-Analytic Therapy' (1919), he distinguishes between 'psycho-analysis' or 'interpretation work' and what he calls 'psycho-synthesis' there. What he has in mind is the coming together of the patient, as inner conflicts he had shelved are resolved and he becomes progressively himself. He says, 'psycho-synthesis [should be] achieved without intervention' (1950, vol ii, p. 395).

Freud talked of the aim of analysis as 'making conscious the unconscious', 'removing the repressions', 'filling in the gaps in memory'. 'They all amount to the same thing', he said (1949a, p. 363). He also later talked of the achievement which psycho-analysis aims at as: 'where id is there ego shall be' (1933, p. 112). We can add: 'where super-ego is there ego shall be'. Here we should remember that the divisions Freud marked within the personality – ego, id and super-ego – are dissociations. As these are healed through 'psycho-synthesis' or 'integration' in the resolution of the long-standing conflicts, what comes together is at the same time transformed. Thus, as Melanie Klein points out, the super-ego is transformed into genuine conscience (1948, p. 68), and dissociated sexual impulses are transformed in being assimilated into relationships of love. Sexuality becomes part of ('fused with' as Freud puts it – 1949c) love and, as such, something that the person stands behind. Aggressiveness, too, is turned away from hatred, revenge, or the staving off of attacks anticipated by a person in his insecurities; for these are reduced as their bases disappear. It is put in the service of the pursuit of constructive interests. It becomes the liveliness with which these are pursued, the vigour with which the person puts himself into them. It is thus transformed from a destructive force which rules the person to an expression of the conviction with which he puts himself into what he pursues in the face of obstacles.

The ego too is transformed into the self which the person finds. Freud had thought of the ego as the seat of reason dissociated from the centre of energy and emotion in the id. It guides the person, but cannot move him. To do so it has to divert the id's energy by inhibiting its aim by means of repression which it carries out 'at the behest of the super-ego'. That is, the person, as ego, is torn between what is imposed on him from outside and desires he has not made his own. He feels helpless before each of them. From a position of weakness he deals with this situation by identifying himself, in part, with the outside demands and by denying the forbidden desires which nevertheless continue to exercise him however much he shuts his eyes to them. He thus fails to come together in himself and the conflict is simply preserved by being put in cold storage or, to change the metaphor, covered up – like Pompeii, as Freud puts is, whose burial has been its preservation (1979, p. 57). What is thus preserved becomes a fixed structure of the personality – ego, id and super-ego – which shapes the person's day to day responses and conduct.

In the course of the transformations I indicated the person becomes more genuine in his morality and, at the same time, his sexuality is channelled into personal relationships and loses its impulsive character. He comes out of his retreat in the beleaguered ego, where he was doing his best 'to serve its three harsh masters' (1933, p. 108) and establishes new relations with his former masters. As he loses his servility to them they, in turn, lose their uncompromising harshness. He now can be at one with them in their newly acquired character and the divisions within him disappear.

In thus making his own the values he had used as reaction-formations to his sexuality, in accepting the latter and growing with it, in putting his aggression into his convictions where it is transformed, the person acquires self-mastery and autonomy. He can now dispense with repression and, in the new orientation he develops towards others, he loses his ego-centricity. In the considerations that enlighten his life he is no longer split from his feelings; he is affectively related to the norms of reason which provide the framework for these considerations. Consequently he is affectively behind his judgements, deliberations and decisions. In this way, alongside the super-ego and the id, the ego too is transformed: it is transformed into a locus of convictions, commitments, affections, loyalties, concerns and interests directed outwards to people, values, activities, and matters of significance. It is in the way that he engages with these, takes them into his life, that the person is *himself*. This is the *self* I spoke of earlier and into which the ego is transformed.

I said that the analyst's efforts are directed to *enlightening* the analysand about himself through the interpretations he gives him. As the analysand takes in these interpretations, assimilates them, he becomes conscious of the way he thinks and feels about things including himself. This goes together with giving up evading these and keeping them at bay. This is both an enlargement of consciousness on his part and an enlargement of self – a change in him as he gives up defences and owns ways of thinking and feeling which he has so far disowned. Here his will is engaged and changes in direction.

Coming to see something new *about* oneself is certainly a step in the direction of self-knowledge, but whether or not it adds up to self-knowledge depends on what one does with it, how one takes it into one's life. Moving towards greater self-knowledge is thus a change in the self; it involves more than the intellect or the understanding; it involves also the emotions and the will. One may know what one is like, but unless one is oneself *in* or *behind* what one is like one will not have come to self-knowledge – and there are certain ways of being in which one cannot be oneself. I made this point earlier in connection with character.

Thus self-knowledge is not knowledge *about* oneself and there is a big difference between 'learning *about* oneself' and 'learning to *be* oneself'. Thus a person who *knows* himself is one who is in touch with himself. That is he *lives* what he feels about things; he has made his feelings his own. That means that the direction of his life, within the limits of contingencies that he can do nothing about, is his: he is *in* the life he lives, *behind* his responses to things. We say that he *knows* what he feels about things in just this sense, namely that his feelings inform his convictions and his responses. He *knows* what he wants in the sense that he is himself in the things he seeks. That is, what he wants are things he can make sense of in terms of values, concerns and interests that are *his* in the sense that he has made them his own. He *knows* his own mind in the sense that the mind he makes up is his. That is he decides things for himself. He *knows* what he thinks about things in the sense that he thinks for himself: his thoughts are his, they are not second-hand.

Coming to know oneself is indeed a coming to *know*: coming to know one's own mind, to know what one thinks, feels, wants. I have pointed out what these expressions mean colloquially. This is something we need to take seriously. Yet philosophers and psychologists tend to forget it and turn the knowing in question into a knowledge of what is already there – a knowledge of what one is like: of one's character, one's inclinations and inhibitions, of the way one habitually reacts to things. This short-cuts the transition from insight to the kind of change in which a person comes to himself and leaves the connection shrouded in mystery: why should knowing what one is like make one different? Why should such knowledge be enough to cure the patient? Surely knowing something, whatever it may be, is one thing, changing it is another. Surely changing it is something over and above knowing it even when one does not like what one finds out. One is misled by the grammar of 'know' and 'find' here, as well as that of their intentional object, namely what I called 'the self' as this expression occurs in 'oneself'.

If I am right, then, it is clear that coming to *know* oneself is coming to *be* oneself – just as Plato pointed out, coming to know goodness is coming to *be* good, that is coming to goodness in *oneself*. It is equally clear that coming to *be* oneself involves coming together in oneself, so that one can put more of oneself into what one does and how one lives. Hence in coming to self-knowledge, in the sense of learning to be oneself, one moves towards greater autonomy. Equally since such a person's feelings and responses to things are more and more *his* in coming to be himself he becomes authentic. We see that coming to self-knowledge *is* changing in oneself; and the self to which one comes in so changing is one in which one's inner divisions are healed. In coming to such wholeness one inevitably finds greater autonomy and authenticity.

We can further see why such a person is said to have self-knowledge. He is not deceived in himself, he is authentic or true, and he is at one with himself – all marks of knowledge, except that here the lack of deception, the authenticity or truth, the oneness, characterize the self. Thus the knowledge the person has characterizes the person *in himself* and *not* his beliefs about himself. In *this* self-knowledge is like wisdom, innocence and certain forms of self-deception. The wise person, the person who has what Plato called 'moral knowledge', is wise in himself and virtuous. The innocent person is child-like: he is someone who has not learned to lie, he is trusting like a child. A person who, in Tolstoy's words, 'lives a lie', is someone deceived not *about* himself but *in* himself. He will come to self-knowledge in realizing that his life is a lie, in taking this to heart, and in turning away from it. As his life changes so inevitably does *he* change – in himself, in his mode of being.

I said that in psycho-analytic therapy the analysand will benefit from the analyst's insight into him when he can make it his own, come to see what is conveyed to him for himself. The transition from such insight to self-knowledge involves the patient in giving up his defences, which the analyst would have pointed out, taking this insight into his life and coming to terms with it there. This means working on it affectively within the context of his life – dealing with his anger, depression, feelings of having been neglected, rejected, betrayed, or of having failed in one way or another. This will involve, for instance, revising his view of what he is angry about in the light of the perspective of newly discovered feelings in himself which he has come to own – a perspective which had not been available to him before. It will involve him in going to the root of his anger, of his feelings of failure, appraising what truth they contain, what they say about the way he has lived, accepting that truth, reconciling himself to it, and seeing how and where he can go on from there, what he can still make of what he has – for he may have overlooked, denied or underestimated that.

It is *here* that the prospect of change in analysis lies, change in the direction of self-knowledge. But this is something that has to come from him – otherwise whatever he comes to will not be *his* and so will not be self-knowledge. He comes to it in the way the insight he comes to engages him affectively. It is in this engagement that the divisions within him are healed.

What a person is like, I argued, is a mixture of what he has made of himself in relation to what has been his lot and of the lot which has been his and was not his doing. He has, I argued elsewhere, participated in and contributed to his own development. What he has made of himself can, in principle, be undone, the vicious circle that keeps him in the same spot can be reversed, and he can continue to go on from there. Obviously there is a time and a place for things in a man's life and what he has missed may not be restorable, and much of what has been his lot may not be alterable. Even then he can change his attitude to it, come to see it from a new perspective. In doing so he will change in himself. This may reduce what he has found painful in it or it may increase the pain. But in either case it will bring him relief and the change towards making something of his life despite what is unalterable there. It will bring him greater freedom within its limits. Indeed, insofar as his lot cannot be altogether divorced from the significance it has for him personally, with his change of attitude towards it his lot will change with him in certain respects. This is the sense in which coming to know oneself alters the self one comes to know, alters it in the direction of greater wholeness, authenticity and autonomy. These comprise the values or ideals of psycho-analytic therapy. The analyst helps the patient to achieve these in helping him to come to greater self-knowledge and, as a corollary, he respects the patient's independence and autonomy.

As for the pain and distress the patient suffers, this too is bound to have a mixed source. Certainly insofar as some of it comes from the perspective of feelings that will change in the course of analysis it will be reduced. Equally too insofar as some of it comes from the conflicts and difficulties that beset him in his current life and which are the product of what he has been clinging to, as he lets go of it so will the distress bound up with it diminish. On the other hand, there is much in life to hurt a person and cause him pain, particularly a person who is open to life. One who is open to what life has to offer will inevitably be also open to its many pains. Thus in the last paragraph of *Studies in Hysteria* Freud considers the following objection:

> You say yourself, that my suffering has probably much to do with my own relation and destinies. You cannot change any of that. In what manner, then, can you help me?

Freud replies:

> I do not doubt at all that it would be easier for fate than for me to remove your suffering, but you will be convinced that much will be gained if we succeed in transforming your hysterical (neurotic) misery into everyday unhappiness, against which you will be better able to defend yourself with a restored nervous system.
>
> (Freud 1950b, p. 232)

For 'a restored nervous system' here we can read 'a person who is more himself than he was, has come to a greater unity in himself and has thus gained in toleration of pain and in self-mastery'. By 'against which you will be better able to defend yourself' Freud means, 'you will be able to face it and bear it without going to pieces', 'take it on the chin instead of tying yourself up into knots in trying to soften its blow or avoid its full impact'.

3 Conclusion

I have tried to show that Freud's determinism, when cleared of its confusions, is an expression of his vision of the extent of self-division, evasion and self-deception in human life and of the failures of autonomy in individual lives that are inevitably bound up with these. But this is by no means a denial of the reality of free will and responsibility. On the contrary as failures of autonomy they presuppose the possibility of human freedom. Indeed, Freud believed that individual human beings are ultimately responsible for this state of affairs in their own lives. He held that often a person has in himself the resources to heal the divisions within him if they can be made accessible to him. Through the inner work they make possible he is able to come together and find a direction of will in which he is himself. The work which makes this possible engages him: he is not a passive recipient of it.

The engagement of these inner resources means the engagement of more than a dissociated reason. As repressed emotions become accessible, the inner work they make possible involves such things as the working through of guilt, forgiving, making amends, the giving up of grudges, the exercise of patience and the tolerance of pain. It is in this way that inner divisions are healed and in the courage and strength that the person finds in the process he can advance along this path towards greater autonomy.

12

SARTRE

Freedom as something to which man is condemned

1 Freedom, consciousness and human existence

We normally speak of a person or a people as free, or a wheel as moving freely *in particular cases* in opposition to *others* where, for instance, an individual is ruled by voices from his past which he dare not disobey, or a people is in slavery to an occupying power, or again where a wheel is prevented from moving freely by rusty ball bearings or a brake that is catching it at one or two points. Such claims are empirical and contingent.

Sartre, on the other hand, is not speaking about particular cases – one case or type of case in contrast with others. He is concerned with the character of human existence *as such* in distinction from other forms of existence. His claim that human beings are unconditionally free, that is whatever their circumstances, is an *ontological* claim: 'freedom is the being of man' (Sartre 1943, p. 516) – it belongs to the very character of human existence. As such it cannot be limited, restricted or lost.

He argues that human reality has a 'being for itself'. In contrast, what has a 'being in itself' is what it is by virtue of the properties it possesses, including its causal properties. These give it a positive being. It reacts, moves or changes as a result of causes or forces which impinge on it. It reacts to its surroundings which thus impinge on it causally because of its particular constitution or make up. That is something given. Thus a thing that exists in itself has no say in what happens to it: its destiny is not its own, its history is not its own, it is not capable of owning anything. Sartre attributes this to its lack of consciousness.

A person, on the other hand, is capable of making choices and these make a difference to what happens to him; choices furthermore are open to revision. A person makes choices in the light of his appraisals of situations he meets in the course of his life. His actions are thus not triggered causally, they are responses to the significance he sees in things in the way he takes this significance into his life personally. Given this significance he responds to things in the light of his wishes, projects and commitments.

So in Sartre's view, man does not have a fixed nature, one that is given to him independently of who he is. Neither is the environment in which he acts – his 'behavioural environment' as Gestalt psychologists called it – one that is determined causally. What impinges on his life has a significance which is subject to his appraisals. He is, in this sense, what he makes of himself: whatever his circumstances, his past, his heredity, his upbringing, his bodily condition, his health, his physical appetites and inclinations. It is up to him, Sartre claims, what he makes of them in the light of his values – values which are themselves subject to his appraisal.

Sartre emphasizes that man is a conscious being. He means that man is capable of thinking, appraisal and judgement about his surroundings and the situations in which he acts, about himself and his actions, about his past and the future. He is therefore capable of making choices, forming intentions and projects, and so of determining the direction of his life. This is very different from casual determination. He, himself, thus determines what he does and has a say in what happens to him. Only conscious beings are capable of choosing and their freedom lies in this. But Sartre's claim is stronger than this: where the course of what happens to a man is determined by his choices, freedom, Sartre claims, is inescapable. First because whichever way a man goes the course of his life is the result of the choices he makes or evades making. In the latter case it is still *he* who does the evading. He is thus responsible, whether or not he admits it. Secondly, it is always open to him to shoulder responsibility for it and do something about it. Choices can be revised, evasions remedied.

Committing oneself for the future in what one does and says, in one's choices, convictions and loyalties, is the grain or tissue of human life. It differs radically from causal determination. A certain course of events which is causally determined can be changed by the manipulation of causes; and for various reasons, including one's ignorance, this may not be possible for people at a certain time and in a certain place – for instance a disease which may be incurable at present may become curable in the future. In contrast Sartre sees commitment for the future to be a tie which lacks substance and whose only strength is the strength of the person's determination in the sense of resolve. To those opposed to it it may be stronger than steel; but the man himself can give it up if he so chooses. Whether he does so or not is up to him. There is nothing to tie his hands; he is free.

He may, of course, be opposed to giving it up; he may not want to. He may not be the kind of man who breaks a promise lightly. But his integrity is not something external to his will that prevents him from doing so; it is the very expression of his will, of his commitment for the future. There is nothing that bolsters it, nor anything that makes him incapable of going against it if he so wills. This is part of the 'nothingness' or 'lack of positive being' which Sartre attributes to man. There are, of course, cases where a man is *unable* to give his life the direction he would like it to have. For instance, doing so may involve a certain cost he is unwilling to pay. He may deceive himself about this cost and then wonder why it is that he is unable to give his life a direction which he finds attractive. Clearly such a man is divided in himself. Sartre would say he must decide whether what he wants is sufficiently attractive to him to make it worthwhile for him to pay the cost of pursuing it. Here too there is nothing standing in his way except part of himself; what is in question is a conflict of *commitments*. Once more nothing ties his hands; he is free.

What Sartre is speaking about is the freedom which is indistinguishable from the *being* of man. If that were a 'positive being', if man's being were given to him from outside, causally determined by his heredity, upbringing and circumstances, then he could not be free. It is precisely because man lacks such positive beings that he is free: because his consciousness is nothing in itself but like the visible space of a mirror is constituted wholly of what is reflected in it; because his intentions, plans and commitments for the future have no substance or 'genuine duration', as Wittgenstein puts it; because his character is nothing over and above what he can own – his adjustments, his defences, his commitments, his habits, his inclinations. He is free, secondly, because his situation impinges on him through his consciousness. Sartre's idea is that his consciousness constitutes a 'gap' between man and the world: it makes it possible for a man to appreciate his situation and form projects which he realizes in his actions. That is the world affects man only through his consciousness of it and this conscious-ness is not a causal link in a chain of causes. His consciousness thus being nothing in itself constitutes a 'gap' between man and the world. In his appraisals of the situations that face him man is an agent employing various criteria of appraisal. That is he acts on the basis of considerations which he owns. Secondly, in the intentions he forms and in the actions he takes he commits himself for the future: the way he goes on from these is not causally determined. There is thus a similar gap between his present and his future, his present intentions and his future executions of them.

We see that when Sartre claims that man is inescapably and absolutely free he is repudiating causal determination in an original way by making a fundamental distinction and a radical break between man, in the character of his existence, and the rest of nature. This is reminiscent of Kant's distinction between the world of phenomena in which causality reigns supreme and the world of noumena or intelligibilia, or even of signifi-cances, in which the will, at one with reason, is autonomous and, therefore, free. Both Kant and Sartre knew, of course, that man is not always autonomous and that autonomy is something which man achieves: it is an achievement and needs to be sustained. But Sartre, unlike Kant, claimed that not to have achieved autonomy is to have evaded it and that such a man is equally free.

Sartre might have described autonomy as 'relative freedom' in the sense that it is contingent and admits of degrees. Indeed far from thinking of it as inescapable, he thought of it as something rare. This is what he is thinking of when he says, 'we were never more free than during the German occupation ... The circumstances [which he describes with force], atrocious as they often were, finally made it possible for us to live, without pretence or false shame, the hectic and impossible existence that is known as the lot of man' (Sartre, 1949, Vol III, pp. 11–12). He means that whereas easy circumstances often encourage smugness and a sleepy life, in situations which force us to take a stand we come to ourselves and assume responsibility for what we say and do. As he puts it:

> Because the Nazi venom seeped even into our thoughts, every accurate thought was a conquest. Because an all-powerful police tried to force us to hold our tongues, every word took on the value of a declaration of principles. Because we were hunted down, every one of our gestures had the weight of a solemn commitment (ibid. p. 52).

It is in our convictions and commitments that we are ourselves. If we had no convictions, no loyalties, if we cared for nothing outside ourselves, there would be nothing for which to assume responsibility. We would just blow with the wind of the moment or be driven with our ego-centric jealousies, grudges, ambitions: we would have no autonomy, no will of our own, that is no will owned by us. Rather we would be owned by impulses of the moment or by cravings which rule us: we would have no inner unity and so no centre from which to act. The freedom to which we refer in such connections is conditional: we can have it or lack it. To attribute it to a person in relation to something he says or does, or the way he lives, or to deny it of him, is to make an empirical claim. Whereas the freedom Sartre attributes to human beings *as such* is, as he claims, absolute. Even when we evade and deny the responsibility it confers on us we are free.

2 Absolute freedom in the face of obstacles, necessities and an irrevocable past

Sartre, then, argues that as conscious beings we have a unique form of existence: (i) we have no positive being, our being or nature is not given to us from outside, fixed independently of what we make of ourselves, and (ii) the environment or circumstances of our life do not impinge on us causally, but through what we make of them in our appraisals, through the significances we attribute to them. Though he criticizes Descartes' conception of consciousness and rejects his dualism (see Dilman, 1993, chapters 5 and 6) he develops Descartes' notion of our *activity* as conscious beings in an original way worth serious consideration. This is the Cartesian view of the will as immune from causal determination and, therefore, as self-determining.

Secondly, Sartre equally puts Descartes' view of the will's illimitable freedom independently of the body's susceptibility to causal determination in a new light and develops it in an interesting way. This is Sartre's view of the will's inalienable freedom in the face of conditions which constitute obstacles, constraints and compulsions on a person's actions, and of various inevitable contingencies or necessities which are part of his world. Thus having argued that man, in his capacity for choice, is not subject to causality, Sartre next argues that while compulsions and constraints can, though they need not, reduce a man's autonomy, they cannot take away his freedom, or in any way limit it.

Thus the man who acts in panic may do something which he not only regrets but for which he may blame himself. Fear, Sartre holds, does not compel the man in the way that one part of a moving mechanism compels another part to move. A man has always a choice: he need not give in to his fear, he does not have to obey an order, however it is backed. He does not even have to submit before torture. If he does, *we* may not judge him adversely, we may excuse him; but the fact remains that it was *he* who gave in, who was panicked into submission, and he may not forgive himself. In the film *Rome, Open City*, the Italian engineer Manfredi spits into the face of his torturer; he dies but does not betray his friends. This is a supreme expression of the relative freedom Sartre speaks of in 'La République du Silence'. What it shows for Sartre is that it is *possible* for man to act in this way even under such extreme pressure on his will.

He claims that a man can always incorporate a compulsion into his situation and instead of being panicked into yielding to it take a decision, make a choice, in this adverse situation. He may thus voluntarily submit his purse to a highway robber who is holding a gun to his head. Sartre's claim is that it is open to him to do so as a human being. We may say, whether or not it is so depends on the individual in question: does he have courage, is he able to keep a cool head under such circumstances? Sartre obviously appreciates this. But he would say that if he has courage that is not because he is made that way; and if he does not, it is up to him whether he can find courage in the future on a similar occasion. It depends on how he chooses to live, on the things he chooses to give himself to and, consequently, on what he finds in doing so. That is how a person changes direction affectively, changes the commitments which constitute his character.

Sartre argues that the obstacles we meet in life are not imposed on us irrespective of our choices and commitments. A steep rock, he says, is an obstacle to a mountaineer because of his chosen project. It is not so to a mere passer-by or a rambler. It is our freely chosen projects that make an obstacle an obstacle. If, for instance, I describe myself as lacking physical strength or stamina, those two are not absolute characteristics of my body.

My body has these qualities relative to the challenges I accept, the difficulties I create for myself as a sportsman. If I had not chosen to be a sportsman I would not describe myself, my body, in these terms. So there is no such thing, Sartre says, as freedom *in the abstract*, only in a situation, one which owes its being to my freedom. I am in a situation which challenges my physical capacities to the limit only because I chose to be a sportsman, a mountaineer. I may be unable to climb this rock; but I can give up the challenge. I can take up a different occupation.

Obviously this is not an option when it comes to being decent when I find that it conflicts with certain things that I want in life – or at any rate it may not be so for a particular individual. I shall return to this point in the final section of this chapter. But it is true that if certain of my desires count as temptations for me they stand condemned by my values. Sartre concludes:

> Human reality encounters resistances and obstacles which are not its own creation everywhere; but their character as resistances and obstacles comes from the capacity for free choice which defines human reality.
>
> (1943, pp. 569–70)

Sartre takes a similar line with regard to those inevitable contingencies of human life – the time and place of a person's birth, his nationality, his parents, his upbringing and past, his place in society, his sex and other physical characteristics which define a human being in his unique individuality. Since they do not belong to a person by choice and yet are part of him, they pose a special problem for Sartre's conception of human freedom as absolute and illimitable: here is it not something which is not mine by choice which seems to give direction to my life? Sartre puts the problem dramatically: 'I am thrown in the midst of certain brute existents, into a worker's world, French, from the Loire or the South, a world which offers me its significances even before I have had time to unseal them.' His answer is: 'I *exist* my place.' In other worlds, though I am thrown into it, I do not just happen to be there. I grow in it, I choose from it, I make it mine. It is the sustenance I derive from it that enables me to grow, to have interests and concerns, affections and attachments, and therefore things that I love, value and want, as well as things that I abhor and must oppose, and so have choices to make. It is this place which thus enables me to engage with my surroundings and it is in these engagements that I become a person in my own right.

Take the case of my parents. It is true, of course that I could not have been born to different parents, since with different parents I, the person speaking to you now, would not be *me*, the person I am. But the fact that I am the person I am and have the parents I have is completely *fortuitous* nevertheless. That is why Sartre says that I am *thrown* into the world. Depending, however, on what attitude I adopt towards this fortuitous fact, I can make my parents *mine* in what I call 'the strong sense' and be my own person. Or, alternatively, I can see them as people I am chained to or of whom I feel ashamed and thus disinherit myself spiritually. There is no paradox here, for there is a difference between *separating* myself from my parents in the process of becoming myself and *exiling* myself from them affectively and thus disabling myself from entering life's relationships as a person who, in his feelings, matters to someone, as someone with a secure sense of worth. So while I have no choice in the matter of what parents I am born to, it is *I* who make them what I make of them. I am responsible for the way I take them into my being and so for what I am in my relationship with them.

Thus, as in the case of obstacles, Sartre argues that my freedom is logically prior to such contingencies as my place, where and when I was born and of what parents, and that it is up to me what to make of them. They cannot, therefore, constitute a limitation to my freedom. Of course my place may appear to me as a restriction. But this is because of what I have made of it, because of the ends I have chosen; and I am free to revise the choices I have made. If I am born to a poor family and do not have the means to satisfy certain ambitions, I can work hard so as to be able to pay my way, or I can give up those ambitions. If I complain about my lot, then I am in bad faith. Certainly I do not have to look on poverty as something of which to be ashamed.

Poverty is remediable, but what if I am an outcast, an untouchable? What if I belong to a people for whom certain of my rights are not recognized? Sartre's answer is that I do not have to recognize these attributions. I can reject that whole way of thinking as a mythology, I can fight it whenever I meet it. I do not have to submit to it, I am therefore free. This is not to deny what is mine by birth, but to reject the sense that other people attribute to it.

Of course, I live in a world which belongs to others and is shaped by them. 'A man comes into being (Sartre writes) in a world that gives itself to him as already conceptualized, ploughed, explored, laboured in every sense ... But this does not constitute a limit to the freedom of those who belong to it. Rather it is in such a world that man must be free, only in such a world that he can be free'(1943, p. 603).

Sartre means that the world into which each person is born and in which he grows up, is shaped by the language and culture that develops among men. This includes a great mixture of elements which range from the concepts of our thinking, the criteria of our assessments, our values and standards of behaviour, to customs, habitual modes of behaviour, mythologies and prejudices. We would not have a place on which to stand, from which to assess and criticize, to choose, accept or reject, were it not for at least some of it. It is because we have such a place that we can make our own something that has not come into the world through us, or defy and reject it.

Sartre speaks of these as 'circumstances' that we must take account of in 'choosing ourselves'. They are *circumstances* of my life, however, only when I am alienated from them – when I regard them as prejudices, superstitions, taboos. Otherwise they constitute the *framework* within which I make choices and find myself. This is hardly what one would call 'choosing ourselves' as Sartre does. It is nevertheless a process through which we shape ourselves, participate in our own development. Thus Sartre is saying that in neither case is a person shaped by something he has nothing to do with, even when it exists independently of him and has not come into being through him.

What is crucial for Sartre is that I am *not forced* to go along with any part of this, that it is not *imposed* on me: I am not shaped by something I have nothing to do with if it exists independently of me and has not come into being through me. I do not have to be the way I am; I am not a manufactured product. But from this it does not follow, as Sartre holds, that I choose myself – another point to which I shall return.

Sartre rightly emphasizes the importance of a person's special relation to the future in his commitments for his identity as an individual. The future is open: whatever will be has not yet taken place and, therefore, may not take place. Sartre says that a person is his projects and commitments, and these (we have seen) do not tie his hands when he is behind them. He is therefore free. But a person is equally his past. Without a history his actions would be gratuitous acts, in Gide's sense, and Sartre denies that this is a paradigm of autonomous action. The kind of freedom Sartre is speaking of has the possibility of autonomy written into it as well as, of course, that of its antithesis, namely bad faith. His point is that for either of these to be possible a person must have a history, a past in which a certain continuity is discernable; and this underlies the possibility which characterizes human existence.

The problem with what comes to me from other people was that it exists independently of my will. Sartre's answer was that I can reject it, if I so choose without denying what I owe to it. The problem with my past or history is that it is over and done with, and, in that sense, it too exists independently of my will: I cannot have a different past, a different history. So now can I be different now, *act* differently? And if not, how can I be free?

Sartre's answer is similar to the one he gave in connection with the contingency of my place: 'Nothing comes to me from the past that is not chosen by me. We do not receive our past ... One has to *be* one's past, to *live* it – now.' There is, of course, an 'immutable element' in the past. For instance, that I have had whooping cough as a child cannot be changed. But there is also an element that is 'changeable', namely the significance of the brute facts of my past in relation to myself in the unity I have. Thus the date of my marriage is in the past and so is the assumption of its tie. This limits my possibilities and dictates my conduct: but that is because my values and projects being what they are I maintain my conjugal tie, remain true to my past promises. These limits, however, are not limitations to my will, for I own those values, I am behind those projects: it is I who maintain my conjugal tie. My doing so is something that shows itself in my future conduct: I do not hold these values unless I go on from the promises I make in certain ways. Thus (as Sartre puts it) 'the urgency of the past comes from the future.'

Sartre, who has a taste for paradox, says that each of us chooses his past. He means *now*. Thus we remain loyal to it, for instance to the promises we made, or we break with it, for instance in giving up grudges we have nursed, in forgiving past offences. This is something we do *now* and what it amounts to, whether for instance it is genuine or not, shows itself in how we go on from it. Hence the relevance of the future to our past via our present commitments.

Of course Sartre does not deny that one can be a slave to one's past. For instance a person may be unable to turn his mind away from a past loss or he may dwell on some past hurt obsessively without knowing how to stop. But there are ways of letting go of the past without forgetting or rejecting it: if one can let go of it, it will let go of one. Sartre does not go into such cases, but he would have said that in such cases it is the person who holds on to something in the past and he does so now.

I agree with Sartre that if my past is alive in my present life it is *I* who live it, although there are different ways in which I may do so which need to be distinguished. For instance, I may live it in my loyalty to commitments I made in the past, in the affection I hold for figures from the past. Or I may act out my past conflicts in my present relationships, fight my childhood battles with figures in my present life – what Freud called 'transference'. In the first kind of case I maintain my autonomy; indeed my loyalties to the past are my strengths. In the second kind of case, however, my relation to the past is one of slavery – one in which there is no gaoler other than myself. And as Freud has shown, transferences can be resolved, men can be liberated from their bondage to the past in some such transferences, without their being forced to reject or disown their past. Doing so involves 'working through' the emotions in which they have remained stuck on events and relationships in the past – real or imaginary.

I said 'working through' – for instance I have to work through my feelings of resentment to be able to give up my grudges, to work through my feelings of guilt to be able to forgive myself, to work through my grief before I can reconcile myself to a loss and find a new life. This is my way of putting it; not Sartre's. His emphasis on man's 'nothingness' while right if understood properly is apt to hide the resistance to change that man encounters from all directions. And the weight he puts on choice in his conception of the way a man changes makes it look too easy and rational. This is his Cartesian heritage, however much he may have dissociated himself from Descartes in his criticisms of Cartesian dualism. Still I believe that in his fundamental insight that what stands in the way of a person's changing and moving towards greater autonomy is the person himself. Sartre is right. This is an insight he shares with Freud, however diametrically opposed they may be in their language.

3 The burden of freedom, bad faith and autonomy through self-knowledge

I have commented on the *inescapable* character of the freedom Sartre attributes to human beings. He holds, however, the responsibility it confers on men to be a burden to them which they want to escape, but in vain. That is why he speaks of freedom as something to which we are 'condemned'. The attempt to escape it results in what he calls 'bad faith', in which men lose their *autonomy* while retaining their *freedom* – the freedom to change, to grow up, to accept responsibility and to find greater autonomy. Sartre holds that the road to such autonomy is through *self-knowledge* and that coming to self-knowledge is not coming to the knowledge of a pre-existing self, waiting to be discovered, but coming to oneself – which is a process in which a person shapes himself in participating in his own development. Once more in all this, despite appearances to the contrary, Sartre is close to Freud.

Men cannot escape their freedom, Sartre holds, since it is part and parcel of their existence as conscious beings. But the responsibility that goes with it is something they can avoid accepting. Indeed, it is part of man's freedom that he does not have to accept or shoulder this responsibility. Sartre's view is that whichever way a man turns he is *inevitably* responsible because he is free. But he is free not to accept it. Because the responsibility is there as a consequence of his freedom, not accepting it is an *evasion* and a deception of oneself. Sartre calls it 'bad faith'.

To shoulder this responsibility means thinking for oneself, making one's own way in life, judging by one's own standards, and when things go wrong taking the consequences. It is not an easy path to take, since it involves separating oneself from others. One is on the side of what one believes to be right, not on the side of others. Whether one's lights coincide with those of others is a purely contingent matter and so, therefore, is their support. One needs the strength to stand on one's own feet, and that can be a lonely business. Besides, not being able to unburden on other people or on circumstances the blame for what one embarks on when things go wrong makes taking decisions an awesome thing. For one does so in the full knowledge of one's responsibility.

Hence to shoulder this responsibility takes courage and means becoming independent, separating oneself from others in a certain way. One can still belong with others and enjoy their support, but one does not belong in the way that a cog belongs to, or forms part of, a certain mechanism, or the way a sheep belongs to a herd. In human terms this spells insecurity: one does not chug along with the rest, doing as others do. One's fate is in one's own hands; at least one has to deal with the hazards of life, or fate, on one's own.

To accept responsibility is an acknowledgement of one's own inescapable freedom. Such an acknowledgement is not a purely intellectual thing, it involves commitment to proceeding in the direction I have indicated. Sartre characterizes this affective apprehension as *anguish*. In anguish one acknowledges the responsibility which inevitably flows from the freedom which is one's lot.

For the reasons I have indicated many people, if not most, would rather not face the responsibility which it takes anguish to face. They would rather deny that they are free, pretend that they are not. They would rather be like children, have things taken care of for them, do what they are told and let others deal with the consequences.

Sartre gives the example of a young woman who allows herself to be courted, even encourages her partner by leading him on, but without taking the plunge and committing herself to a particular engagement. She wants and reaps the benefit of the courtship in terms of the pleasure she finds in it while pretending it is something that is simply happening to her. She is afraid to stand behind her response, to own it, take responsibility for it. That would make her vulnerable to blame, ridicule, rebuff and even exploitation. She is afraid of this and is not prepared to take the risk, but she is unwilling to give up what she wants either. To put it differently, she pursues certain ends deviously, without acknowledging responsibility for them. This characterizes the pursuit itself, her conduct. Her project involves a contradiction; it is in conflict with itself – like someone who is trying to learn to swim but insists on keeping one foot on the ground. We would describe her as 'double minded'; Sartre describes her as 'in bad faith'.

A businessman may say, 'I signed the contract in good faith'. In other words, he believed that the deal would be mutually beneficial and he was prepared to stand by the contract. He did not, for instance, mean to benefit from it at his partner's expense. It was not his intention to use this contract to stave off an impending bankruptcy or to obtain some further benefit. This is the meaning of 'being in good faith'. The attitude and conduct of Sartre's young woman is the very opposite of this. She lets her partner think that she is not opposed to the courtship and will meet him halfway when she is ready, while having no intention of doing so.

She is in bad faith not simply with her partner, however, but *in* herself as well. She wants her partner's attention, encourages it and enjoys it, while evading any acknowledgment of responsibility, pretending to herself that she is both indifferent and passive. Her bad faith with her partner characterizes her mode of being or existence. Because she evades recognizing what she herself wants and her responsibility for what she does she is *self-deceived*. She is not just deceived *about* herself, this deception coming from her; she is also deceived *in* herself. Her unwillingness to accept the responsibility which is hers characterizes her mode of being – her whole character and approach to relationships.

Because she is unwilling to enter openly and without reserve into engagements to which she is attracted, because she will not stand behind or own her responses to what she wants, she is unable to find either growth or sustenance. Her avoidance of responsibility thus keeps her from being herself and from attaining autonomy. The source of her plight thus lies within her, it is her own immaturity. She both pursues what she wants and at the same time neutralizes it. It is this which curtails her autonomy. It is this conflict which she must resolve if she is to come to herself and have greater autonomy.

One thing is clear, namely that refusing to accept responsibility for how one is and what one pursues inevitably curtails one's autonomy, insulates one from fuller contact with one's surroundings, principally the people around one, and keeps one from growing, coming together in oneself and thus finding oneself. I believe that this is at the centre of Sartre's so-called 'existential psycho-analysis' and I believe also that *this* central idea is one that is shared by Freudian psycho-analysis. Sartre, like Freud, believes that it is through self-knowledge that men can be *liberated* from this self-inflicted plight – self-knowledge which opens up the possibility of making certain decisions, decisions which cut through inner conflicts which tie their hands.

Coming to such self-knowledge is for the person to work his way out of his self-deception. Doing so involves giving up certain attitudes, the pursuit of certain ways of dealing with various vulnerabilities, certain ways of adjusting to one's fears and insecurities, changing in certain ways. One comes to know oneself in what one becomes, provided that the direction in which one moves as one changes is towards becoming oneself. Freud spoke of the way, during psycho-analysis, conflicts which have been shelved and disowned come up for resolution as they become accessible. As he put it: 'they come up for decision'. This comes nearest to what Sartre has in mind when he says that it is through the choices he makes that a person turns away from bad faith.

4 Freedom and choice

We have not considered Sartre's criticism of scientific psychology; but his main criticism is that it treats man as having a 'positive being', that is as a thing whose being is determined from the outside. His view, we have seen, is that man does not have a positive being and determines his own being himself. He determines his own being through the choices he makes in the way he commits himself for the future. But the commitments do not bind him: to commit oneself is not to place oneself on tracks, so to speak, that stretch into the future, thus keeping one moving in the same direction. It is I who keep to my commitments, sustain my choices, 'reassume my conjugal tie'. I am free not to do so – in contrast with a train that has to run on rails. Causes precede the effects which they determine; unless further causes intervene the effects are a foregone conclusion. In contrast, in human life, 'the urgency of the past – e.g., of my promises, my vows of loyalty – comes from the future' (1943, p. 580).

A man who commits himself in the decisions he takes, the projects and intentions he forms, the plans he makes for the future, the engagements he enters into, can change his mind. The intention does not have a positive being, a substance, it is not like railway tracks that determine the direction and destination of the train. As Matthieu puts it in *Le Sursis*: 'There is nothing, I am nothing: I am free.' This is how Sartre expresses it in *L'Être et le Néant*:

> For a human being, to *be* is to choose himself; nothing comes to him from without or from within himself that he can receive or accept [or better: that he has to receive or accept]. He is wholly and helplessly at the mercy of the unendurable necessity to make himself be, even in the smallest details of his existence. This freedom ... is the being of man, that is to say his non-being.
>
> (1943 p. 516)

I want to consider the way Sartre makes man's freedom pivot on *choice*: 'to *be* is to choose oneself', 'the inescapable necessity to make oneself be'. In contrast many writers have pointed out that not everything is open to choice for an individual. In *Anna Karenina* Kitty Scherbatsky thought that she could be like Varenka, that she could emulate her saintliness. As Tolstoy puts it: 'she had deceived herself in supposing that she could be what she wanted to be' (Tolstoy, 1956, p. 256). She herself recognizes this, returns to the life she had turned away from, and in it she finds herself. Within its limits she prospers morally, regains her freedom and finds happiness. The words I quoted from Tolstoy are not an expression of determinism. When Schopenhauer says that 'no man becomes this or that by wishing to be it, however earnestly' he is expressing the same insight. As Guntrip, a psycho-analyst puts it:

> The psyche has, one might almost say, a kind of solid substantiality of its own which we cannot alter at will, and which we have to begin by accepting and respecting. Thus, we cannot ourselves, by wishful thinking, become anything we would like to be, we cannot

by an effort of will make ourselves *feel* differently from the ways in which we discover that we do feel. We do not choose what we shall feel ... At any moment we are what we are, and we can become different only by slow processes of growth ... Our conscious mental operations do not convey the full force of this stubborn durability of psychic reality, since it is relatively easy to change our ideas, to alter our decisions, to vary our pursuits and interests, and so on; but we can do all that without becoming very different basically as a person.

(Guntrip, 1977, p. 218)

This point is well illustrated in Tolstoy's depiction of Father Sergius' struggles with himself to live up to his ideals (Tolstoy, 1960). The struggles involve failures, renewed attempts, learning from one's failures, self-criticism, seeing the error of one's ways, and *time* – time for assimilation, time for growth to take place. In this connection Simone Weil speaks of 'attente', that is waiting, which takes patience, humility and attention. She contrasts it with obstinacy and willing.

When Sartre speaks of 'choosing oneself' this almost sounds like 'choosing one's persona', that is how one will appear to others, the image one will present of oneself to others. Sartre does not mean it this way, but it is significant that choosing calls up such an image. What Sartre has in mind is sometimes referred to as 'radical choice', that is a choice in which one makes a radical break – choosing new values for instance. If this means choosing the very ground on which one has to stand in order to make a genuine choice it would be like lifting oneself up by one's bootstraps, in other words an impossibility.

No doubt certain crucial choices have a role to play in the kind of person one becomes, choices one is faced with at the crossroads of one's life: choice of school, of friends, marriage, profession, whether to make a stand or not in a critical juncture of one's life. But one has to have come a long way before one can have such choices to make. Hence one could not have come there by means of the choices one has made. I think that what Sartre is *trying* to say is that a person *participates* in his own development. Much comes to him from outside, as Sartre himself points out. But he has the possibility of owning it, of making it his own. The criteria of assessment and judgement that become his in what he learns enable him to criticize, to assess what comes to his life, what attracts and entices him.

To begin with, in our early life, we are passive recipients: we copy, imitate, absorb, believe (as Wittgenstein puts it) by swallowing what we are told. It is this which gradually enables us to be critical, choosy, to develop tastes, likes and dislikes, and in time values which inform our affective responses, our actions. In what we learn, especially in the ways of feeling we come to, in our loyalties and values, in the things we come to

203

care for, love and develop an interest in, we become individuals, we come to ourselves – unless our responses to the fears, anxieties, insecurities, neglects, exploitations and abuses that form part of our lot arrest our development, close us into ourselves so that we stop learning. Sartre is right about our having an important part in all this, about our contribution to it, and so about our responsibility for who we are and where we stand. But I think he is wrong in putting the emphasis wholly on choice.

Again I think there is something right and very important in what Sartre means when he says that we lack positive being. But in his proper emphasis on this he neglects what Guntrip in the passage I quoted calls 'the psyche's solid substantiality'. What is in question is not the kind of solidity of things which Sartre argues we try to emulate in our bad faith – as in the example he gives of his waiter. No, the solidity Guntrip speaks of comes from the convictions, commitments, loves, tastes, interests, loyalties in which we are ourselves – including our loyalties to the past, to the place where we were brought up, even to all that we know and are used to. There is, of course, no contradiction between Sartre's 'nothingness' and this 'substantiality of the psyche'. Yet in his zeal to avoid Descartes' mental substance Sartre neglects this 'substantiality of the psyche'. Its antithesis is 'nothingness' in a different sense – a nothingness which comes to haunt Ibsen's Peer Gynt. But there is nothing inevitable about that nothingness and it has little to do with ontology (see Dilman, 1993, chapter 4).

I have two further criticisms relating to the burden which Sartre makes choice carry in human life. He claims that not to choose is itself to make a choice. This is to run together cases that need to be distinguished from each other. There are cases where we speak of a man as having drifted into a course of action, or as having yielded to pressure, or as having acted in fear or panic. Drifting is the opposite of making a choice; it is to evade making one. Again yielding to pressure or losing one's head and acting in panic is very different from choosing to do something one would not otherwise do because of adverse circumstances. People vary whether to excuse or not someone who loses his head or yields to pressure.

Sartre's view is that a man has always a choice: he need not give in to his fears, he does not have to obey any order, however it is backed, he does not even have to submit before torture. We have seen that in these words he is expressing a logical or grammatical point: fear or panic does not compel a man in the way that steam compels the piston to move. But he is also expressing a moral view which belongs to him personally: 'whatever happens to me comes by me ... I must therefore be without remorse or regret, as I am without any excuse' (1943, p. 641). As the expression of a moral attitude these words cannot be justified by any articulation or elucidation of the logic of human existence. Lucidity with regard to the character of human existence does not commit one to a particular moral attitude with regard to other people's actions or our own.

Finally I want to return to Sartre's argument about the relativity of the obstacles we encounter to the choices we make: the rock poses a challenge to me, constitutes an obstacle for me, as a mountaineer or rock-climber, a project which I chose. If I am physically unsuited to climb it, I can take up a different occupation. He writes in his essay on Descartes: 'to be free is not to be able to do what one wants, but to want what one is able to do' (1947b, p. 319). 'Thus (he says) with an ability that varies from person to person and is limited, man exercises absolute freedom' (p. 320). Sartre's idea is that what are obstacles to a man's will are the result of choices he has made himself: 'I want to climb the rock', 'I won't hand him the money', 'I will make a go of my marriage'. I may not be free to succeed, but I am always free to give up trying to make a go of what is an obstacle to my will. The obstacle exists independently of me, but my will is my own and free. I characterized this as Sartre's Cartesian heritage.

I referred to Kitty in *Anna Karenina* giving up trying to be like Varenka: she recognized her limitations and within those she found genuine freedom. All right. But consider a different example, close to Sartre's heart. During the occupation of France a young man joins the 'resistance'. Given the significance of the situation, the occupation of his country, not of his making, he feels it to demand of him that he joins the fight against Nazism. He joins the resistance and is one day captured. Under interrogation by the Gestapo who torture him he betrays the position of his comrades.

He never thought of himself as a hero, but he did not think of this as a reason for staying at home. So he joined the resistance freely and with his eyes open. He wanted to carry through what he joined the resistance to do. But he failed. Unlike Kitty he was not deceiving himself, he was not in bad faith. His tragedy – and I use the word advisedly – was that he was not up to carrying through what he felt called upon to do in the circumstances in which he found himself as a result of his choice. He chose to join the resistance, certainly, but there is a sense in which being the man he is he could not have done otherwise. He was responding to a call which he did not choose; it chose him so to speak. His response to the call was a supreme act of freedom. A response to such a call is very different from forming or choosing a project. He failed: he was unable to resist the extreme compulsion of torture.

The words I quoted from 'La Liberté Cartesienne' fit this kind of case ill. Certainly it is 'in the field of his freedom' that the young man in the above example met the torture to which he was subjected. It was not up to him to measure up to it. He joined the resistance with his eyes open, as I put it, and there is no return from where it has got him. Have we not reached a limit here to what Sartre describes as his 'absolute freedom'? The fact that someone else in his place could have resisted torture does not change this. Here I don't think we can say that *he* could have done otherwise.

13

SIMONE WEIL
Freedom within the confines of necessity

1 The duality of man

Most of the thinkers we have considered speak of a certain *duality* in man. In Homer's *Iliad* men are presented as the plaything of power: both those who wield it and those who are its victims. As Simone Weil puts it in her essay on the *Iliad*:

> Such is the nature of force. ... It petrifies differently but equally the souls of those who are its victims and those who wield it. ... The battles are not decided between men who plot and calculate, make and execute decisions, but between men stripped of their faculties, transformed and fallen down to the level sometimes of inert matter which is nothing more than mere passivity and sometimes of blind forces which are nothing more than mere motive power.
>
> (Weil 1963, p. 32)

On the other side we have 'justice and love or compassion for which there is absolutely no place in the scenes depicted ... but which nevertheless impregnate it, the *Iliad*, with their light'. In other words they belong to the perspective of its author. That is on the one side we have the desire for power and respect for those who wield it, and on the other side, and at an entirely different level of soul, we have compassion and the love of justice. But they do not exist in the same space.

In Sophocles' *Oedipus* we have a man who is wholly helpless before what fate has in store for him and we have a chorus who laments his fate.

Plato in the *Phaedrus* represents the soul as a chariot being moved by two horses which pull in different directions: one obedient to reason and the other one impulsive and wanton. In the *Gorgias* Socrates opposes Callicles who sees life and freedom in giving free reign to impulse and self-assertion. Callicles identifies freedom with licence and thinks of its antithesis as repression (p. 492), whereas Socrates points to a different alternative: freedom can only be found in self-mastery. In the *Phaedo* he argues that it is through self-denial that self-mastery is achieved. A person who has achieved self-mastery is someone who *owns* his desires and passions. Consequently these are no longer activated by outside circumstances; they are responsible to his considerations and judgements. They no longer exist in dissociation from the centre from which he acts; he is behind them. As for self-denial, it is turning away from thinking of oneself and learning to think of others – developing concerns for things outside oneself.

In the *Phaedo* Socrates represents this duality in terms of the body and the soul. One should not confuse this with Cartesian dualism, for what is in question are two opposite directions in which a person can face: the carnal and the spiritual. Self-denial gives him access to a new dimension of reality: spiritual reality in context with which a person finds his soul. The self which he finds in finding his soul is to be contrasted with the self to which he dies, or which he denies, namely the ego – the self as in 'selfish' as opposed to the self as in 'self-knowledge'.

Kant too speaks of two different spheres of existence: the phenomenal and the noumenal world. In one man's will is subject to inclination and as such divided from reason; in the other it is at one with reason and as such autonomous and, therefore, free. Here, according to Kant, a person finds freedom, oneness with morality, and happiness together.

Schopenhauer recognizes three forms of human motivation: egoism, malice and compassion, but holds *egoism* to be the overriding force of motivation. The will is aggressive in its self-affirmation and only by the will's denial of itself, he believes, will compassion establish itself in a person's life. Evil arises out of self-affirmation and goodness is to be found in turning away from egoism (see Hamlyn 1980, p. 134). We have seen that Schopenhauer denies that we can change by willing to be this or that. But he holds that we can deny or turn away from willing and as a result attain a freedom which does not pertain to willing. I have not discussed this question, but I suspect that what is in question, 'not willing', is itself an attitude of will, namely one of patience and acceptance in contrast with a Cartesian exertion of the will – as we have seen in Spinoza.

The conception of such an attitude is absent in Freud and Sartre, though I do not think that no place can be found for it in psycho-analytic therapy – quite the contrary. Still both Freud and Sartre hold conflict to be inherent in human life: 'Conflict is of the essence of our relations with other people' (Sartre 1943, p. 502). 'The conflict that is at the heart of our relations with other people cannot be resolved' (ibid., p. 479). We can, however, choose to give up wanting the impossible, a lasting communion with another, and settle for less, or choose to live our relationships with the other to the full through our engagement in conflict. I think this is Sartre's view. He takes a similar view in connection with our relation to ourselves: we want to be free, to savour the fruits of our freedom, yet we want to evade the anguish of the responsibility this confers on us. We often settle for bad faith; but we can choose to live 'without pretence or false shame, the hectic and impossible existence that is known as the lot of man' (Sartre 1949, Vol III, p. 12). Sartre thus sees the freedom of man, in the sense of autonomy, to lie in the opposite direction from Spinoza and Schopenhauer, namely in an attitude of defiance.

Freud, on the other hand, finds it in the kind of inner work which is psycho-analytic therapy. As I see it, the aim of such therapy is the *resolution* of inner conflicts and divisions, as opposed to opting to adopt one side of the conflict and throwing in one's lot with it – following its call 'without remorse or regret' as Sartre puts it. Nevertheless while such resolution is at least the ideal of psycho-analytic therapy, in his 'theoretical' reflections Freud is constantly a prey to philosophical dichotomies: reason and passion, nature and culture, the id and the ego. The nearest he comes to a reconciliation between what he thus divides in these concepts is giving up the pleasure principle in favour of the reality principle. He conceives of this, however, inadequately in rationalistic terms: one accepts the discipline of morality, making concessions to others, since one needs them and has to live with them. One does so voluntarily out of enlightened self-interest.

The duality which Freud is thus unsuccessfully trying to articulate is the opposition between two affective attitudes and orientations: one which belongs to childhood and is characterized by an immature dependency on others and one which is characterized by a mature autonomy. Freud was impressed by how much the former attitude and orientation persists in adult life – as was, of course, Sartre too. Indeed, those conflicts which Sartre sees as inherent in human life are rooted in the persistence in adult life of just such an orientation.

Freud thought that we can be helped to grow up and out of such an orientation, even if only belatedly, through self-knowledge. Simone Weil, on the other hand, emphasized how much of what belongs to our very nature or make-up as human beings is stacked against the possibility of such a change and, therefore, how rare is what Freud sees as possible in some degree, and Sartre sees as impossible: the reconciliation of personal autonomy with lasting communion with others in genuine reciprocity. She writes:

> When a human being is in any degree necessary to us, we cannot desire his good unless we cease to desire our own. Where there is necessity there is constraint and domination. We are in the power of that of which we stand in need, unless we possess it.
>
> (Weil, 1959, p. 154)

And again:

> When a human being is attached to another by a bond of affection which contains any degree of necessity, it is impossible that he

should wish the autonomy to be preserved both in himself and the other.

(ibid., p. 156)

Thus she speaks of friendship, when it is pure, as 'a supernatural harmony, a union of opposites' (ibid., p. 154). By 'supernatural' she means that it goes against the grain of our nature and so she describes it as 'a miracle'.

I now turn to this duality in Simone Weil's thought between the natural and the supernatural.

2 Gravity and grace

In Simone Weil's thinking there is what one may call a 'moral psychology', that is reflections about how men act normally, their illusions about themselves, their cravings, their expectations from others, the relations in which they stand to the values in which they measure and judge other people's lives, the way these values enter their own lives and the role they play there. She sees them as subject to *necessities* which are regular and law like and which make their actions and reactions predictable. She speaks of these as governed by laws which she likens to Newton's law of gravity, laws of moral gravity, and hence as being subject to the mechanisms of gravity – 'mechanism' in the sense in which Freud spoke of 'defence mechanisms'. The term 'gravity' has a special significance in this connection: it pulls men down morally, makes them 'base', constrains them to act from 'low' motives.

Men's moral actions – here she speaks of a 'social morality' – are the result of an equilibrium which they find in their relations with others in the circumstances which prevail. In times of stability and with social arrangements that ensure people more or less similar powers men respect each other, observe rules of justice, co-operate with each other, punish those who have transgressed such rules of law, etc. The conception in question is very near to Freud's view of 'civilized' behaviour. But where the circumstances change in a person's or group's 'favour' a new equilibrium is reached. The same person who previously respected others now starts taking advantage of them. She mentions the way the Athenians, a civilized people, treated the defenceless people of the little island of Melos and quotes Thucydides in his account of this incident:

> The human spirit is so constituted that what is just is only examined if there is equal necessity on both sides. But if one is strong and the other weak, that which is possible is imposed by the first and accepted by the second.

(Weil 1959, p. 98)

When the men of Melos said that in the case of a battle they would have the gods with them on account of the justice of their cause, the Athenians replied:

> As touching the gods we have the belief, and as touching men the certainty, that always by a necessity of nature, each one commands wherever he has the power (ibid.).

This is an instance of what she calls 'laws of moral gravity'. She gives us a devastating picture of normal human behaviour, which she illustrates richly with examples from history – men doing spectacular things, even going to their deaths, from low motives, seeking 'justifiable' retribution for a hurt or loss inflicted, with an anger and resentment they would condemn in others, trampling on and abusing others. What she says about human weaknesses and insecurities, about the human thirst for compensation, consolation, reward and justification, the way it corrupts people's morality, our natural reaction of wanting to return the evil done to us, the way we project our own evil onto others, the way we shun commerce with the weak lest we partake of the weakness ourselves, the way we try to be as full of ourselves as we can manage or get away with – all this and more is full of insight. There is much in what she says that coincides with Freud on identification, introjection, projection, defence and evasion.

What distinguishes her from Freud primarily is that there is nothing in Freud to correspond to her upper level, namely the supernatural and, connected with this, no explicit value judgement. What she says about psychology at this level corresponds very roughly to what in human psychology falls within the domain of Freud's pleasure and reality princi- ples properly understood. The object of her reflections are her own experience, struggles and suffering, and her very wide knowledge of history, including the history of philosophy and of religions.

Her moral psychology, as I said, has an upper level. But this is not simply, so to speak, an additional floor or level in which human beings move. As a matter of fact she holds that very few of them do so. It is a vantage point from which she considers human psychology and behaviour. What she sees comes into focus from its perspective. What she calls 'laws in the domain of the spiritual' are, by and large, her articulations of conceptual connections in terms of which she captures a great deal of moral wisdom. Here are a few examples I put in my own words – each sentence should be preceded by 'in the domain of the spiritual':

To desire good is to possess it.

(As she puts it: 'if one desires the good one obtains it, so long as one's desire is pure and it is really the good that one desires, the real good' – Weil 1950, p. 93.)

One cannot possess the good without being transformed by it.

The good one comes to possess grows within one (Weil 1950, p. 277).

Goodness is its own reward.

One who possesses goodness cannot be harmed by evil, so long as he does not let go of it.

Possessing the good does not protect a man against suffering: purity attracts evil and destroys it by converting it into suffering.

One cannot receive the good without self-renunciation.

One cannot fall into goodness; one only falls into evil.

One cannot do evil willingly and knowingly.

This is simply a small sample.

I attributed a two-tier 'moral psychology' to Simone Weil. What she is concerned with here are the moral and spiritual capabilities and weaknesses of human beings. In what I called the first tier, we have reflections on human nature, that is on human weaknesses in the face of various circumstances of life which can be seen as testing them. Here she sees them as subject to the same 'laws' and 'mechanisms' of 'moral gravity'. She holds that all human beings, without exception, have to contend with them in themselves. I said 'contend with': they can yield to them if they are not aware of anything else. They are what she calls 'necessities', and in yielding to them they allow themselves to be pulled down so that their behaviour, even when it outwardly conforms to such values as justice and concern for others, comes from mixed motives – including those of self-interest. This is at best. At worst they are pulled down into evil – and, as she says, they then lose all sight of the good ('the light of the good'). Then in what they do they are 'like tiles blown off the roof by the wind'. 'Their only fault,' she says, 'is the initial choice by which they became those tiles' (Weil, 1968, pp. 176–7). What is in question, as we shall see in the following section, has little to do with the Sartrean concept of choice.

As I said 'human nature', as Simone Weil depicts is through a variety of examples, is what comes into focus through her *moral* perspective. They are presented in terms of concepts the connections between which constitute the laws that hold in the domain of the spiritual. What these 'laws' depict is not the nature of man or 'human nature', but *the nature of goodness and of spiritual reality*. Just as physical reality enters into human life, inevitably so – human beings live their lives in contact with physical reality: they handle physical things, build houses, sit in the shade of trees, walk on the ground, etc., etc. – so *can* spiritual reality enter into individual lives. I say 'can' since an individual can live his life in oblivion of it. But there is a sense in which it enters human life as such, namely in the sense that any individual life can be seen from its perspective – as Simone Weil sees it. But to do so one must oneself be aware of it, it must enter into one's own life, at least to some degree.

We have seen Simone Weil sees human beings in their very nature as subject to 'forces' which pull them down morally. She thinks that they have a choice as to whether they allow this to happen or not in the sense that it is each individual who yields or submits to these forces – forces which are part of each individual as a human being. He does not have to submit. This is the freedom he has and loses in submitting. This is her conception of *moral gravity*. In contrast coming into relation with goodness and spiritual reality is rising morally. Here Simone Weil uses the simile of wings. She says that all that an individual has to do is to refuse to submit and to keep his eyes fixed in the right direction; he will then rise not through his own efforts but 'by God's grace'. I shall say something about what this comes to later.

3 Free will and necessity

We have seen that Simone Weil holds that when man submits to the force of moral gravity in himself he falls and becomes subject to necessity. He becomes blind to the light of the good and acts in bondage to necessity. As she says, when one comes into contact with evil, whether as subject or object, it activates the mechanisms of moral gravity in one: one risks becoming an 'object', and acting without light and under compulsion. The person who comes in contact with evil as object or victim, that is when evil is done to him, is sorely tempted to return this evil where it came from, that is to seek revenge. Unless he has had contact with goodness and can keep his eyes turned in its direction, that is unless its light is kept from being eclipsed by the temptation, he will react automatically. It is in this reaction, in the execution of what he is tempted to do, even where it involves planning and biding his time, that he behaves 'like an object': a loose cannon. He is subject to necessity, he is not free.

Here she speaks of 'le transfert du mal' (Weil 1948, p. 78) – the transfer or projection of evil. Thus she says evil is 'multiplied':

> Except for those souls that are near enough to saintliness, the victims of force [she speaks of evil and force as belonging to the same family] are sullied by it just like its agents. The evil that is in the handle of the sword is transmitted through its blade. And the victims who are thus brought into contact with it and who lose

their head in the process of the change which such contact effects in them, do as much evil or more, and then soon fall back into their original passivity.

(Weil 1948, p. 176)

The opposite of what holds in the human world where moral gravity is sovereign is true when individuals gain access to the spiritual world: the mechanisms of moral gravity convert suffering into evil; purity on the other hand converts evil into suffering. Purity, she points out, is invulnerable to evil, but not to suffering (Weil 1948, p. 124). And again: one who possesses good, so long as he can keep it, cannot be harmed by evil. But that does not mean that he is protected from suffering. On the contrary, purity attracts evil (as she puts it) and destroys it by converting it into suffering. She cites Jesus as the supreme example of this: all the violence of the Roman Empire collided with Christ and in him was converted into pure suffering.

Again as she puts it: the false God, the God of this world, of Christianity stripped of the supernatural, changes suffering into violence – I would mention what is going on in the Middle East at present, she mentions Marx. The true God, the God that belongs to the spiritual world is hidden or absent from *this* world, the world of moral gravity, changes violence into suffering.

I have been talking of Simone Weil's view of the way when someone comes into contact with evil, whether as subject or object, he risks being turned into a thing so that his will is no longer his, is on loan to evil, in the service of the mechanisms of moral gravity. I considered the case when he is the object of evil, the victim of violence. When he is the subject, that is when he allows evil to enter his soul, it takes root there and spreads like cancer: he is transformed by it. All vices are subject to moral gravity – as she puts it, in words identical to those of Socrates: no one is evil voluntarily. For deprived of light – the light of the good or moral knowledge – one's will is no longer one's own: one does not own it, it owns one. In a passage from which I have quoted, she says:

When a man turns away from God [from the good] he simply gives himself up to the law of moral gravity. He then believes he is deciding and choosing, but he is only a thing, a falling stone. If we examine human society and souls closely and with real attention, we see that wherever the virtue of supernatural light is absent, everything is obedient to mechanical laws as blind and as exact as the laws of gravitation.

(Weil, 1968, p. 176)

Her belief is that when a person is alienated from spiritual values, when he has no such values, he cannot be himself and is not free. For he is then subject to forces which replace his will. He is obviously still a human being but these forces work through his will. His will has been invaded, occupied, it no longer belongs to him. That is what she means by 'he believes he is deciding and choosing, but he is only a thing, a falling stone'. In a way he is *deciding, choosing, making plans*, but *he* is not the author of these decisions, choices, plans.

Ce que la nature opère méchaniquement en moi: j'en suis pas l'auteur. (Weil 1948, p. 63)

I am not the author of what nature operates in me mechanically.

Obviously 'mechanism' and 'mechanically' are metaphors. They characterize the decisions, choices, and the mode of the person's pursuit of aims and ends: they are dictated by considerations to which he can see no alternative; he is ruled by them.

Simone Weil, like Plato, sees these as emanating from the ego, which has a quasi-automatic tendency to expand. There is in the soul, she says, something like a phagocyte; it causes it to expand and fill in all the space which the circumstances allow it. Thus, for instance, someone who is obsequious before the strong will impose his will on the weak mercilessly. Only where there is a balance in power with those around him he will observe their rights. When he is insulted or hurt he will feel ignored, pushed down, humiliated; he will want to redress the balance which he feels has been altered against him in that he has been made to feel small, treated as if he did not count, did not exist. So he will want to get his own back on the other, making him feel small in turn. He will want to return to his previous height in his own feelings. If, for instance, the conventions of the life he lives demand that he gives someone a present or makes some concession, he will expect something back, even if only a show of gratitude, which will compensate for and restore the loss, fill in the void it has left within him.

All desire for reward, compensation, consolation which mars so much of our moral actions, she says, has at its root this tendency of the soul to expand, its inability to bear the void created in it by what comes out of us, by what we give, or by the hurt and humiliation we receive. It is the desire to feel important, to feel one counts, that one's existence is recognized, that it makes a difference to others. All evil, she says, is a form of expansion – one hurts others, one imposes one's will on them, one appropriates what is theirs by force or by deception, one menaces them, one thus forces one's existence on them: one is noticed, one assumes power, one feeds on what belongs to and is felt to nourish others, and so one grows in one's own eyes.

214

All this Simone Weil believes is a lie, for such expansion is a whistling in the dark; its fruits contain no real nourishment. The power, for instance, one hopes to obtain by means of it is ephemeral. In reality no one possesses power in the way he thinks he does. He is in fact a slave to the power he thinks he manipulates; the power he exercises is not *his*. When he meets someone more powerful he will come down to earth and feel his own weakness and insignificance. Everything that is thus menaced by time, she says, secretes a lie to protect itself. What is a lie is the idea that one is something: that one is owed all that one wants, that one has a right to all the good things in life, that one is the salt of the earth, the centre of the world, immortal. Freud called it a phantasy of omnipotence. He said that we grow out of it to some extent, though to a large extent it persists in the unconscious and shows itself in the way we behave. Simone Weil identifies it with the desire in us to say 'I', as she puts it. She says that this 'I' is almost the whole of us. She writes:

There is no love of truth without an unreserved consent to death [the death of the I, the self, the ego]. The cross of Christ is the only gateway to knowledge.
(Weil 1948, p. 64, translation mine)

To escape the necessity which moral gravity imposes on us we have to bear the void, resist expanding. She thus calls humility the queen of virtues. Humility, she says, is the refusal to exist outside God – in other words in oneself, in identification with one's ego. This involves giving up those attachments on which our ego feeds. In them the ego extends itself and in what it receives from them it grows and is also protected. To give them up is to be naked. In our dependence on what we thus receive and need we are subject to the mechanisms of moral gravity: we are not free. She defines 'free action' as an action that is not subject to the mechanisms of gravity, an action that contravenes the laws in accordance with which they operate, one that goes against the grain of what they dictate.

We possess nothing in the world, except the power to say 'I'. It is this that we should give to God: the only free act.
(Weil 1948, p. 35, translation mine)

So long as we persist in saying 'I', that is living in identity with our ego, we remain anchored in the world of moral gravity. By 'giving that to God' she means giving it up. Doing so is to turn to God; it involves giving up our attachments, dying to ourselves, to the ego in us. This is something each individual can do for himself, though as she points out it takes work – inner work – to be able to do it, i.e. to turn away from the self, the ego, and hence in the direction of God. It is the only free act, she says: pulling up our anchor from the world of moral gravity. The rest is accomplished by God's grace.

Why the only free act? It is the only crucial choice: there are only two directions we can give to our life – that is from Simone Weil's religious, spiritual perspective. If we turn to or remain facing in one direction, we are subject to moral gravity and we have no freedom. If we turn in the other direction our actions will be subject to moral necessity. She says, there are two forms of compulsion, that of moral gravity, such as when we seek revenge in hatred for the harm someone has done to us, and that of the love of the good, such as when we put ourselves out for someone out of compassion. In the former case, she says, our hatred or, in other instances, our greed or our jealousy turns us into a thing, an object; in the latter case she says, we are a slave to the good. Paradoxically, in such slavery we are free.

Why free? I am putting it in my own words: because in giving up our ego we find ourselves, in acting from a love that is pure we are ourselves. It is in giving ourselves to goodness that we come to ourselves. What is in question is the asymmetry between good and evil, between love on the one side and greed, hatred and envy on the other side. Love, she quotes Kierkegaard, is not diminished by being given. The more one gives the more one has; one is enriched. Hatred, in contrast, empoverishes. So does greed. The more one wants for oneself the less one has by comparison to what one wants; the more one keeps the less one has. For it is in giving that one is nourished – in one's soul.

She distinguishes between two kinds of slavery. Affliction, she says, destroys the 'I' from outside: one can no longer say 'I', and one obeys 'like a dog'. She means that one becomes servile. She speaks here of an egoism without an 'I'. Here obviously one is not oneself, one is not free. In slavery to the good one renounces the 'I' oneself, its destruction takes place from inside. Here one obeys the good out of love; one's devotion to it is not servile. In one's slavery to it one is therefore free.

Why slavery then? She means a slavery of love in the sense that in one's love there is no thought for oneself and one is wholly at the disposition of the object of one's love: the good. There is no question of doing otherwise than what it demands. So she also speaks of necessity, what is a moral necessity for one, which she contrasts with the necessity of moral gravity. The former elevates, gives one wings, as she sometimes puts it; gravity on the other hand pulls one down – in the direction of baseness and evil – it lowers one morally. As she puts it: the 'I' contains no source of energy which would enable a person to elevate himself. The energy of the 'I' is self-assertion. It finds expression in exertion, effort, in the pursuit of ends. We find it, she says, in pride for instance: in the proud person there is a lack of grace. Thus what is achieved by effort and self-assertion is contrasted by what is received by God's grace.

Thus when one acts from moral necessity one is impelled to act; one is not attracted by any ends that one is pursuing. When, for instance, a person helps someone in need out of compassion he does not do so in order to do good. Of course he acts as an intentional agent: he intends to relieve the other's discomfort or to provide him with what he needs and uses his intelligence to do this in the best possible way in the circumstances in question. But in his compassion there is no question for him whether or not to go to the other's help. It is in this sense that he is impelled. He acts, as she puts it, by renouncing the fruits of acting. He does not do any weighing; his mind is fixed on one thing which is not open to choice for him. This is a way of speaking with which we are familiar: 'Why did you jump and put your life at risk?': 'I had to; I could not just watch him drown.' 'Why did you join the resistance?' 'In view of what the occupying power was doing in my country I could not do otherwise. I had no choice.' Simone Weil quotes the Breton seaman: 'Fallait bein!' – one had to. She describes this as the purest kind of heroism.

In contrast, to help someone in need 'in order to do good', she says, is to act for a reward – an external end, one to which one's action becomes a means. Goodness, however, when it is pure, is its own reward. For this to be the case, one must not have goodness in mind – thus the Breton seaman. One must act because one cannot bear to watch someone in need or distress, for instance, without putting oneself out, doing something to help him.

Here one is fully in or behind what one does, and one is, therefore, free. Whereas where a person acts from hatred, malice or greed, this is not so. He is deprived of the light of the good – moral knowledge – and is subject to the mechanisms of gravity; so he is not the author of his actions. He is not free. As I quoted her: a free act is one that is not subject to the mechanisms of gravity.

4 Freedom in a world of necessity:
Simone Weil and Spinoza

Simone Weil, we have seen, contrasts moral and natural necessity. Natural necessity operates on human beings from within and from without. When it operates from within, she refers to it as moral gravity because it pulls people down morally. It works through the self on the self – in the sense of ego. Its source and object is the self; the nature in question is 'human nature'. To be free we have to renounce the self. This takes work.

Natural necessity operates on human beings also from without through its determination of outside events which encroach on their lives. This includes the work of physical gravity, but is not confined to it. What is in question is the domain of the natural laws of the physical sciences. Men's control over the events they produce, or rather which are produced by causes in accordance with them, is limited. Human beings since time imm-emorial have suffered natural disasters, earthquakes, famines, pestilences, including those that are the result of human – often other people's – neglect, irresponsibility, greed and selfishness.

Simone Weil speaks of these natural necessities that encroach on and affect human lives from without as at once a veil of God, one which screens Him from us, and also a mirror (Weil, 1968, p. 194). It mirrors God's absence from this world, his way of not interfering with it out of love. For God's love finds expression, she argues, in the way He retires from his creation. The nearest model of this is to be found in the way saints retire from *this* world or renounce the self: two sides of the same coin.

'God's abandonment of Christ (she writes) at the supreme moment of the crucifixion: what a gulf of love on both sides' (Weil 1948, p. 192). This gulf is an expression of His love which is mirrored in natural necessity. It is created by God's retirement from His creation out of love so as to force human love to become supernatural – or at least to provide the possibility and opportunity for this to be so. Christ remained faithful to God in his love while he believed he had been abandoned. His fidelity was 'une fidelité à vide' – in the void, that is without the consoling belief that God was with him.

God's absence is thus something positive. In His way of hiding Himself He loves us. Natural necessity which is His absence is at the same time, therefore, a gateway to God. It makes it possible for human beings to love Him without any thought of return. We are free, she says, to walk through that gateway or to turn away from it: 'the only free act.' If He did not hide Himself from us thus, she says, if He were not absent from His creation, our love of Him could not be supernatural. In that case what we love would not be Him; it would be a worldly God that we loved.

So, she says, we must love this necessity which is a mirror of God, we must make ourselves passive and obedient to it like matter. In other words, we must accept what befalls us, be patient in the face of adversity. To fight it, to try and assert ourselves in the face of it, to pit our strength against it, is futile. Only in giving up our natural inclination to resist it, to complain in our failure, to seek some consolation or compensation for it, only in consenting to it, shall we be free. This is what she means by 'obeying necessity', 'making ourselves as docile as the waves' which the wind blows on the sea. In this respect her views are very reminiscent of Spinoza.

To accept and obey natural necessity which thus encroaches on our lives from without is to renounce the self. For to assert ourselves against it, to complain, seek consolation and compensation is to cling to the self – the ego. In the case of the natural necessities that operate from within, the mechanisms of gravity, what she says we ought to do is not to yield or submit to them, but to turn away from the self through which and on which they operate in us. In both cases, however, the way to freedom lies in the same direction: in both obeying natural necessities and giving up our attachments to this world we renounce the self and, therefore, do the same thing.

Simone Weil identifies *the will* ('volonté') with effort, exertion, self-assertion and 'finalité' or the pursuit of ends (as in 'effort of will', 'wilfulness', 'having a strong will'). So she says that all forms of good that are absolutely pure escape the will – that is cannot be attained by willing. She means that we come to the good not by design, not by aiming to be good, but by consent, service, obedience, patience and attention. These two, however, are attitudes of will – as in being willing and in containing oneself. One may call them forms of passivity, but not of mindless vacuity. It often takes courage and renunciation to consent and to be patient. It takes self-discipline to obey and to attend, to concentrate one's attention. One comes to such courage and self-discipline by inner work. As she puts it: to receive and express truth takes work, whereas one receives what is false without work (Weil 1948, p. 63). Thus what is authentic, whether it is an attitude or an action, what one says, paints or writes, has to come from one, and this takes work. What is not authentic, what one acquires or produces by imitation, takes no work. One's goodness has to be authentic, otherwise it is mere conformity. Thus one does not fall into the good – as she puts it. What one falls into is morally low, one comes to it by *yielding* to the mechanisms of gravity.

This has to be contrasted with *obeying* natural necessity; to be able to do so takes work and renunciation. It is that which brings one into contact with the good or God – she speaks of these interchangeably. That contact transforms a person without the person doing anything except to maintain that contact. It is this which Simone Weil calls 'grace' – the grace of God: the fruit of loyalty to goodness. The change in the self that comes from it in time is internal to such loyalty and cannot be produced *at will*. Such a change is an elevation of the soul; it is in the opposite direction from the one in which moral gravity pulls the soul.

5 Conclusion

There is of course a great deal here that needs further discussion and elucidation. Simone Weil's thought is profound but clear. She often expresses it in the form of paradox; but her paradoxes are always apt and extremely illuminating.

As far as her conception of human freedom goes, she holds, like Plato, that it lies in the direction of goodness or, and this comes to the same thing, the purity of a person's love of the good. It is in moving in the direction of oneness with goodness that one comes to oneself, that is finds authenticity, so that one's actions come from oneself. But one moves in that direction –

which movement is an inner transformation – not by 'willing' but by the grace of God. That is what one receives, what one comes to, is not the result of any striving or exertion on one's part; it is what is wrought in one by the goodness with which one maintains contact. One cannot, therefore, take any credit for it and one should look on it as a gift with gratitude. The moment one takes credit for it one loses it, for taking credit is the reappearance of that part of the soul which says 'I', and that is a change in the opposite direction: being caught up in the mechanisms of gravity and losing one's freedom.

14

G E MOORE

Free will and causality

1 G E Moore on free will and determinism

In chapter 6, entitled 'Free Will', of his little book *Ethics*, Moore is concerned with the apparent conflict between the general law or principle of causality and the claim (he might have said 'common sense belief') that we have free will. He calls it 'the free will controversy' where, he says, 'it is ... often assumed ... that the question at issue is solely as to whether everything is caused, or whether acts of will are sometimes uncaused' (p. 130). Speaking for himself, he says, 'it is extremely doubtful whether free will is at all inconsistent with the principle that everything is caused' (ibid.). Determinists assume that if everything is caused we cannot have free will. Libertarians share this assumption and so claim that acts of will sometimes have no cause. He writes:

> All that is certain about the matter is (1) that, if we have free will, it must be true, in *some* sense, that we sometimes *could* have done, what we did not do; and (2) that, if everything is caused, it must be true, in *some* sense, that we *never could* have done, what we did not do. What is very *un*certain, and what certainly needs to be investigated, is whether these two meanings of the word 'could' are the same (p. 131).

He argues that they are not.

He starts by considering one of the common arguments which determinists use to deny the existence or reality of free will:

P.   Everything that happens has a cause – is caused by something that preceded it.
C.   Hence what happens, in any particular case, was *bound* to happen, so that nothing else *could* have happened instead.

Moore argues that there is a sense of 'could' in which the above argument is valid, i.e. that its conclusion does really follow from its premise. He says that if we have free will, it must be true that we *could* have done things which in fact we did not do, had we so chosen. Therefore to defend our conviction that we have free will we can do one of two things: (i) we can question the premise (does one have to accept the law of causality in the sphere of human intentionality?) or (ii) we can investigate what precisely follows from its acceptance. Moore chooses the second alternative. Like Freud, he does not question the range which the determinist who denies the reality of free will assumes for it. He argues that its acceptance does not put our 'belief' in the freedom of the will in jeopardy.

The determinist *implies*, Moore says, 'that there is *no* proper sense of the word "could" in which it is true that a man *could* have acted differently' (p. 127). This, he says, is simply not true; there is such a perfectly good sense. 'All that we are maintaining (he writes) is that, in *one* perfectly proper and legitimate sense of the word "could", and that one of the very commonest senses in which it is used, it is quite certain that some things which did not happen *could* have happened' (ibid.). He then proceeds to give a proof of this which is, not surprisingly, very similar to his 'defence of common sense' which has been characterized as a 'defence of ordinary language' by Norman Malcolm (1963, pp. 182–3):

> It is impossible to exaggerate the frequency of the occasions on which we *all* of us make a distinction between two things, neither of which *did* happen – a distinction which we express by saying, that whereas the one *could* have happened, and other could *not*. No distinction is commoner than this ... If so, it absolutely follows that one of the commonest and most legitimate usages of the phrases 'could' and 'could not' is to express a difference, which often really does hold between two things *neither* of which did actually happen (p. 128).

In other words, whatever follows from the principle of causality, it remains true that we do make a distinction between things that have happened and could not have happened otherwise and things that have happened and could have happened otherwise. In other words, *sometimes* whatever it is we have done we need not have done it, we could have done something else. We did it because we chose to do it; we could have chosen to do something different instead. Moore puts this by saying that 'could' here in 'he could have done otherwise' means 'could, if he had so chosen'.

He gives a few examples. One of these is the following:

> I *could* have walked a mile in twenty minutes this morning, but I certainly could *not* have run two miles in five minutes. I did not, *in fact*, do either of these two things; but it is pure nonsense to say that the mere fact that I *did* not, does away with the distinction

between them, which I express by saying that the one *was* within my powers, whereas the other was *not* (p. 128).

After giving two further examples, he says: 'it is surely quite plain that we all of us do *continually* use such language: we continually, when considering two events, neither of which did happen, distinguish between them by saying that whereas the one *was* possible, though it didn't happen, the other was *im*possible. And it is surely quite plain that what we mean by this … is something which is often perfectly true. But, if so (he concludes), then anybody who asserts, without qualification, '"Nothing ever *could* have happened, except what did happen", is simply asserting what is false' (p. 129). 'It is, therefore, quite certain that we often *could* (in *some* sense) have done what we did not do' (ibid.).

So Moore says that though the determinist's argument from causality is perfectly valid it does not impugn our belief in free will expressed in the words 'there are occasions on which we *could* have done otherwise than what we did'. For the word 'could' that occurs here has a different meaning from the one it has in the determinist's conclusion: the word 'could' is 'ambiguous' (p. 130). However, he says, *if* someone were to convince him that it had only one sense, the one in which it does follow from the principle of causality that nothing could have happened other than did happen, 'we should, I think, have to give up this principle, because the fact that we often *could* have done what we did not do, is so certain' (ibid.). This is precisely what Wittgenstein does by distinguishing between two grammatical spheres of discourse: one in which the principle or 'general law' of causality holds and one in which we explain what we are concerned with in terms of reasons (see *BB*, p. 15).

Thus for Moore 'we have free will' means 'we could have acted differently if we had chosen to act differently' (p. 134), and this is perfectly compatible with causal determinism. People fail to see this because they confuse causal determinism with 'fatalism' – 'the view that *whatever we will* the result will always be the same; that it is, therefore, *never* any use to make one choice rather than another' (p. 132). Moore rejects this: 'reasons of exactly the same sort and exactly as strong as those which lead us to suppose that everything has a cause, lead to the conclusion that if we choose one course, the result will *always* be different in *some* respect from what it would have been, if we had chosen another; and we know also that the difference would *sometimes* consist in the fact that *what* we chose would come to pass' (ibid.).

A second reason, Moore points out, why people think that causal determinism excludes a belief in the reality of free will is this: they are led to think that we should regard the voluntary commission of a crime in the same way in which we regard the involuntary catching of a disease. They think, wrongly, that they are committed to doing so by their acceptance of causal determinism. They are led to think this because they take 'could not' to mean '*would* not, even if he had willed to avoid it' (p. 133). In other words, they do so because they think that the principle of causality implies the ineffectiveness of the will – the idea that the will is an epi-phenomenon.

Finally, Moore points out, quite rightly, that some people will not regard what he has argued to be sufficient 'to entitle us to say that we have free will' (p. 135). They will say: 'Granted that we often *should* have acted differently, if we had chosen differently, yet it is not true that we have free will unless it is *also* often true in such cases that we *could* have *chosen* differently' (ibid.). This, we have seen, is precisely what Schopenhauer argues: 'I can do what I will' – indeed I do what I will. 'I can will what I will' – which is a tautology: I will what I will. But from none of this does it follow that I could have willed differently – as opposed to I would have acted differently. In other words, unlike Moore, he takes causal determinism to imply the determination of our actions through the determination of our will or choices.

Moore has two answers to this; the first is unsatisfactory because it involves an infinite regress, the second would have been satisfactory if he had been able to develop it. His first answer is that 'by saying that we *could* have *chosen* to do it [which is what Moore said] we may mean merely that we *should* have so chosen, *if* we had chosen *to make the choice* ... There certainly is such a thing as making an effort to induce ourselves to choose a particular course; and I think there is no doubt that often if we *had* made such an effort, we *should* have made a choice, which we did not in fact make' (pp. 135–6).

His second answer is as follows:

> There is another sense in which, whenever we have several different courses of action in view, it is *possible* for us to choose any one of them; and a sense which is certainly of some practical importance, even if it goes no way to justify us in saying that we have free will. This sense arises from the fact that in such cases we can hardly ever *know for certain* beforehand, *which* choice we actually *shall* make; and one of the commonest senses of the word 'possible' is that in which we call an event possible when no man can *know for certain* that it will *not* happen. It follows that almost, if not quite always, when we make a choice, after considering alternatives, it *was* possible that we should have chosen one of these alternatives, which we did not actually choose (p. 136).

Schopenhauer rejects a similar argument which may be called an argument from consciousness: it *seems* to us that the future is open as far as our actions are concerned and that it is *I*, the agent, which determines it in what I *choose*. But as Spinoza pointed out if a stone, a projectile, moving through the air had consciousness, it too would think what we think.

Moore's argument may be called an argument from ordinary language, and it may seem to be open to the same objection. However, the objection is answerable and finally Moore is right: often when I am faced with a number of alternatives it is by the choice I make that I determine what I will do. It is, of course, as the person I am, given my past, my bringing up, my experiences, my culture, that I choose. But that does not mean that what I do is determined by causes external to my will, causes which nevertheless operate on my actions through my will – in the sense that I am the product of what made me the way I am with my will a part of that. That is what Schopenhauer thought, wrongly, when he said that Spinoza's stone would be right in thinking that it moved as it had chosen, implying that our predicament is that of the stone – despite the distinctions he makes.

Supposing that the stone has consciousness is, of course, a literary device, like the animation of animals, to make a point. However, man's predicament or mode of existence is radically different from that of the stone, and human language is an important part of what contributes to make this difference. What we say in that language, the way we speak about ourselves and our actions cannot, therefore, be external to our mode of existence and to our conception of ourselves. It is in this sense that Moore's arguments from ordinary language have something important in them.

2 J L Austin's criticism of Moore

In the first half of a paper entitled 'Ifs and Cans', originally a lecture to the British Academy in 1956, reprinted in his *Philosophical Papers*, edited by Urmson and Warnock, J L Austin criticizes Moore. He starts by stating Moore's position on his example 'I could have walked a mile in 20 minutes this morning, though I did not, but I certainly could not have run two miles in 5 minutes':

> Moore argues that there is much reason to think that 'could have' in such cases simply means 'could have *if* I had chosen', or, as perhaps we had better say in order to avoid a possible complication (these are Moore's words), simply means '*should* have if I had chosen'. And if this *is* all it means, then there is after all no conflict between our conviction that we often could have, in this sense, done things that we did not actually do and the determinist's theory: for he certainly holds himself that I often, and perhaps even always, should have done something different from what I did do *if I had chosen* to do that different thing, since my choosing differently would constitute a change in the causal antecedents of my subsequent act, which would therefore, on his theory, naturally itself be different. If, therefore, the determinist nevertheless asserts that in *some* sense of 'could have' I could *not* ever have done

anything different from what I did actually do, this must simply be a second sense of 'could have' (about which Moore has no more to tell us) different from that which it has in the 20-minute-mile example (pp. 154–5).

This second sense, I venture, if it is at all applicable to human actions is one in which 'can' means 'can only' and 'cannot' signifies logical impossibility: 'I *can* on each occasion I do something *only* do what the full causal picture at the time dictates. A situation in which that causal picture is realized is *bound* to elicit the same action each time it recurs.' If we include the agent's choice in the causal picture then the reality of free will or choice becomes compatible with determinism at the cost of the vacuity of determinism. If, on the other hand, to avoid such vacuity, we make the agent's choice dependent on causes or chains of causes external to it, then the reality of free will is transformed into a mere semblance or appearance of free will – in reality an illusion. I think the former is Moore's position and the latter Schopenhauer's.

Austin sums up Moore's position as follows:

1 'Could have' simply means 'could have if I had chosen'.
2 For 'could have if I had chosen' we may substitute 'should have if I had chosen'.
3 The if-clauses in these expressions state the causal conditions upon which it could have followed that I could or should have done the thing different from what I did actually do (pp. 155–6).

He then raises three questions:

1 Does 'could have if I had chosen' mean the same, in general or ever, as 'should have if I had chosen'?
2 In either of these expressions, is the *if* the *if* of causal condition?
3 In sentences having *can* or *could have* as the main verb, are we required or entitled always to supply an if-clause, and in particular the clause 'if I had chosen'? (p. 156).

He answers all three questions in the negative.

In connection with (1) Austin points out that the two expressions do not mean the same thing. What a man *could have* done is what was open to him, what was within the domain of choice for him, what he was *capable* of doing – given his knowledge, his powers, his values and loyalties. What he *should have* done is what on reflection – in retrospect – he judges would have been the right thing or the proper thing to do, or the one that would have furthered his pursuits or his self-interest. Austin further points out, quite rightly, that it is not clear what 'I should have, if I had chosen' means, if anything. He then thinks of special circumstances in which that expression has a colloquial use: 'If I had chosen to run a mile in 20 minutes this morning, I should (jolly well) have done so' – meaning if I choose to do something I don't let difficulties daunt me and put me off: I stick to my decision (pp. 156–7). He adds, again quite correctly: 'I should certainly not myself understand it to mean that if I had made a certain choice my making that choice would have caused me to do something' (p. 157).

In connection with (2) Austin points out that 'Moore did not discuss what sort of *if* it is that we have in 'I can *if* I choose' (ibid.). He contrasts it with the causal *if* in 'I pant *if* I run' by contrasting the inferences we are allowed to draw in each of the two cases.

> From 'if I ran, I panted' it *does* follow that 'if I did not pant, I did not run', but it does *not* follow either that 'I panted whether or not I ran' or that 'I panted' period. These possibilities and impossibilities of inference are typical of the *if* of causal condition: but they are precisely reversed in the case of 'I can if I choose' or 'I could have if I had chosen'. For from these we should not draw the curious inferences that 'if I cannot, I do not choose to' or that 'if I could not have, I had not chosen to' (or 'did not choose to'), whatever these sentences may be supposed to mean. But on the contrary, from 'I can if I choose', we certainly should infer that 'I can, whether I choose to or not' and indeed that 'I can' period … So that, whatever this *if* means, it is evidently not the *if* of causal condition (pp. 157–8).

Not only is the *if* here not the *if* of causal condition, but it is appropriate only in special situations – that is (in Austin's words) the 'can' here is not 'constitutionally iffy': not conditional. I have the capacity whether or not I choose to exercise it: I can run a mile in 20 minutes period. I might add 'if I choose to', for instance, in the face of a challenge which I don't want to take up. Otherwise the 'if I choose to' is redundant and adds nothing to 'I can', since what I can do is what is open to choice for me.

The important point is that the exercise of these human capacities is subject to choice and that we choose by weighing up reasons. The outcome of our deliberation is not causally determined; nor is the choice we make the cause of our action. 'I choose to do it' means '*I* determine what I do, given what *I* consider important, etc.' The existence of free will means that there are occasions when I can say this, without self-deception, and mean it. Our language recognizes the possibility of there *being* such occasions.

To return to Austin, he then goes on to examine 'I shall if I choose' in the same way. He argues that it is different from 'I can if I choose'. He contrasts 'I shall ruin him *if* I choose' with 'I shall ruin him if I am extravagant'. To put it in my own words, in the first case it is *I* who would be ruining him and my words are a threat or a warning to him. In the latter case it is my extravagance that will ruin him. The connection between my extravagance and his ruin is causal. The only thing I can do if I do not want him to be ruined is to stop being extravagant. In my extravagance his ruin is not the object of my intention, though if he were ruined as a result of my extravagance I would be responsible. In the former case, if I were to carry out my threat, if he did not accede to my demands and thus, in my eyes, gave me reason to carry it out, it would be *I* who would deliberately bring about his ruin. Here his ruin is the direct object of my intention. In executing that intention I aim to bring about his ruin. This is not a matter of capacity ('I can') but of will ('I shall'). The threat, 'I shall if I choose', is conditional, but the intention, once I have decided, is not ('I shall').

An intention, however, is not a cause, and to change one's mind is not to remove or counteract a cause. We can say that the hunger of the starving man caused him to steal food, meaning that it was so great that he could not resist doing what in normal circumstances he would never do. He was acting like an intentional agent under duress. This is at least one kind of example of 'cause' that applies to the actions of an intentional agent. Here it is the will that yields to what we speak of as causing him to do something. The intention, on the other hand, is an expression of the will which is not under duress. As Austin puts it, the 'I shall' in 'I shall ruin you if I choose' is not an assertion of fact, not a prediction, but an expression of *intention*. 'Shall' here is not used as an auxiliary to express a future tense – as in 'I shall ruin him if I am extravagant': a future consequence of my extravagance (p. 159, p. 161).

Here also the 'I shall' is not iffy; it is categorical. 'I intend to marry him if I choose' or 'I shall marry him if I choose' is a categorical expression of intention and the 'if I choose' is redundant (p. 162).

Thus Austin concludes, in neither 'I could have if I had chosen' nor 'I should have if I had chosen' is the *if*-clause a 'normal conditional' clause, connecting antecedent to consequent as cause to effect (p. 165). Under (3) he argues that the verb 'could have' in Moore's 'I could have if I had chosen' is a past *indicative* and not a past subjunctive or conditional. We have already seen his argument for his claim that the *if*-clause is normally not required and is, indeed, redundant.

So what does Austin's criticism of Moore amount to? At one level, insofar as Moore's defence of the existence or reality of free will against the challenge of causal determination is 'a defence of ordinary language' Austin shows Moore to be rather careless and cavalier with ordinary language. In the chapter we are concerned with Moore defends what he would call 'the common sense view' that we have free will, which implies that there are occasions on which we could have done otherwise than we did. He defends it against the deterministic argument that since everything that happens has a cause, whatever happens in a particular case was bound to happen –

nothing else could have happened instead. His defence depends on an alleged ambiguity of the phrase 'could have' in connection with 'happened', 'done'. Austin criticizes Moore's analysis of this phrase.

Let us be clear, Austin has no philosophical axe to grind. He is not interested in defending determinism. His interest is confined to seeing that the job Moore is engaged in doing is done well. He is at one with Moore in thinking that it is an important job. He shares Moore's respect for ordinary language and has respect for Moore's seriousness and for the vulnerabilities which make his errors worthy of note: 'in philosophy, there are many mistakes that it is no disgrace to have made: to make a first-water, ground-floor mistake, so far from being easy, takes one (*one*) form of philosophical genius' (p. 151).

At another level, and *indirectly*, Austin shows that the exercise of our capacity for choice is neither a cause nor a condition of our actions. Choosing and intending are expressions of will, and the will characterizes human actions: the connection between what we will, e.g. intend, and what we do is *internal*, or, as Wittgenstein put it, 'willing, if it is not to be a sort of wishing, must be the action itself and cannot be allowed to stop anywhere short of the action' (*PI*§615). It can, of course, be 'trying, attempting, making an effort' *to do* something. But even when the attempt is a failure and the effort leads to no action it cannot be identified without reference to the action which the agent does not succeed in doing. Thus the action is still internal to its identity. This is something Moore is not clear about in the way he tries to reconcile 'I could have done otherwise' with 'the principle of causality': 'to say that *if* I had performed a certain act of will, I should have done something which I did not do, in no way contradicts this principle; (pp. 131–2). Moore here treats the 'act of will' as an additional cause which alters the causation of the action and hence as externally related to it.

3 The principle or law of causality

I should like first to ask what Moore supposes the sense of 'could not have' to be in the conclusion 'nothing could have happened other than what did happen' which he claims follows from 'everything that happens has a cause'. Next, secondly, I want to consider the range of 'everything' in the premise of the argument Moore is concerned with: is it meant to apply to human actions and intentional agency?

Moore takes 'nothing else could have happened' in the conclusion to mean 'what did happen was *bound to* happen given that the causal condition for its happening was fulfilled'. As he puts it:

To say this [*viz* that absolutely everything that happens has a *cause* in what precedes it] is to say that it follows *necessarily* from something that preceded it; or, in other words, that, once the preceding events which are its cause had happened, it was absolutely *bound* to happen (p. 129).

There is the suggestion of an *inevitability* here which makes it seem that free will is an illusion: causes determine what we do irrespective of what we will. Moore escapes this conclusion by taking what we will or choose itself to be a cause of what we do: we could have done otherwise than we did *if we had chosen otherwise*.

Moore seems to think that *left to itself* whatever happens is *absolutely inevitable*: causes determine the outcome absolutely or necessarily. But human actions are not left to themselves, the agent determines them through his own causality by choosing. If his actions are inevitable, they are inevitable only *relative* to his choices. I think it is this distinction that lies behind Moore's two senses of 'could not have' – an absolute and a relative or conditional sense.

But really 'absolute inevitability' is nothing other than 'logical necessity' and that sense does not apply to causality. For *in principle* whatever can be predicted on causal grounds can be averted. A causal prediction does *not* claim that something will happen inevitably. What is it that makes us speak of something we predict as *inevitable*? We say, for instance, that given how far his cancer has progressed and how little we know about this kind of cancer, he only has three months left to live. Within three months his death is *inevitable*. That is we expect such and such to happen: a causal prediction. When we say 'it is inevitable' we are *adding* to the prediction: we know and have no way of averting what we predict. Outside logic all inevitability is relative – necessarily so.

Someone, like Laplace, may say: 'if we had *full* knowledge, if we knew *all* the causes that bear on what we take to be an accident, we would see that it was absolutely inevitable'. But then he is appealing to an *ideal* which could never be realized in reality. 'In logic', Wittgenstein writes, 'nothing is accidental' (*Tract* 2.012). In contrast, accidents cannot be excluded from real life.

Mathematics works in a closed vessel so to speak (Rush Rhees) and the statement of a mathematical problem includes all the factors that are relevant to its solution. Therefore nothing that can turn up can interfere with that solution. When one repeats an experiment it is otherwise; all sorts of things can go wrong and influence the result. The scientist tries to find out what could influence the result and by trying to keep these factors constant attempts to secure uniformity in the results obtained in repeating the experiment. But this attempt to produce a closed system is always limited in real life. Whereas the necessity that belongs to the result of the repetition of an operation is not subject to any sort of interference. One of the characteristics of a formal method is that *accidents are excluded*.

(Dilman 1973, p. 150)

A particular action can only be *relatively* inevitable – e.g. given the enormous chip he carries on his shoulder he is *bound to* react unfavourably to any request on your part to tone down those actions of his which are infringing on your rights, however nicely you ask. This is a *factual* claim about him as an agent and his actions: it is to say that in this respect *he is not in fact a free agent*. It *may* be true or false, and so if true it could have been false. This is a claim about a particular person; and it cannot be deduced from the law of causality.

But what does the law of causality claim anyway? And why should we adhere to it where human agency and intentional actions are concerned? In the *Tractatus* Wittgenstein says of it that it is not a law but the *form* of a law (6.32) and that what it excludes cannot even be described (6.362). He is thus contrasting it with a genuine causal claim or hypothesis, for instance one that states that there is a causal connection between smoking and lung cancer. What does it exclude? Answer: people smoking regularly without contracting lung cancer. If a great many such people were found we would either have to give up, or perhaps amend, our hypothesis, or we would have to find some special conditions holding in the case of such people which account for their not contracting lung cancer despite their being heavy smokers. What does the so-called law of causality exclude? That lung cancer may have no cause? But what does that mean? As Wittgenstein suggests, we can hardly make sense of that – a disease without a cause (6.362). There are no exceptions to it in the sense that where we have not been able to find a cause we continue to search for one: we never say, 'this – e.g. disease – has no cause', but only 'as yet *we* do not know its cause'. Whether or not it has a cause is not open to investigation; what we investigate is 'what is its cause?', 'what causes it?'

As Rush Rhees once put it: ' "some things happen without any cause" is shocking when it is said in connection with causal enquiry, because it seems to be a statement in the grammar of causal investigation'.

Someone may ask: what about indeterminacy in quantum physics? This is a question of scientific debate. But the debate is as to whether there is a point in sticking to methods here which have served the scientist well in macro-physics. As Wittgenstein puts it: 'Certain events would [may] put me into a position in which I could not go on with the old language-game any further' (OC §617). By 'could not' he means 'would not want to', 'would not see any point in'.

To return to Wittgenstein's remark that 'what the law of causality excludes cannot even be described', in other words that we cannot make any sense of something happening without a cause in macro-physics. Its making no sense is bound up with the kind of *concepts* in terms of which we think *here* – a disease, a fire, a flood, the movement of an object. But elsewhere, where we speak in a different grammar, use different concepts – a human action, a voluntary movement, a piece of thinking that a person engages in – causal questions may not arise. Freud said in a lecture: 'gentlemen, are you asking me to believe that there is anything which happens without a cause?' But in his investigations what he could make no sense of was human behaviour, in a wide sense, that did not issue from some purpose or intention: 'by abandoning a part of our psychic capacity as unexplainable through *purposive ideas* we ignore the realm of determinism in our mental life' (Freud 1954, p. 193).

By a purposive idea he means a reason, an intention, the intelligibility of an affective response in terms of the perspective internal to a particular emotion. When such a 'purposive idea' is owned by the agent the action comes from him, he is behind the affective response: he is the author of the action or response. When the 'purposive idea' exists in dissociation from him, he is not behind the action which issues from it, the reaction in which the emotion finds expression. He lacks autonomy; he is divided in his will. But – and this is the rationale on which psycho-analysis as a form of therapy is founded – the division can be healed, the form of behaviour of which the action or reaction forms a part can be modified.

Thus one could say that Freud *adapted* the law of causality to the domain of individual psychology. He gave it *a similar role* there as the one the general law of causation plays in macro-physics. In its adapted form, far from rejecting free will, it acknowledges its reality while recognizing the phenomena of self-division and the way it limits individual autonomy.

What Moore does not recognize in his criticism of the argument from what he calls the principle of causality is the limitation of its scope to a grammatical dimension of our language, to a sphere where a whole category of concepts are operative. This is what Wittgenstein had in mind in *The Blue and Brown Books* when he indicated a distinction – admittedly in somewhat crude terms – between cause and reason. We have met this distinction in many of the writers we have considered.

Does this mean that causality has no application to human beings, that it does not enter into human life as it were from the inside? Of course it does. We are flesh-and-blood beings and our ability to carry out all our activities as intentional agents depends on the proper functioning of our bodily organs – our organs of perception, our nerves, our brain, our muscles, our heart, our digestive organs, our glands, etc. Anything that goes wrong in their proper functioning can affect our activities adversely in all sorts of ways. It is through causal intervention that what has gone wrong here is rectified and our everyday autonomy restored to us in our usual activities – our ability to see, read, articulate our speech, walk and move about, handle things, think and reason coherently, our moods, etc. Unless, for instance, our brain functions properly we cannot think coherently; and if we are overwhelmed with depression owing to some deficiency in our endocrine system we may not be able to appreciate, see clearly many of the situations in which we act. These are some examples of the way causality impinges on our lives from the inside, so to speak, restricting the exercise and sphere of our activities. However none of this is incompatible with our possessing free will, that is with our capacity as human beings to choose, make decisions, determine our own actions.

4 Conclusion

All that Moore does in the chapter we have considered is to hold on to our conviction that we have free will in the face of an argument from causality which seems to threaten it. He insists that we have the capacity to choose and that when we choose it is we who determine our action and not some external cause – a cause that by-passes our will, is independent of it, a cause which would make our will ineffective. Of course, we can only choose what we know to be in our power to do. Good. But he throws little light on the apparent conflict between causality and free will. His aim is deliberately very limited but so is, though not deliberately, the light he is able to shed on the problem.

I agree with Austin that he shows real philosophical receptivity to the problem and, if I may add, purity of dedication in the whole-hearted way he works on it and aims at clarity. But his contribution, nevertheless, remains limited.

'I could have done otherwise' is an expression of regret in which people take responsibility for what they have done: 'I should have known better.' But there is, of course, an explanation for why I did what I did, and not something else – for instance 'I was tempted and fooled myself into thinking that it would be all right.' If I were to be tempted in the same way *and* also again fool myself I would do the same thing. This is not an articulation of determinism, but the statement of a tautology. It in no way excludes the possibility of my learning a lesson from what I recognize in retrospect and so acting differently in the face of the same temptation. Somebody may say: 'Yes the same temptation, but you now know or see what you did not know or see the first time. So you are not in the same situation, when you act differently.' This is simply to repeat the tautology from which no deterministic conclusion follows. When Schopenhauer and Freud gave us examples of people who continue to repeat the same pattern of behaviour, despite their resolution to avoid it, they were saying something that could be otherwise, something that is not always the case, not the case with everyone – even though it may be more common than we are willing to recognize or admit. This is not philosophical determinism.

15

WITTGENSTEIN
Freedom of the will

1 Science and the freedom of the will

A lecture on Freedom of the Will, delivered by Wittgenstein in Cambridge, probably in the academic year 1945–46 or 1946–47, was published in the Journal *Philosophical Investigations* for April 1989. The main question Wittgenstein discusses there is whether advances in scientific thinking and scientific discoveries need undermine our conviction in the reality of free will.

He points out that what people say in particular cases and what they articulate in general terms varies from person to person depending on their experience and perspective. In other words (i) cases need to be distinguished and what we say in each will depend on the case: 'the man is free', 'the man is not free'. The attribution and denial go together; either is possible and makes sense because the other is possible and makes sense. The possibility of distinguishing them is important. (ii) Secondly, even in the same case different people may say different things. One may say 'the man is responsible, he could have chosen otherwise', another may say 'the cards were stacked against him, I would not hold him responsible'.

In any case, Wittgenstein points out, 'these statements are not used as scientific statements at all, and no discovery in science would influence such a statement' (p. 97). He then qualifies this: 'What I mean is: we couldn't say now "if they discover so-and-so, then I'll say I am free". This is not to say that scientific discoveries have no influence on statements of this sort' (p. 97). On the following page he makes up the following example:

You might feel: 'One thing I know: if people are hungry they want to eat. Cold nearly always produces a reaction of wanting to get warm etc.' You might for instance say: 'What the newspapers now say is nothing at all. It is the economic condition of the people which is important.' Once you find this out, or hear it from someone, the natural reaction is to think, 'now it's all done'. It is

234

as if you had explained everything, when all you have done is get hold of an explanation which may not have explained anything at all. The discovery dazzles you (p. 98).

He adds: 'A discovery might influence what you say on the freedom of the will; if only by directing your attention in a particular way' (ibid.).

A good example is one that I have already touched on in connection with both Schopenhauer and Freud. Their genuine perceptions led them to the conviction that free will is an illusion, that against certain causes which make for a fixity of character our choice and our resolve is totally ineffective. Schopenhauer takes the example of the Earl of Northumberland in three of Shakespeare's plays. He does not play a leading part in any of these plays; he appears 'with a noble and knightly grace' and talks 'in language suitable to it'. Yet successively he plots against and brings down the king to whom he pledges his loyalty. He concludes:

> In any action the intellect has nothing to do but to present motives to the will. Therefore it looks on as a mere spectator and witness at the course which life takes, in accordance with the influence of motive on the given character. All the incidents of life occur, strictly speaking, with the same necessity as the movement of a clock.
>
> (Schopenhauer 1951, p. 56)

Freud multiplies such examples:

> One knows people with whom every human relationship ends in the same way: benefactors whose protégés, however different they may otherwise have been, invariably after a time desert them in ill-will, so that they are apparently condemned to drain to the dregs of all the bitterness of ingratitude; men with whom every friendship ends in the friend's treachery; others who indefinitely often in their lives invest some other person with authority either in their own eyes or generally, and themselves overthrow such authority after a given time, only to replace it by a new one [in one way like the Earl of Northumberland, in another way like Freud himself in his youth]; lovers whose tender relationships with women each and all run through the same phases and come to the same end, and so on. We are less astonished at this 'endless repetition of the same' [he comments] if there is involved a question of active behaviour on the part of the person concerned. ... Far more striking are those cases where the person seems to be experiencing something passively, without exerting any influence of his own, and yet always meets with the same fate over and over again. One

may recall, for example, the story of the woman who married three men in succession, each of whom fell ill after a short time and whom she had to nurse till their death.

(Freud 1948, pp. 22–3)

He then refers to an example from literature, Tasso's *Jerusalemme Liberata* where a trend of fate is given a romantic portrayal. The hero, Tancred, unwittingly slays Clorinda, the maiden he loved, who fought with him disguised in the armour of an enemy knight.

After her burial he penetrates into the mysterious enchanted wood … Here he hews down a tall tree with his sword, but from the gash in the trunk blood streams forth and the voice of Clorinda whose soul is imprisoned in the tree cries out to him in reproach that he has once more wrought a baleful deed on his beloved.

(ibid., pp. 23–4)

I give this as an example of a discovery, a genuine one, which made Freud think that it supported his mental determinism – in Wittgenstein's words: influencing what he said on the freedom of the will by directing his attention in a particular way. Freud's pleasure-principle which, in reality, was an articulation of his discovery of the role which 'phantasy' plays in a person's life (see Dilman, 1984a, chapter 3) got confused in his mind with philosophical hedonism. In the same way the 'repetition-compulsion' on which he focuses in *Beyond the Pleasure Principle* is taken to substantiate philosophical determinism. It makes it seem that the will is ineffective and free will, therefore, an illusion. This is a familiar movement of thought. One is dazzled by the discovery of a familiar difficulty or by its scope – concerning changing in oneself, trusting or coming to know another person, maintaining contact with another and sustaining a reciprocal relation with him or her, or acting unselfishly. One then turns it into an impossibility: 'one's character is unalterable' (Schopenhauer), 'one cannot know another person' (Proust), 'mutual respect and reciprocity in human relations are impossible' (Sartre).

Wittgenstein, in his lecture, is interested in the way *scientific* discoveries dazzle us, particularly because of the prestige science has with us. Thus Freud's: 'are you asking me, gentlemen, to believe that there is anything which happens without a cause?' The questions Wittgenstein comments on are: Does experience have anything to say on the question whether or not we have freedom of choice? What is the scope of prediction where human behaviour is concerned and does its possibility, even if limited, exclude free will within those limits? Do regularities in human behaviour imply that free will is an illusion? Is human behaviour subject to any laws of nature, and if so, do those laws compel people to behave in the ways that accord with any such laws? Does the existence of such laws, if they exist, imply that how we behave and how we shall go on to behave is 'laid down somewhere', 'written down already' – fatalism. 'We are the way we are because of the way we have been brought up': does this mean that we are not responsible for the way we act and for the things we do? Does it mean that we cannot behave differently from the way we do? What is the criterion for 'I could have *done* something else or have *chosen* otherwise than I did'?

Wittgenstein merely comments on these questions in what is only a brief lecture. He is only interested in opening up the mind of his audience to looking at what raises these questions in new ways. He writes:

> When sometimes I have looked frantically for a key, I have thought: 'If an omniscient being is looking at me, he must be making fun of me. What a joke for the Deity, seeing me look when he knows all the time.' Suppose I asked, is there any good reason for looking at it in this way?
>
> I want to impress on you that given a certain attitude, you may be for reasons unknown, compelled to look at it in a certain way. A certain image can force itself upon you. Imagine, for instance, that you are not free, or that you are compelled (p. 91).

'It is one of the most important facts of human life that such impressions sometimes force themselves on you' (ibid) – for instance that what is going to happen is already written down, say genetically. Wittgenstein wants to make us aware of these for what they are, to weaken their force, to show us other ways of looking at things. He raises questions about what we say when we are under the influence of such an impression – e.g. What is the criterion for 'I could or could not have done otherwise'?

He writes: 'All these arguments might look as if I wanted to argue for the freedom of the will or against it. But I don't want to' (p. 93). These are *philosophical* theories and they call for criticism and ultimately for dismantling. He quotes Bishop Barnes: 'Constant and inevitable experience teaches me that I have freedom of choice' (p. 98). Wittgenstein comments: 'He could have said: "that I have choice". If he had said this we'd agree. We say that human beings choose things, we often say they choose to do one thing or another thing' (ibid.). As he later put it in *Philosophical Investigations*: 'philosophy only states what everyone admits' (§599). In *Zettel* he contrasts this with what we are in constant danger of doing: producing myths (§211) – for instance the myth of the mind as a machine: 'The thief who steals a banana moves as inevitably as a stone falling.' ... You might say (in the case of the thief): "There is a mechanism here, but a very much more complicated one" '(p. 88).

2 Wittgenstein and Simone Weil: the thief and the falling stone

We have already discussed Simone Weil's remark that criminals are like tiles blown off the roof by the wind and coming down with the pull of gravity. What is in question is what she calls 'moral gravity' and she says that we are all subject to it, like the falling stone. We yield to its attraction and in doing so give up our autonomy. We are susceptible to the attraction of moral gravity because of the direction in which we are facing: the perspective from which we see things, the perspective which defines the reality in which our lives unfold, the world in which we move about. But while that reality is part of the human world, an important part of the landscape of our lives, one with which everyone without exception has to negotiate, it is not one to which individual lives have to be confined. The more an individual's life and conception of things is confined to it the less free he is.

Here 'moral gravity' and its 'mechanisms' and 'the falling stone or tiles' are *metaphors*. Human beings are clearly represented as radically different from falling stones. The way a stone is attracted by the earth is radically different from the way a thief is attracted by the money he steals. Money attracts him in a different sense from the one in which the earth attracts the stone. Money is attractive to the robber because of what he sees in it, because of the significance it has for him; whereas the earth is not attractive to the stone – period. The stone has no consciousness: it can see nothing and nothing could mean anything to it. With the metaphor of moral gravity Simone Weil brings into focus the way human beings, on account of their natural susceptibilities to 'worldly things', are pulled down morally. They are susceptible to them because of that part in them which says 'I' – the self-assertion of the survival instinct in us turned ego-centric. They yield to these susceptibilities because they blind them to any alternative. In Simone Weil's words, they dim or shut out all moral light of the good.

Simone Weil, as we have seen, is not a philosophical determinist, she is a thinker who articulates her moral vision of the way 'moral ignorance' (Plato) and the evil which often follows from it *imprison* men. It is in this sense that the thief and the criminal are imprisoned and therefore not free: they know not what they are doing, they can see no alternative to their actions and behaviour.

Wittgenstein is not concerned with this question when he considers the proposition that 'the thief who steals a banana moves as inevitably as a stone falling'. He is concerned with the philosophical determinism which claims that 'every event has a cause' and that the mind and human behaviour constitute no exception to this. Natural laws, causality, govern everything that happens there too, and the person is subject to this in what he wills. It is not he who determines what he does, how he behaves, but causes and laws external to him. He is governed by these laws just as the motion of the falling stone is governed. But how is the falling stone governed then?

> The action of a machine – I might say at first – seems to be there in it from the start. What does that mean? – If we know the machine, everything else, that is its movement, seems to be already completely determined.

> We talk as if these parts could only move in this way, as if they could not do anything else. How is this – do we forget the possibility of their bending, breaking off, melting, and so on? Yes; in many cases we don't think of that at all. We use a machine, or the drawing of a machine, to symbolize a particular action of the machine ...

> 'The machine's action seems to be in it from the start' means: we are inclined to compare the future movements of the machine in their definiteness to objects which are already lying in a drawer and which we then take out. – But we do not in general forget the possibility of a distortion of the parts and so on ...

> When we reflect that the machine could also have moved differently it may look as if the way it moves must be contained in the machine-as-symbol far more determinately than in the actual machine. As if it were not enough for the movements in question to be empirically determined in advance, but they had to be really – in a mysterious sense – already *present*. And it is quite true: the movement of the machine-as-symbol is predetermined in a different sense from that in which the movement of any given actual machine is predetermined.
>
> (*PI* §193)

Wittgenstein said: 'in logic and in mathematics process and result are equivalent' (*Tract.* 6.1261, *RFM* I §82). What this means is that results here are not produced by any process in nature – in the way that processes in the battery produce electricity. Indeed they are not 'produced' at all. If there are any processes here, they are the steps we take in our calculations or deductive reasonings. But they do not produce the result, they discover it for us. That result which may be new to us, is not new to logic or mathematics; it is given with the premises of the argument or the data of the mathematical problem. What will take place in the future can never be given or determined by what is or has been the case in this way, and the idea that it can be is, in part at least, the result of taking the shadow which mathematics casts on the real world, in the way it enters our descriptions of it, for the real thing so described.

Thus when in ballistics we say 'this bullet would inevitably go that way, as inevitably as if it moves on rails', Wittgenstein questions the 'inevitably'. The results of our calculations may be described as inevitable to mean that *if* such-and-such conditions obtain then such-and-such a result would follow *necessarily*, *provided* that nothing new is introduced into the equation. It is the *conclusion* that is 'inevitable', in the sense that it follows inevitably, provided that 'accidents are excluded'. Indeed here 'inevitable' is the wrong word. Something that we anticipate may not happen because something we do not anticipate may happen to stop it. This is taken for granted in the predictions we make. But when we describe what we anticipate as 'inevitable' we mean that we know no way and have no way of preventing it. Wittgenstein's point is that there is nothing inevitable about what we anticipate on the basis of any law of nature.

He asks how this applies to the case of the thief and what are the points of similarity between the thief and the stone: are there natural laws in the case of the thief? (p. 88). Elsewhere Wittgenstein has discussed in detail the radical difference between natural events and human behaviour. Here, he writes:

> If we say, 'there are also natural laws in the case of the thief', we have no clear idea at all.

He then adds:

> There is the point of view of the biologist and the psychologist, who more and more insist that they have made more and more progress; that it is only a question of time ... (ibid.).

Wittgenstein has always been sceptical about these disciplines as human sciences. But if such scepticism is fully justified, as I believe it is, it does not follow that we cannot, on the basis of our experience of life, make some general observations about the human condition, the kind of things human beings have to contend with, their weaknesses, their ingenuity and the pitfalls of their ingenuity. These observations may have something to teach us if they come from someone wise. I think that what Simone Weil says about the law and mechanisms of moral gravity is of this kind. It comes from the experience and observations of someone who has read very widely and reflected both on history and on the nature of good and evil. So the idea of 'laws of moral gravity' has little to do with the pretensions of the 'human sciences' which Wittgenstein exposes.

He asks: 'who would insist on there being a similarity between the thief and the stone?' He mentions three categories of people: (1) the scientist – e.g. an experimental psychologist, (2) someone who holds that punishing wrong-doers is pointless and even counter-productive, (3) someone who believes that we turn out the way we are brought up to be: 'it is all as inevitable as machinery'. All three positions involve conceptual confusions; but it is mainly those that come from misunderstandings of such scientific ideas as 'laws of nature' that Wittgenstein is concerned with and the closely connected notion of 'regularity'. Wittgenstein comments:

> There is no reason why, even if there was regularity in human decisions, I should not be free. There is nothing about regularity which makes anything free or not free. The notion of compulsion is there if you think of the regularity as compelled; as produced by rails (p. 87).

We may speak of a wheel or of a top as spinning freely if it encounters no resistance, if there is nothing to obstruct or interfere with its movement. Yet the movement has regularity and 'obeys', as it is colloquially expressed, Newton's laws of motion. Similarly, in the realm of human behaviour, we may say of someone that he regularly votes for a particular party, that he gets up regularly at seven in the morning, or that he is very punctual in keeping his appointments. There is no suggestion here that he is not free, that his behaviour is compelled, that he is in a rut of which he cannot get out. The regularity in his voting may come from his convictions and the stability of his personality. As for regular habits that serve one well, they are not anything that enslave one. Obviously there is a radical difference between the regularity and lawfulness of nature and the regularities to be found in human affairs and human behaviour. But in both cases we can distinguish between regularities that issue of compulsions of one kind or another and regularities where this is not the case. In the case of people and their behaviour there is not one contrast, but many, that are relevant to the question whether an individual is acting freely or not, but one of these is the contrast between stability of personality and rigidity of character. Thus where a person's behaviour issues from settled beliefs we could say that he is behind what he does. In contrast, actions which issue from a rigidity of character are dictated by a person's anxieties and by the fear that compels him to avoid facing those anxieties. His character is a straight-jacket: in its expressions we see what he is like, but we also see a person who has failed to come to himself.

3 Wittgenstein and Schopenhauer: determination of our decisions

You sometimes see in a wind (Wittgenstein says) a piece of paper blowing about anyhow. Suppose the piece of paper could make the decision: 'Now I want to go this way.' I say: 'Queer, this paper always decides where it is to go, and all the time it is the wind that blows it. I know it is the wind that blows it.'

That same force which moves it also in a different way moves its decisions.

In this sense, there is a certain outlook: 'We are all the time being determined. We think we decide, but all the time we are being shoved about, our decisions too. This means that we are misled into thinking that we do what we want' (p. 90).

Wittgenstein comments that 'normally, unless we philosophise, we don't talk this way' and then he asks: 'is there a case in which we would actually say that a man thought he decided, but actually didn't decide?' (ibid.).

He makes up an example in which he is made to walk this way and that by a remote control mechanism – much in the way that toy boats and airplanes are steered by remote control. He is, however, thus controlled through his will. He is then asked: 'were you dragged about? were you free?' and he answers: 'I was free.'

The example is very similar to Spinoza's stone which is granted consciousness. Spinoza had said: 'man is ignorant of the causes by which he is led to wish and desire'. That is why we think we do what we want and so imagine we are free when we are not. Thus we are in the same position as the stone that someone throws into the air. If it had consciousness it would think it was flying through the air of its own volition, it would take the course of its movement as the fulfilment of its own desire. Commenting on this Schopenhauer said that in that case the stone would be right in thinking it was moving of its own free will. For that is precisely our case and we say that we do what we do of our own free will in the same situation. That is, therefore, what 'acting of one's own free will' must mean. When we reflect on what is involved in such cases we shall see that this expression is a misnomer.

Why is it a misnomer? Because in all those cases where we say that people act of their own free will, their will is not their own; it is determined by outside causes. Outside causes as opposed to what? Themselves.

All right. But what does 'by themselves', 'by himself' mean? We have seen various philosophers have said: 'the person is the cause of what he does', 'the action is self-caused', 'the will is its own cause' or 'the act of will has no cause; the action originates in the will'. These expressions can be misleading, however, and in any case they raise again the question they were meant to answer. What we need to be clear about is how it is that certain reasons and considerations – and there are different kinds – come to weigh with people and how it is that they take them into account when acting or when refraining from doing what they want to do. Wittgenstein brought out how it is that here we have a whole dimension of action and change that is different from events and their causality. The reality of both the will and the self – implied in our use of personal pronouns – is to be found in this dimension – or to put it in a slightly different way: the will and the self have their reality in this dimension.

But in that case how can what a person wills – his decisions and intentions – be caused? Caused by a mechanism regulated with a crank (p. 90)? Strictly speaking, it seems to me, this is an impossibility. We can electrically stimulate various centres in the brain to bring about certain movements of the body. But the person would be a by-stander to these movements and he would not think of these as voluntary movements. Perhaps by simultaneously stimulating some further centres in the brain we can make him *think* he was moving these parts and doing so with such-and-such an intention – in the way that, perhaps we could give a person certain drugs and produce in him paranoiac fantasies that root themselves in real situations. But the two cases are not alike and I cannot make sense of what we are supposed to imagine here.

Be that as it may, the fact remains that we can take Wittgenstein's example 'allegorically' to remind us of cases where a man's decisions and desires are manipulated by others, controlled from outside, so that their decisions are *not theirs*. This is in fact what Wittgenstein suggests: 'Actually, there are cases which come pretty near to this' (p. 90). Well, in such cases, do people decide in reality? We could say, they decide, but 'their decisions aren't theirs'. The seeming contradiction in this way of putting it can be removed: 'other people decide for them; and so they do not really decide, they only go through the motion of deciding – they are self-deceived'. There are many different cases here. I shall mention a few. A person is a slave to certain trends or conventions. He has no thoughts of his own when it comes to choosing what to buy, what to wear, what to say in certain situations. He does not choose, he follows the trends or conventions mindlessly. He is clearly an intentional agent, like any other human being; but he hasn't got a mind of his own. We can also say: he hasn't come to himself, he is not himself. A person who does not have a mind of his own cannot be himself.

A slightly different example is the case of a person who is very suggestible: he is persuaded to act a certain way not through reasoning or argument, but by suggestion through bogus argument – by propaganda for instance.[1] Here we talk of the *manipulation* of people through the manipulation of their will – precisely the kind of case that Wittgenstein wanted. The subject of such manipulation thinks he chooses, acts and speaks for himself, when he does what others want him to do and speaks the way others want him to speak. If and when he comes to see this he will, in that respect, move towards coming to himself and say: 'what a fool I have been! how I have been duped!'

A third and more extreme case is that of post-hypnotic action.[2]

These cases are to be *contrasted* with normal cases, and what we say in them have sense in the way they *deviate* from the normal cases. They have their place in the same grammatical dimension as the normal ones. That is why we cannot say: 'what we will is *always* the result of outside causes', so that 'those who think that they act out of their own free will dream with their eyes open'. In Spinoza there is an important qualification to this which restores a limitation to the scope of human freedom. For he claims that in giving up our ego and making those outside causes our own by accepting them (by making God's will ours) we can move from a state of bondage to a state of freedom.

Thus Wittgenstein points out that in our everyday speech we recognize these limitations and contrasts: 'normally, unless we philosophise, we don't talk this way'. Therefore, so long as we keep a lively sense of particular cases in their variety and do not obliterate the contrast in wanting to redraw the line between human freedom and human bondage, we can intelligibly say:

> In many more cases than we are willing to recognise we have not come to ourselves and do not own our will: our will is not determined by ourselves, but by outside causes – other people, propaganda, manipulators, dissociated parts of ourselves (Schopenhauer, Freud). In many more cases than we recognise we don't have a mind of our own, we act without lights (Plato, Spinoza, Simone Weil).

Wittgenstein says that in such statements 'we are comparing the case of a human being with those *special* cases where we *would* say that a man was determined: where we would say that he thought he was deciding freely but was actually compelled' (p. 91). He then asks: 'why should anyone be inclined to compare ordinary cases with such a very special case?' There is obviously not a single answer to this question. But in one kind of case, at any rate, it may be that one has been struck by similarities, sometimes even hidden by our ordinary ways of speaking, which reveal a new aspect. It may move to the foreground and dominate our vision. Such similarities may be suggested to us by the force of a literary portrayal of character. 'Think,' Dostoyevsky writes, 'of the thousands of intelligent people who, having learnt from Gogol about Podkolyosin, at once discover that scores of their friends and acquaintances are awfully like Podkolyosin' (Dostoyevsky 1955, p. 499). In seeing this likeness they come to see these friends and acquaintances in a new light.

A caricature can thus reveal a new aspect in a politician for instance.

It is for us, from then on to keep that insight without turning the politician into a caricature of himself in our thinking. This is what we have to be on our guard against in philosophy too.

4 Choice and causality: 'He was brought up to think as he does'

We have seen that where Bishop Barnes says 'I have freedom of choice', Wittgenstein prefers to say that as human beings we have the capacity for choice and decision: he could have said: 'that I have choice' (p. 98). He then raises the question whether our choices and decisions can be causally determined? His answer is: they can, but only in *special* cases: They cannot *all* be determined; in the *normal* cases they are not.

We can say that normally and in the absence of any qualification it goes without saying that a choice is free in the sense that our notion of the kind of freedom human beings have is bound up with what we *understand* by 'choice' and 'decision'. Thus we can even say that a choice or decision is *in itself*, or *intrinsically* free: for it is what a person determines *himself*. When it is not free it is not *really* a decision – i.e. it is not really one that the person *himself* takes. He is deceived in thinking otherwise. He simply goes through the motion of deciding and does what has been decided for him. He does not decide, he conforms to a ready-made decision. This, I take it, is what lies behind Wittgenstein's taking 'freedom of choice' to be a pleonasm. But it does not preclude Wittgenstein from considering whether it is possible for a person to *think* that he chooses or decides when in reality he does not do so: can he think that *he* determines what he is to do when in fact this is determined by outside causes?

Someone may say: even when the will is determined by the person himself it is determined by outside causes, causes about which he could have had no say. For what the person wills or resolves to do in a particular situation depends on what he values and what he wants, or more briefly, on what he is like. *That*, in turn, depends on what culture he was brought up in, who his parents are and what they were like in his childhood, and various other contingencies that encroached on his life during his formative years. In short, always and inevitably, the will is determined by outside causes, though this can never appear to the individual when he makes choices, takes decisions, and acts.

Wittgenstein simply mentions someone speaking like this: 'He was brought up in this way, not this way. It is all as inevitable as machinery' (p. 89). However he does not discuss it. We have considered this question in connection with Sartre's reply to it. I want to add something to it now with which, I am confident, Wittgenstein would have agreed. Obviously, when I make a choice or take a decision I *inevitably* do so as the person

I am. What is crucial to my freedom or autonomy, however, is whether I am *myself* in the person I am or the character I have.

I said *inevitably*: if I am a conformist in my character my decisions will be motivated by my need to conform; if, on the other hand, I have deeply held convictions I shall act from those convictions. Where I always do the done thing I have no mind of my own. What I do then can hardly be described as coming from me or be an expression of my will. I have no will of my own; I have not found or come to myself. I am, more or less, a product of my upbringing. What I do is determined by my upbringing; it does not come out of my considerations and weighing.

In contrast, even though my values come to me from outside and I acquire them in the course of the upbringing I receive, I can take part in this upbringing – not at first but as soon as I am in a position, through what I have learned, to contribute to it. Even if at first I simply accept, indeed swallow, my parent's values and precepts, what I learn gradually enables me to reflect on them, come to understand their significance in relation to the situations with which life confronts me. While I weigh those situations in terms of these values, at the same time those situations weigh those values for me in the light of other forms of significance I pick up in the course of my upbringing and other contacts. It is in this process that I begin to come to myself, come to have a self I can come to, and at the same time come to own the values or reject them in favour of others I come in contact with and make my own. To put it slightly differently, in the values I make my own I come to myself; in coming to myself I acquire the capacity to make my own the values I come in contact with in my upbringing. These are the two sides of the same coin. I am then no longer a product of my upbringing. In the course of it I acquire a mind of my own and a will that is mine. I do so thanks to what I *learn* from those who bring me up. Admittedly, my categories of thought come from the language I speak and that belongs to the culture in which I grow up. But I learn to use them to think for myself. I acquire the capacity to weigh and accept or reject what I am given. As I said, more and more I participate in this process of learning and growing up, that is in my own formation, as I acquire independence of thought and come to myself. I thus come to own myself, and it is as myself, as an individual, that I think, consider, take decisions and act – as opposed to as a mere product of my culture and particular circumstances, as the *kind* of person who has received such-and-such an upbringing.

The argument, therefore, that the will is inevitably determined by outside causes even when it is determined by the person himself, because the person himself is a product of the causes that shape him, is fallacious. It ignores the crucial distinction between cases where a person is an individual and cases where he is little more than the product of outer circumstances, a type – typical of someone who has been brought up in such-and-such circumstances.

If then a person chooses for himself, can he or can he not choose other than he does? This is a question which, we have seen, Moore discusses, and Schopenhauer raises. So does Wittgenstein: 'Suppose I had shown someone how it is impossible to resist certain temptations ... Suppose someone said: "But his choice was free. He could also have chosen to do the opposite. His guilt lies in the very fact that he chose in the way which seems so natural"' (p. 93). Wittgenstein argues that unless it makes sense to say 'he could have done otherwise' it would make no sense to say 'he could not have done otherwise'. He gives the example of someone drunk: 'alcohol increases the temptation to do certain things colossally'. Another example he gives is this: if I have a bad headache and there is a very tiresome person it may be very difficult for me to be patient with him. Yet another one is this: 'Look how he has been brought up. He is not strong in character' (ibid.). We thus give excuses for not holding the person in question responsible for something he does which he, himself, knows he ought not to do. In the last case we have someone who has not come together in himself. His upbringing has been *deficient*; it has not provided him with the support, encouragement and discipline to help him to deal with inner conflicts. Consequently, what he wills 'he does not will entirely', there is not enough of himself to put behind his belief that he ought not to do what he is tempted to do.

In the case of the alcohol example, he finds 'dutch courage' to do what he is otherwise tempted to do. The alcohol distances him from considerations that normally stop him doing what he is tempted to do. It stops him thinking of the morrow, of taking seriously the consequences of yielding to the temptation.

What we have are *special* cases which are different in degrees from the normal cases where we would not say 'he could not have done otherwise'. It is by contrast with the normal case that we speak this way, use this kind of expression. If we asked someone who refused to take a bribe whether he could have done otherwise, whether he could have chosen to take a bribe, it would not be clear what we were trying to ask him. Are we suggesting, perhaps, that he is morally corrupt and that it is out of fear of the authorities that he has turned down the bribe? In the absence of such a suggestion the question does not make sense. If his choice or action comes from conviction, if he does what he wants without reservation or qualification, the question does not apply. He did what he wanted to do – period: he had a choice and he did what he wanted. He did not give way to pressure. The action came from him.

Suppose someone insists: 'all the same, could you still have made a different choice?' The answer to this is: 'why should I? I have no regrets about what I chose. I did not do so under duress, I did not give in to pressure, and I am happy with the outcome.' I may even add: 'if the same opportunity were to arise again I would make the same choice, do the same thing.' This in no way shows, as Schopenhauer seems to think that I could not choose differently.

It is only in *special* circumstances that it does so. He is a thief who goes to gaol. He says that he will not steal again. He comes out, the opportunity presents itself, he forgets his resolution and steals again. Here we would be inclined to say: 'When he said he would not steal again he was fooling himself. When tempted to steal, he cannot resist the temptation, he cannot do otherwise than yield, otherwise than steal. The temptation overwhelms him and leaves him no choice.' What we have here is a *weakness* of character, a defect or deficiency, which with insight into his character could be spelt out.

Once more what is important to recognize is that in the latter case we have a weakness, a defect, a deficiency, which makes sense in contrast with the former case.

5 Freedom and predictability

At the end of his lecture Wittgenstein raises some questions about the compatibility between prediction and choice. 'Prediction,' he says, 'is incompatible with choice in the case where you yourself predict what you will choose' (p. 98). If I say, 'At 5 o'clock I shall leave this room', this is *not* a prediction; it is the declaration of an intention (see *PI*§631). How could we turn this into a prediction? 'At 5 o'clock I shall want to leave this room'? This is not a prediction of what I shall *do*. 'At 5 o'clock I shall be overcome by an irresistible urge to leave this room'? Still this does not say what I shall do? Suppose I add: 'and I shall not be able to resist the urge; I know from past experience'. Now this is something I predict; but it is no longer something I choose or do voluntarily.

Let us now try it in the third person. I can predict that at 5 o'clock he will leave the room. I can support this as follows: he comes to see us every Friday and leaves at 5 o'clock. Here prediction is not incompatible with choice or a voluntary action. Indeed I can predict what he will choose, knowing his taste, how he will vote, knowing his political affiliation. *He* cannot do so; but not because he does not know. For him not to know this is for him not to have made up his mind.

Wittgenstein imagines someone predicting 'my exact process of choosing' (p. 99) – i.e. my deliberations: e.g. he will walk into the shop, ask to see different ties, he will say to himself that the striped one is vulgar, the green one is ugly, etc., and finally choose the red one. He may add: "I have often seen him do this and always end up with the red one."' It looks now as if my deliberations are not really deliberations but some sort of ritual and that I have no choice. Perhaps my mind is made up, fixed in advance. But the point is, however it has come to be so made up, it does not move. Elsewhere Wittgenstein had imagined someone with a fixed smile on his face, one which does not alter with circumstances. He said that in such a case the man would no longer be smiling. It is the same with a mind made up in advance and insensitive to circumstances. Such fixity is something very different from resolve, where I know my own mind and you cannot change it for me.

So where I have a choice and what I shall do is subject to deliberation, before I make up my mind I do not know what I shall choose, what I shall do. Wittgenstein imagines someone putting this as: 'then our choice simply depends on our ignorance; if we weren't as ignorant as we are we should have no choice' (ibid.). But not knowing what I shall choose to do is not like not knowing whether or not it will rain tomorrow. It is to have an open mind, not to have decided or made up one's mind. Perhaps if one had the information that the weather man has, one would know that it is highly probable that it will rain tomorrow. Not to know here is to lack this information which is there to be had. But in the case where I have not yet made up my mind there is no such information of which I am ignorant. Unless my mind can be open in this sense so that I can myself make it up I can have no choice. This is what the philosophical determinist denies: the human mind, like everything else in nature, is causally determined, like the rain that is going to reach the West coast of Britain by dawn tomorrow.

It is not clear to me whether at the end of his lecture the words that are put between quotation marks are words spoken by Wittgenstein or by his alter-ego: 'if I had prophesied to Mr Malcolm what he was going to choose tomorrow and he had read my prophesy, then he would not deliberate' (pp. 99–100). If Malcolm *believed* such a prophesy then his mind could not remain open and then he would have been left with no room for deliberation and no possibility for choice. But for that very reason he could not believe it: 'How do you know what I shall choose?' 'You always choose a red tie.' 'Maybe. But this time I have some misgivings and I want to think.'

If this was not possible, if one could know what someone will choose in the way one sometimes knows that it will rain tomorrow, this 'would simply change the business' (p. 100). In other words this would be a radical change in the character of human life, and then there would be no logical space in it for choice and for what we call 'free will'. But then we would no longer be the kind of beings we are and this would do more than 'simply change the business'.

Wittgenstein gives the following analogy:

> If Moore and I play chess or roulette and someone else could predict what was going to happen (telling us), we would just give up playing roulette. Suppose someone said: 'This is no game of chance at all. What makes us think it is a game of chance is only

our ignorance', I could contradict this and say: 'No. It is a game of chance now that we are ignorant; if in the future we were no longer ignorant it would no longer be a game of chance.'

We can't even say that if prediction was possible Moore and I would not play the game. You might say: the point of the game would then be different. And the point of choosing would be if we had a prediction of it.

I would say: You can call it a different game or not call it a different game ... (p. 100).

Let us suppose that it was possible to calculate by means of a calculating machine what I shall choose and do in a particular situation. Someone feeds in data about my brain as I face that situation. He finds out what I shall choose to do in this way and his finding is confirmed by what I in fact choose to do. Here my mind is open in the sense that I do not know 'what I shall choose to do'. That is I do not know what is *fixed* and calculable – as in the case of a game of roulette. But my now knowing what I shall choose to do before I choose and make up my mind is, as I pointed out, different. 'I don't know' there means that nothing is fixed yet. It is *I* who am going to do the fixing. Thus if our case is to be parallel to the roulette case it must be an illusion that *I* fix what I am going to do, make up my mind, since it is already fixed *before* I choose. Therefore I do not *really* choose. Can it nonetheless *seem* to each one of us that we do?

If so, we would all be automata, thinking we were intentional agents whose actions issue from their choice. That is a Cartesian demon may now be deceiving us, making us believe we were the author of our actions when in reality our choices and actions were fixed, determined by our brain processes at the time we confronted particular situations. But then what would it be to find out that we were thus deceived? It would have to include my being able to use such a machine as I have imagined to calculate and on that basis predict my own 'choices' and actions. But my decision to use the machine and my doing so would now have changed the situation confronting me, the one in which I act. It will have introduced a new datum to be fed into the machine. Feeding that datum would further change the situation in which I have to make a choice and act, and so on *ad infinitum*. Our imaginary example thus creates a tail-catching situation for me in which my tail is always one step ahead of my reach. In that case how can we say that in reality what I shall choose is fixed *before* I make my choice though I cannot ever find out that it is so? Does it not follow that what we can at least find out in theory in the case of a roulette game, we cannot find out here even in theory?

Someone may say: each of us can know in advance what *others* will choose and do, but no one can know this in his own case, since if he is told, this will make a difference to the choice predicted by others. Hence the fact remains that we have imagined a case, a possibility (so he maintains), in which each of us are necessarily ignorant of what we shall choose to do. Given such ignorance, we do genuinely choose, though we know from the case of others that what we choose is a *fait accompli* – the die is already cast.

This, however, will not give us what we want. For what each of us is necessarily ignorant of in this example is not the kind of 'not knowing one's own mind' which the possibility of choice presupposes.

I conclude that the roulette case offers a misleading analogy for what we want here. Roulette's being a game of chance does depend on our ignorance – on our being unable to calculate the outcome of each spin. But our having the capacity to choose does not depend on our ignorance in *this* sense. What we need is not this kind of ignorance but our mind being open in reality so that it is each one of us that closes it in making a choice, taking a decision, forming an intention or resolution.

6 Conclusion

Wittgenstein has done more than most philosophers I know to bring out and clarify what is radically distinctive about human existence. What is called 'free will' is part of this distinctive existence – of what is characteristic of human action, of the capacity of human beings to make choices, form intentions. What is in question is not a capacity which some human beings have and others lack – like athletic prowess. It defines human existence. That is why in his lecture on Freedom of the Will, considered in this chapter, Wittgenstein says that 'freedom of choice' is a pleonasm. What we have is the capacity of choice and therefore of ourselves determining what we do. But that does not mean that our choices and actions cannot be interfered with or determined from outside. These are *special* cases, however, which constitute instances of different forms of weakness, deficiency or failure on our part. They deviate from norms which we take for granted in the way we speak about human actions, norms that are written into our speech and the concepts belonging to it. These special cases have their place in the same grammatical dimension as the normal cases. We may fail to act freely in *many* different ways, and even perhaps more of the time than we are prepared to recognize. But in them we fail as *human beings* and, therefore, *as intentional agents*.

It is this which the pretensions of the sciences tend to obscure or blind us to. It is on this which Wittgenstein in his lecture is concerned to shed light: whether advances in scientific thinking need undermine our conviction in the reality of free will, that is in our distinctive capacity for intentional action. Wittgenstein's answer is that it does not have to, but that all the same it has tended to dazzle us and make us think that like any other natural object we too are inevitably the plaything of forces external to us – forces which determine us in our very will, in who we are and what we will, so that in reality our willing itself is an illusion.

Wittgenstein's treatment of this idea is very much like his treatment of the argument from illusion in the sphere of knowledge. He says that he does not want to argue for or against the freedom of the will. These are *philosophical* theories and as such they call for criticism and ultimately dismantling. The dismantling is the untying of knots our thinking gets into which produce myths, so that we can admit what everyone admits in the sense of taking it for granted in the language we speak.

So Wittgenstein raises such questions as whether we are subject to general laws in the way that a falling stone is, for instance, subject to the law of gravity. In other words, are our actions determined in the same way that the movement of a falling stone or a projectile is determined? Clearly Wittgenstein's answer to this question is in the negative. No doubt 'laws of nature' do not compel the behaviour of objects subject to it in the way that legal laws compel us to observe certain rules of behaviour on pain of punishment. One could say that they describe certain norms or ideals which enable us to predict the behaviour of objects in particular circumstances. There are regularities here as there are various kinds of regularity in human behaviour. But we need to distinguish regularities which issue from compulsions and regularities which do not.

Obviously the recidivist thief and the falling stone are very different from each other. The thief is an intentional agent. If he cannot resist stealing however many times he is punished this does not mean that we cannot blame him. Nevertheless, I point out, when Simone Weil compares him to tiles blown off the roof by the wind and claims that he is subject to the 'laws of moral gravity' she is not saying something with which Wittgenstein would disagree. She is using a metaphor to make a comparison which, as we have seen, we find in both Plato and Spinoza.

What about our decisions – could it be that they are always determined by external causes without our knowing it? Once more, could it be that we are like a stone flying through the air which has been granted consciousness so that it thinks that where the wind blows it is where it wants and chooses to go? This was a question Spinoza raised. We have considered Schopenhauer's answer to this question that if the stone could and did think so it would be right. Schopenhauer meant that this is precisely how it is with us when we say that we have free will: 'this is that human freedom ... which consists solely in the fact that men are conscious of their own desires, but are ignorant of the causes whereby that desire has been determined'. In other words we call it 'acting of one's own free will', but wrongly.

This is like saying, what we call 'reality' is a form of deception – the deception of human beings by Descartes' demon. The answer to this is that a deception that we all share and can never see through is no deception. If it makes sense to say that someone is deceived it must be possible to say what, by contrast, would constitute his not being deceived, his coming to see through the deception. The answer in this case that 'if human beings came to see *that there were no physical objects*, even though everything in their life and perceptions remained exactly as it is now, they would see that they were being deceived' is no answer at all. It is no answer, because what it gives with one hand it takes away with the other. Wittgenstein shows how this is also the case with the stone that is granted consciousness. A person may think that he is doing what he has chosen to do when in reality he is being manipulated and does what others want him to do. But for this to make sense it must be possible for him, by contrast, to do what he himself chooses to do. Wittgenstein gives many different examples.

He then comments on the argument that each one of us is the product of his upbringing so that whatever he, himself, chooses to do, that it chooses as himself, is determined by the way he was brought up. He points out that this argument is fallacious because it ignores the crucial distinction between cases where a person is an individual, that is himself, and cases where he is little more than the product of outer circumstances. The question is how he stands in relation to his upbringing and to what he was brought up on. There are different possibilities here.

Wittgenstein pursues the question further in connection with the possibility of predicting human behaviour: what are its limits and is it compatible with the possibility of choice? Does our choice simply depend on our ignorance? This is linked with Schopenhauer's comment on Spinoza's suggestion.

Wittgenstein gives the example of a game of roulette. Perhaps here what number will come up is causally determined and could theoretically be calculated if we could know all the relevant conditions that obtain before each spin. Its being a game of chance depends on our not knowing these – on our ignorance. Wittgenstein then imagines a calculating machine which calculates what someone will choose and do in particular situations from data about his brain states fed into it. So here what he is going to do is fixed before he chooses. It follows that he does not *really* choose, that at best he goes through the motions of choosing. All right, so he is an automaton with consciousness – like Spinoza's stone flying through the air. There are two questions here: (i) Could *I* be such an automaton? (ii) Could we *all* be such automata, mistakenly thinking we were intentional agents? That is, could a Cartesian demon now be deceiving us, making us believe falsely that we were the author of our actions? Wittgenstein shows how this is a senseless supposition.

In reality, of course, what we can predict about others is very limited –

for instance, we can predict that someone will vote for a certain party at the coming elections, but normally not the sequence of the things he will say during a conversation. This has to do with the difference between a conversation and a drill for instance. I said 'normally'. If what he said in this way was predictable then we could not carry out a conversation with him. There are of course people who to some extent approximate this. We would say of them, if only metaphorically, that they were 'brain damaged'. Conversation would not exist in a community of such 'brain damaged' people.

As for predicting what one will oneself do, that too is the exception rather than the rule – for instance that when one is offered a drink one will not be able to say no. Here we have a variety of cases of compulsion and addiction. These are cases which constitute 'the abnormal'. Normally, when I say what I will do next, I am not predicting my behaviour; what I do is to declare my intention. Here it is *I* who make what I say come true by *doing* what I say I will do. What I do is not something that happens to me, something I observe or predict. As I said, my will may on certain kinds of situations be determined, and I may even not recognize this to be the case. But this does not make me an automaton, for it is as an intentional agent that I am being manipulated, it is in my will that I am a captive to something external to it. Furthermore this in general must be the exception rather than the rule. Otherwise I could not even *think* that I was an automaton; and neither could anyone *say* it of me.

16

CONCLUSION
Human freedom and determinism

1 Sources of the problem

The philosophical problem of 'freedom and determinism' is in reality a cluster of problems with different sources.

(1) Early Greek thinkers were impressed by the extent to which human beings are caught up in forms of compulsion whereby they behave in ways that are *natural* to human beings – greed, selfishness, jealousy, the thirst for power, the desire for revenge for a humiliation or injury they have suffered. They were impressed by the way feuds, wars and injustices perpetuate themselves as human beings become the vehicle of these natural tendencies. They referred to this phenomenon as *ananke* or necessity. They thought of men in their subjection to such natural necessities as like particles of water in the sea during a storm going up and down with the waves. Men are subject to these in their very *will* and on account of their *nature*. Hence they are not aware of their lack of autonomy until they come to grief and wake up to it in their affliction. They make choices, as it seems to them, but their choices are determined not by themselves as individuals but by the nature they share with other human beings. They are thus unfree by virtue of what they are like in their nature – they are owned by it. They act in bondage to patterns into which they fall naturally and from which they cannot extricate themselves.

The difficulty then is to see how men can avoid falling into such patterns and what it takes for them to do so: how is it possible for human beings to resist those natural tendencies in which they are tempted into patterns of action and reaction in which they come to be entrenched? Plato argued that once entrenched in them people cannot see what is outside. He identified those tendencies which feed these patterns with evil and argued that those actions and reactions in which they perpetuate these patterns are *involuntary* because men who are caught up in them know nothing better and see no alternative to them. They lack moral knowledge: knowledge of good and evil.

(2) This problem acquired a new dimension with the coming of age of

Christianity and its theology or system of concepts. If God is omniscient, that is He knows everything, He must know everything that will take place in the future, including our future actions. He must see our future in the way we know the past in our memories, in which case the future must be fixed much in the way that the past is. But then the idea that we ourselves determine what we shall do in the decisions we make must be an illusion. Even if our future is genuinely tied up to our choices, so that our future actions follow from our choices, the two must be fixed together in advance for God to know them ahead of time. So how could He have created us free? There seems to be a contradiction within Christian theology which cries out to be resolved. This was one of the questions which preoccupied both St Augustine and St Thomas Aquinas.

(3) With the rise of the sciences the question of causality came to the fore and the universality of causation became what threatens the kind of agency that is distinctive of man – the kind of agency bound up with man's capacity to take decisions, make choices, and be guided by considerations of reason. This is what is usually referred to as man's 'free will'. Now it seems to be excluded not so much by God's foreknowledge, for that idea has lost its currency, but by causal determination which in its universality seems to by-pass human agency. For if what a man does is the end result of a chain of causes, then it is not *he* who does what he does; it is the causal conditions operating in his life that bring it about. They make him *what* he is and thus move him into action through choices as links in the chain that are mere epi-phenomena. He is like a puppet on a string that has been granted consciousness, as in the case of Spinoza's stone which imagined it was moving of its own volition.

So if human beings are intentional agents and, in that sense, have free will, how can causality be universal? This was certainly Kant's problem. Descartes by-passed it in according man 'activity of mind' over and above consciousness. This activity consists in the will's capacity, as Descartes conceived it, to initiate actions without a cause. Both Hume and Schopenhauer rightly rejected this conception. Having done so Hume reconciled free will with causality by arguing that freedom does not stand opposed to causality but to compulsion. Causality, he argued, is not a form of compulsion. Kant did not find Hume's answer to be any more satisfactory than Descartes' answer.

Descartes was at least right in according a unique status to man's agency even if his conception of the will and its activity left much to be desired. This was something which both Aquinas before Descartes and Kant and Schopenhauer after him appreciated. Two questions which need to be asked and which are discussed in the book are: (i) What does it mean for a person to decide things for himself, act on his own behalf, in contrast with doing so in subjection to something external to him – e.g. in subjection to public opinion or, at an extreme, to hypnotic suggestion? (ii) What place does causality occupy in human life and actions?

(4) Often 'causal determination' incorporates various forms of compulsion and constraint rooted in people's character and affective life. As the perception of their scope widens no room seems to be left for the kind of freedom with which we are familiar in human life and mark in our language. The very distinctions which its marking presupposes come to be lost sight of and, indeed, forgotten or denied, as noted by Wittgenstein in his lecture considered in this book.

Thus genuine difficulties perceived in what it takes for human beings to be themselves in what they do and so to act freely are turned into impossibilities in various ways. For instance, the changes required for such difficulties to be overcome are ruled out of court by ignoring distinctions that are important to make in this connection – thus Schopenhauer: 'men's inability to change is universal and inevitable'. We find the same movement of thought in Freud when he claims that a person's character is formed by about his fourth year of age and generally changes very little as a result of his later experiences. What is in question is an inductive generalization out of which a theoretical necessity is extracted. It runs together the conception of a settled character in the framework of which a person continues to develop and a rigid defensive or reactive character which represents a form of arrested development.

Another example, discussed in the chapter on Freud, of a genuine difficulty which is turned into a theoretical impossibility is the following. Freud represents the id as the horse which the ego rides; it is the source of energy which the ego directs in its – the person's – actions. But the ego is thought of as so divided from the id that it has to serve and indeed placate it in order to be able to tap its 'motive power'. The same situation is thought of as holding in the ego's relation with the super-ego and with what Freud calls 'reality', in other words the requirements it has to observe when pursuing its aims in the arena of action. Thus Freud says that the ego has to serve its three 'task masters' and is not, therefore, 'master in its own house'. In this way the individual's autonomy and hence his freedom comes to be denied. Freud's theoretical conception thus excludes any transformation in the genuinely divided parts that would allow a different kind of relationship between them and a different attitude to the demands and limitations of the situation within which the person has to act.

2 Relative freedom and bondage: autonomy and bad faith

It is nevertheless true that all the thinkers considered on the side of determinism, including Freud, do within the framework of the kind of determinism which they depict, make room for the distinction between bondage and autonomy. They allow for the possibility of individual freedom. Sophocles, for instance, in many of his tragedies represents the individual's destiny as determined or fixed in advance, and human affairs as subject to inexorable laws. Yet though the laws are inexorable he does not deny that freedom is possible within their framework; indeed he holds it to be possible only within it. This is what counts as wisdom for Sophocles: the man who does not recognize and respect them comes to grief; he cannot escape the consequences of ignoring or disregarding them. In that respect he is not free: he is not free to do what he likes and go on from there as he likes. In his failure to recognize this he fails to know himself.

Oedipus' fate is thus sealed in his lack of wisdom, in the kind of 'self-confidence' which makes him blind to his dependence on what lies outside his control, blind to the contingencies that encroach on his life. He is the prisoner of a fate which becomes *his* only because he colludes with it unknowingly in the way he tries to evade it. Paradoxically he cannot escape the fate Apollo predicts for him because he thinks he can escape it. As I put it: Apollo's oracle proposes a future for Oedipus which Oedipus himself disposes – as he comes to realize when it is too late:

> Apollo, friends, Apollo
> Has laid this agony upon me,
> Not by his hand; I did it.

Until then Oedipus has been blind to his contribution to the sealing of his fate. His blindness is a defect in his character and consists in his lack of humility. It makes him think he can take Apollo on and he rises up to the challenge. He believes that he has earned what he has and that in his cleverness he deserves to keep it. He believes that he has the power to control his destiny. Sophocles shows that this is an illusion and that blind change is no respecter of individuals.

Thus in his lack of lights Oedipus is in a collision course with the fate Apollo has announced for him. In this sense his future is foreclosed – not absolutely, but relatively or conditionally: in the way he is. It is in his *reaction* to the oracle that he makes its prophecy come true; it is in that reaction that he is blind. Oedipus' fate thus is an outcome of the interaction between his character, which is made constant by his lack of self-knowledge, and the inexorable laws which for Sophocles characterizes human life.

Sophocles is not a determinist in a modern sense. But should we want to call him that, then he is one in the sense that his thinking goes along the following lines: *if* you go on in such-and-such a way then such-and-such consequences are inescapable. This is a *conditional* statement. If a person deceives himself about the direction in which he is moving, because he is not prepared to change, then he will not be able to avoid those consequences. Such a person lacks self-knowledge in his lack of understanding of the nature of his obstinacy and in his determination not to change his course. Oedipus is thus blind in his lack of humility.

If this is a form of determinism it certainly does not contain a denial of the possibility of freedom: '*if* you go on in such-and-such a way …' does not simply mean 'you *have* to go on that way'. But in order not to have to go that way the person in question has to be different in himself: he needs to change. There is no denial in Sophocles that such a person can change. But the lesson he has to learn for him to change would demand much from him which he may not be prepared to give. What we learn from Sophocles is that where pride is great, self-confidence is blind, and 'rationalism' is deep rooted, the lesson may only be learned too late – after the fall.

On the other side, Sartre, for instance, insists that man is absolutely and unavoidably free. But he does not claim that man necessarily possesses autonomy. Indeed, he represents man as more often than not in *bad faith*, that is as having given up his autonomy in an attempt to evade shouldering responsibility for his life and actions. In other words though each individual is unconditionally and inescapably free, he may nevertheless fail to be himself and as such remain at the mercy of what is external to him. Thus while such a person is inevitably free, in Sartre's absolute sense, he nevertheless lacks relative freedom, that is the kind of freedom which admits of degrees of limitation. He lacks it in some areas of his life, in the course of some of his engagements. So although he lacks autonomy in these respects, so that his freedom is limited, he is still free to stop evading taking responsibility for this aspect of his life and actions. Were he to be willing to do so his life would change and in this new life he would have greater autonomy. He may not know how to do so; but this does not mean that he cannot learn. So Sartre insists that nothing can take this freedom away from the individual.

On the side of determinism Spinoza insists that we are part of a whole where everything that happens is causally determined. It follows that every part of our life is also absolutely determined. But just as Sartre's absolute freedom leaves logical room for the distinction between relative freedom and relative bondage in bad faith, similarly Spinoza's absolute determinism leaves logical room for that same distinction. Neither, therefore, deny that men are sometimes free and sometimes not, and both offer suggestions about how those who lack freedom can recover the freedom they lack. They differ, and differ radically, in their conception of man and in their moral orientation and attitude to life. They differ in their conception of man's relation to the rest of nature. Spinoza's conception is deeply religious. He sees man as a small part of an immeasurably bigger whole and his salvation in a recognition and acceptance of this. Sartre, on the other hand, is anti-religious and fiercely individualistic. He sees man as having a distinctive character that sets him apart from everything else in nature.

Freud too, like Spinoza and Schopenhauer, embraces a position in which he thinks of himself as a determinist. Yet he devotes all his efforts at developing a form of therapy in which men and women can be helped to attain greater self-determination in their lives. I argue that the structures of personality in which he presents human beings as lacking self-mastery ('the ego is not master in his own house') are not immutable; they are dissociations which can be healed. In the healing of these dissociations men come to themselves and acquire self-knowledge and in this self-knowledge they acquire greater self-mastery and so greater inner freedom.

3 Theological dimension: human freedom and God's foreknowledge

Both St Augustine and St Thomas Aquinas, as committed Christians, wanted to show that God's omniscience, which includes His knowledge of what will happen in the future, and therefore His knowledge of people's future actions, does not exclude human authorship of individual decisions and, therefore, human free will.

Augustine argues that not all that God foreknows comes about by necessity. God knows that we shall grow old and we grow old by necessity. He also knows what each of us shall will before we have willed it. But what He thus foreknows comes to pass by our willing; it does not by-pass our intentional agency. That is God does not foreknow what I shall do *whether or not I will it*. He foreknows what *I* shall will. So it is still *I* who decides.

But how does He foreknow what I shall will? Augustine compares it with the way we know the past by memory. I argue that this analogy is false. What has been has already been; it is over and done with. The truth of what I know *now* of the past is determined by what has already taken place. 'What will be will be' may wrongly suggest that the future is equally fixed or determined: 'the future is not for us to see, *che sera sera*'. We cannot see it, but it can be seen by someone who possesses the power of clairvoyance. 'Just as what was the case *is* in the past, what will be the case *is* in the future.' But this is misleading. For '*is* in the future' simply means '*will* be' and what will be *is not yet*. It therefore remains undetermined until it comes to pass. Hence, at least theoretically, it can always be stopped from coming to pass if we know how to do so.

What a soothsayer like Tierisias is supposed to see is the direction in which things are moving or are made to move *plus* the blindness, self-deception and obstinacy of the actors. The insight he possesses is not a form of clairvoyance, and the inevitability of what he sees coming is relative or conditional: it is inevitable *provided* the actors persist in their obstinate self-deception.

God's foreknowledge, however, is neither a form of clairvoyance nor the kind of insight Sophocles attributed to Tieresias. 'God sees what is in store for us' refers to the inescapability of a certain judgement on our life. I compare it with Socrates' judgement in the *Gorgias* that Archelaus *cannot* be happy – no matter what he says, no matter what happens, no matter what he may have. It is an absolute judgement of value. As for 'God knows what will befall each one of us independently of our actions', this means that He knows it in what He has *willed*. In other words the believer is enjoined to accept it unconditionally and unquestioningly. Attributing such knowledge to God is giving expression to certain eternal truths within Christianity.

Once we are clear about the meaning of these truths and see what it means to attribute 'foreknowledge' to God, it will be clear that such an attribution does not exclude free will in human beings but, on the contrary, presupposes it.

Discussing the same problem Aquinas argues that God's knowledge of what I shall do in the future is not really knowledge of the future. For God is not in time and so knows everything timelessly.

I offer the following analogy: what are the roots of a particular equation. The answer *for me* lies in the future, for it awaits my solving of the equation. But the answer I discover is already timelessly present in mathematics; it was true before and independently of my discovery of it. Similarly what God knows is not contingent, but logically necessary, timelessly true. How? Isn't this as absurd as Augustine's suggestion that God's knowledge of the future may be like our memory knowledge of the past?

I do not think so. I argue that what is necessary and timelessly true in Christian belief is God's judgement on our actions, past, present and future, and on our life when it is completed: *that* is what God sees. As for particular events in the future which affect our lives for good or ill, when they are seen as God's will they are seen as unquestionable and, therefore, as what is to be accepted. In Christian belief God's will is eternal. That means that God's will is inescapable and, for the believer, therefore, it is to be accepted. In other words, in seeing what happens, whatever it may be, as what God has willed the believer sees it as willed in eternity or outside time. That, in turn, means that he sees it as to be accepted *unconditionally*. That is, as he sees it, nothing that can happen can change that. The necessities in question belong to the connections in which things are seen as taken within the framework of Christian theology, and so, within Christian belief.

4 Causality and freedom

In 'modern philosophy', by contrast, the possibility of human freedom is argued against causality; if everything that happens has a cause then how can there be any room for free will? Descartes' answer was that not everything is subject to causality; our willing is not. Hume's answer was: being subject to causality is not being subject to compulsion and only that which is subject to compulsion is unfree. Kant's answer was that when the will is subject to causality, in the form of inclination, it is heteronomous and hence determined by something external. As such it cannot be free. But when it is at one with reason and determined by it, it is self-determined and, therefore, free. Spinoza's answer was that everything is subject to causality and hence free will is an illusion. Nevertheless in detaching ourselves from everything that pins us down to a worm's eye view of things, and so coming to see ourselves as part of an infinite whole, we shall stop trying to advance our isolated self-interest. We shall then emerge into a state of freedom in which we are at one in our will with nature so that we are pleased to accept willingly whatever comes our way. I have compared this with someone who out of love says 'your wish is my command'. He is free in obeying the beloved's will. Spinoza's conception of human freedom is thus a religious one: he is ready to accept whatever happens as God's will.

Much nearer to the present, G E Moore argued that our belief that we have free will implies that there are many occasions when we could have done something other than what we did. He further argued that there is a sense in which the truth of this is compatible with the general law of causality which claims that everything that happens has a cause. He unquestioningly accepts that our will must be subject to causality, as Schopenhauer does too. To deny this, both Hume and Schopenhauer argued, is to make our will arbitrary and our actions totally random.

But why should that be the case? The book argues that when a person himself determines or resolves what to do, it is in accordance with reasons that weigh with him that he does so. He is *himself* in what he thus determines in the way he *owns* these reasons. His actions then are not random; yet they are not determined by anything external to him by causes that act on his will. Causality after all is not the only order there is.

Yet even here causality is not suspended. We are flesh and blood beings and our ability to carry out the activities in which we engage as intentional agents depends on the proper functioning of our bodily organs – our organs of perception, our nerves and brain, our muscles, our heart, our endocrine system, etc. Anything that goes wrong in their proper functioning can affect our ability to carry out these activities adversely in various ways – our ability to judge, to see, to move, etc. It is through causal, medical intervention then that what has gone wrong is rectified and our everyday autonomy restored. This is how causality impinges on our lives from inside; this is how the execution of our intentions depends on certain causal conditions being satisfied.

I greet a friend with a wave of the hand. Someone may ask: what made you wave your hand so? I answer: I saw a friend; I was greeting him. The question, what made your hand move so? would be totally inappropriate in this context and could only be asked by someone who, for some reason, thought I was having a fit. The chain of causes which explain the movement when I have a fit have no place in the explanation of the voluntary move-ment involved in my greeting of my friend. Yet without the processes affected when I have a fit I could not greet a friend with a wave of the hand. I could not do so if my arm were paralysed. Here is an instance of the way we are subject to causality, even though as intentional agents we are the author of our actions. It is *we* who thus determine them normally; they are not the effect of causes external to our will. Thus while the will itself is not subject to causality, our willing is made possible by certain causal processes that go on in the body.

In contrast with Descartes then I am saying that our will, as it finds expression in our intentions, choices and decisions, belongs to us, flesh and blood beings, and it is embedded in situations of human life in which we act. We enter these situations as beings with a specific history in the course of which we have learned a great many things and have become the partic-ular individual who judges, deliberates, takes decisions, acts. We bring much of this to bear on the situation in our assessments and considerations before acting. It is as such that we determine our actions in accordance with considerations and, therefore, not arbitrarily: our actions are not gratuitous acts. All the same the exercise of our capacities which thus enables us to act with intention is made possible by the proper functioning of processes in our bodies which themselves depend on the operation of various causes.

If our decisions are determined by us in accordance with considerations is it false that *everything* that happens has a cause? Can there be a cause-less event or happening? As Rush Rhees once put it: ' "Some things happen without a cause" is shocking when it is said in connection with a causal enquiry, because it seems to be a statement in the grammar of causal inves-tigation.' Thus if, for instance, someone were to suggest that some particular disease, say cancer, has no cause, we would not be able to make sense of his suggestion. We would say: perhaps its cause has not yet been discovered, so scientists will go on searching for it. Within the grammar of causal investigation, within the sphere of a whole category of concepts, there is no exception to the general law of causality: *everything* that happens – all motions, chemical transformations, physical and physiolog-ical processes – has a cause. It must have a cause, even if we do not know it. This is so within macro-physics.

Not everything, however, that we speak about, describe and refer to, falls within the grammar of causal investigation. Many things we refer to and find of interest raise other questions for us, questions which cannot be answered in causal terms. Questions about human behaviour and responses are among these. It is not too difficult to show how different is our question 'what made him smile?' for instance, from 'what made him ill?'

What made him smile? We may say: 'surely, there must be a reason; otherwise he is mad'. But then we are not talking of causes in the sense relevant to the general law of causality. This is something Schopenhauer misunderstands, even though he distinguishes between different kinds of causes. He talks of 'motives' in connection with human behaviour as 'causality through cognition': 'as little as a ball can move before receiving an impact, so little can a man get up from his chair before being drawn or driven by a motive'. This makes it seem as if getting up from a chair is something that happens to a man, something to which he is at best a spectator.

He speaks in the same way where a man is pulled in two different directions and finally makes up his mind to go one way or the other. He compares such a man to a top which as it slows down begins to oscillate until finally it falls on the side in which its centre of gravity lies outside its base. In men, similarly he says, finally the strongest motive drives the others from the field and determines the will. The outcome, Schopenhauer says, takes place with complete necessity as the result of the struggle. But the struggle here is not a struggle in which *the person* engages. It is a tug of war between conflicting forces where the stronger one prevails, thus determining the direction in which he moves or is dragged. For Schopenhauer the causality in question, as he thinks of it, may well operate through cognition or consciousness; but in it the person is a mere spectator, a passive by-stander. He does not act, he does not choose.

Indeed, confined to such passivity, human beings are not agents, they are not the author of their actions. Their actions are little more than the actions of chemical agents – the metal that rusts when exposed to moist air. Give the metal bar consciousness, in the way that Spinoza asked us to imagine a stone moving through the air having consciousness – if that were possible at all – and we have the case of human beings as conceived by Schopenhauer.

This is the result of taking the general law of causality to apply without any grammatical distinction. Descartes was surely right in insisting on man's 'activity' in his will; but as both Hume and Schopenhauer pointed out he uprooted the will, in its 'acts', from the person in his character and history. In their attempt to avoid Descartes' mistake they erred on the opposite side: they turned man into a passive by-stander. How can we cut through these opposite errors? Answer: by bringing out the sense in which a person can be *himself* in his character, *own* his past and his emotions, come to a *unity* in himself – a unity in which his reason is not divided from his emotions (as in Kant), his conscience does not stand opposed to his desire (as in Freud).

No doubt he is the individual person he is as a result of much that has come into his life from outside: his parents and upbringing, chance contingencies that have affected him and given direction to his development – much, in short, that he did not choose and could not have chosen. Is it not true then that in acting in character his choices have their origin in what lies outside the sphere of choice for him? And does this not mean that he is determined to act the way he does as a result of what made him the way he is, what produced his individual character – that is of 'causes that have shaped him'? Very briefly, there are two points which the book argues in this connection: (i) that the formation of character is not a causal process, that it involves much learning on the part of the individual and progressively greater degrees of personal participation in what may be called the process of growing up, and (ii) that there are different forms of character, some in which a person is himself and others in which he has not come together in himself, lives a mindless existence, or in alienation from himself. There are many different such types of character.

If, for instance, he is a conformist, his decisions will be motivated by his need to conform. Where thus he generally does the done thing he has no mind of his own. What he does does not come from him; it is not an expression of his will. Indeed he has no will of his own, no will that he owns. We could describe him as a 'mere product' of his upbringing. In contrast, where in the course of his development he makes his own the values which he learns from the example of his parents, and grows up to be a person who holds deeply held convictions, he will act from those convictions. His actions will be an expression of his individual will, not a reflection of his upbringing. There are here a great variety of cases that need to be distinguished.

It has been said – by Moore for instance, but also by many others – that where a person is free or has free will he is not bound to do what he does. It is possible for him to do something other than what he does. What someone who says this means is that such a person is not stuck in a pattern of behaviour which he continually repeats – in ways which Schopenhauer has pointed out. In his examples Moore is nowhere near to appreciating what is in question.

But however widespread such cases may be they do not represent the normalities of life within the language we speak. They are *special* cases which stand out in their particular character by contrast to what is taken as unproblematic in our language. So the question, 'could he have acted otherwise than he did?' or 'could he have chosen differently?', arises only where there is some suggestion of abnormality. Thus imagine someone who is offered to take a bribe and refuses. The question 'could he have done otherwise?' suggests that though he refused to take the bribe he did so out of the fear of being caught. So either there is the suggestion that the person referred to is corrupt, or the person asking the question is himself corrupt – he assumes that everyone has his price and, therefore, can be bought. In the absence of such a suggestion or assumption the question 'could he have done otherwise?' makes no sense. If put to a person in this situation, his answer would be: 'why should I have done otherwise!' He was fully behind what he did in refusing to take the bribe. Moore's question, 'could he have done differently if he chose to take a bribe', is therefore no criterion. This is something Wittgenstein points out in the lecture discussed in the previous chapter.

The book thus considers the contribution of a number of thinkers in Western thought from the time of ancient Greece to the present to 'the problem of freedom and determinism'. It brings out the richness of what is in question and itself contributes to the discussion of the questions raised by these thinkers under its different aspects.

NOTES

CHAPTER 5 ST AUGUSTINE

1 I have discussed what such trust comes to and how it differs from my trust that the chair will not give way under my weight elsewhere – 'Self-Knowledge and the Possibility of Change' in *Rules, Rituals and Responsibility*, ed. Mary I Bockover (Open Court 1991).

CHAPTER 9 HUME AND KANT

1 Compare this with Kierkegaard's notion of 'willing one thing' in contrast with 'double-mindedness', and with Plato's conception of 'philosophical virtue' as opposed to 'popular virtue'.
2 Such a reflection is often a form of self-reflection.

CHAPTER 15 WITTGENSTEIN

1 See Socrates' discussion of this in the first part of the *Gorgias* and Dilman, 1979, chapter 2.
2 See Dilman 1984, chapter 5, section 2.

BIBLIOGRAPHY

Aquinas, Thomas (1944) *Basic Writings of St Thomas Aquinas* Vol 1 – Q82 The Will, Q83 Free Choice (New York: Random House).
—— (1965) 'On Free Choice', *Selected Writings of St Thomas Aquinas* (The Library of Liberal Arts, New York: Bobbs-Merril Co Inc).
Aristotle (1949) *The Nichomachean Ethics of Aristotle* (Everyman's Library, London: J M Dent and Sons Ltd)
Augustine (1964) *On Free Choice of Will* (*De Libero Arbitrio*) (Indianapolis, NY: Bobbs-Merril).
Austin, J L (1961) 'Ifs and Cans' (1956), *Philosophical Papers*, eds J O Urmson and G J Warnock (Oxford: Clarendon Press).
Descartes, René (1927) 'Meditations', 'Passions of the Soul', *Selections*, ed. Ralph M Eaton (New York: Charles Scribner's Sons).
Dilman, İlham (1973) *Induction and Deduction, A Study in Wittgenstein* (Oxford: Blackwell).
——(1979) *Morality and the Inner Life, A Study in the Gorgias* (London: Macmillan).
——(1981) *Studies in Language and Reason* (London: Macmillan).
——(1983) *Freud and Human Nature* (Oxford: Blackwell).
——(1984a) *Freud and the Mind* (Oxford: Blackwell).
—— (1984b) 'Reason, Passion and the Will', *Philosophy*, Vol 59, no 228.
—— (1991) 'Self-Knowledge and the Possibility of Change', *Rules, Rituals and Responsibility*, ed. by Mary I Bockever (Illinois: Open Court).
—— (1992) *Philosophy and the Philosophic Life, A Study in the Phaedo* (London: Macmillan).
——(1993) *Existentialist Critiques of Cartesianism* (London: Macmillan).
Dostoyevsky, Fydor (1955) *The Idiot*, trans. David Magarshack (London: Penguin Classics).
Foot, Phillippa (1954)'When is a Principle a Moral Principle?' *Arist. Soc. Proc.* Suppl. Vol. XXVIII.
——(1958)'Moral Beliefs' *Arist. Soc. Proc.*
——(1958)'Moral Arguments' *Mind*.
——(1961)'Goodness and Choice' *Arist. Soc. Proc.* Suppl. Vol. XXXV.
Freud, Sigmund (1933) *New Introductory Lectures on Psycho-Analysis*, trans. W J H Sprott.(New York: W W Norton).

——(1948) *Beyond the Pleasure Principle*, trans. C J M Hubback (London: Hogarth Press).

——(1949a) *Introductory Lectures on Psycho-Analysis*, trans. Joan Riviére (London: Allen and Unwin).

——(1949b) *The Ego and the Id*, trans. James Strachey (London: Hogarth Press)

——(1949c) *Three Essays on the Theory of Sexuality*, trans. James Strachey (London: Imago Publishing Co).

——(1950a) 'Turnings in the Ways of Psycho-Analytic Theory' (1919), *Collected Papers*, vol ii, trans. Joan Riviére (London: Hogarth Press).

——(1954) *Psychopathology of Everyday Life*, trans. A A Brill (Ernest Benn).

——(1979) *Case Histories* II, trans. James Strachey (London: Penguin Books).

Freud, Sigmund and Breur, Joseph (1950b) *Studies in Hysteria*, trans. A A Brill (Boston: Beacon Press).

Gide, André (1922) *Les Caves du Vatican* (Paris: Gallimard).

Guntrip, Harry (1977) *Personality Structure and Human Interaction* (London: Hogarth Press).

Hamlyn, David (1980) *Schopenhauer* (London: Routledge & Kegan Paul).

Homer (1952) *The Iliad and Odyssey of Homer* (London: Chancellor Press).

Hume, David (1957) *An Enquiry Concerning the Principles of Morals* (The Library of Liberal Arts, New York: Bobbs-Merrill).

——(1967) *A Treatise on Human Nature*, ed. Selby-Bigge (Oxford: Oxford University Press).

Ibsen, Henrik (1966) *Peer Gynt* (London: Penguin Classics).

——(1971) 'The Master Builder', *The Master Builder and Other Plays* (London: Penguin Classics).

Jones, Ernest (1949) *Hamlet and Oedipus* (London: Victor Gollancz Ltd).

——(1974) 'Free Will and Determinism', *Psycho-Myth, Psycho-History*, vol ii (New York: Hillstone).

Kant, Immanuel (1959) *Fundamental Principles of the Metaphysics of Ethics*, trans. Thomas Kingsmill Abbott (London: Longmans).

——(1961) *Critique of Pure Reason*, trans. Norman Kemp Smith (London: Macmillan).

Kierkegaard, Søren (1961) *Purity of Heart*, trans. Douglas Steere (London: Fontana Books).

Klein, Melanie (1948) 'The Early Development of Conscience in the Child', *Psycho-Analysis Today*, ed. Sandor Lorand (London: Allen and Unwin).

Malcolm, Norman (1963) 'George Edward Moore', *Knowledge and Certainty* (New Jersey: Prentice Hall).

Mischel, Theodore (1967) 'Kant and the Possibility of a Science of Psychology' *The Monist* Vol. 51.

—— (1969) 'Scientific and Philosophical Psychology', *Human Actions*, ed.Theodore Mischel (New York, London: Academic Press).

Moore, G E (1947) *Ethics* (Oxford: Oxford University Press).

O'Neill, Eugene (1973) *Long Day's Journey into Night* (London: Jonathan Cape).

Plato (1952) *Symposium* (London: Penguin Classics).

——(1973a) 'Phaedo', *The Last Days of Socrates* (London: Penguin Classics).

——(1973b) *Gorgias* (London: Penguin Classics).

——(1973c) 'Phaedrus', *Phaedrus and Letters VII and VIII* (London: Penguin Classics).

Proust, Marcel (1954) *A la Recherche du temps perdu*, vols i-iii (Paris: Bibliothèque de la Pleiade).

Reich, Wilhelm (1950) *Character Analysis*, trans. Theodore P Wolfe (London: Vision Press).

Sartre, Jean-Paul (1943) *L'Etre et le Néant* (Paris: Gallimard).

——(1945) *Le Sursis* (Paris: Gallimard).

——(1947) 'La Liberté Cartesienne', *Situations* I (Paris: Gallimard).

——(1949) 'La Republique du Silence', *Situations* III (Paris: Gallimard).

Schopenhauer, Arthur (1951) 'Free Will and Fatalism' and 'Character', *On Human Nature, Essays* (London: Allen and Unwin).

——(1960) *On the Freedom of the Will*, trans. Konstantin Kolenda (Oxford: Basil Blackwell).

Sophocles (1968) 'King Oedipus' and 'Antigone', *The Theban Plays* (London: Penguin Books).

Spinoza, Benedict (1960) *Ethics*, ed. James Gutmann (New York: Hafner).

Tolstoy, Leo (1956) *Anna Karenina*, trans. Rosemary Edmunds (London: Penguin Classics).

——(1960) 'Father Sergius', *The Kreutzer Sonata and Other Stories*, trans. Aylmer Maude (Oxford: Oxford University Press).

Trilling, Lionel (1955) 'Anna Karenina', *The Opposing Self* (London: Secker and Warburg).

Weil, Simone (1948) *La Pesanteur et la Grâce* (Paris: Librairie Plon).

——(1950) *La Connaissance Surnaturelle* (Paris: Gallimard).

——(1959) *Waiting on God*, trans. Emma Craufurd (London: Fontana Books).

——(1960) *Attente de Dieu* (Paris: La Colombe).

——(1963) 'L'Iliade on le Poème de la Force' and 'Dieu dans Platon', *La Source Greque* (Paris: Gallimard).

——(1968) 'God in Plato' and 'The Love of God and Affliction', *On Science, Necessity and the Love of God*, trans. and ed. Richard Rees (London: Oxford University Press).

Winch, Peter (1972) 'Moral Integrity', *Ethics and Action* (London: Routledge & Kegan Paul).

Wisdom, John (1965) *Paradox and Discovery* (Oxford: Blackwell).

Wittgenstein, Ludwig (1956, *Remarks on the Foundations of Mathematics* (Oxford:Blackwell) – *RFM*.

——(1961) *Tractatus Logico-Philosophicus*, trans. D F Pears and B F McGuinness (London: Routledge & Kegan Paul) – *Tract*.

——(1963) *Philosophical Investigations* (Oxford: Blackwell) – *PI*.

——(1965) 'Lecture on Ethics', *Philosophical Review*, vol LXXIV

——(1967) *Zettel* (Oxford: Blackwell) – *Z*.

——(1969a) *On Certainty* (Oxford: Blackwell) – *OC*.

——(1969b) *The Blue and Brown Books* (Oxford: Blackwell) – *BB*.

INDEX

Am80364mn
10⊗